Acclaim for
LONE SEEKER MANY MASTERS

"This book will go a long way and inspire seekers from all around the world for many years to come. I couldn't stop until I finished the book. It's a pure delight."

— *Hon'ble Sher Bahadur Deuba, Former Prime Minister of Nepal and President of Nepali Congress*

"Swami Anand Arun churns out another gem in the form of the this book. It is a story of a seeker who has inspired many people to become seeker. It's a story of his spiritual journey which takes into account his experiences and interactions with other spiritual stalwarts."

— *Hon'ble Dr Anil Jain, National General Secretary, Bharatiya Janta Party, India*

"Osho is the pioneer partisan of spirituality in our times. And Arun Swami is to be thanked for having had kept the torch aflame. I am sure Lone Seeker Many Masters is going to be yet another bestseller. The fact that the book is written in English unlike his past bestsellers in Nepali would further augment its worth."

— *Hon'ble Pradeep Giri. Member of Parliament and Central Committee Member, Nepali Congress*

"Lone Seekers Many Masters by Swami Anand Arun is a gateway to enlightenment and spiritual awakening and helps exploring the eternal truth. The beauty of this book lies in its simplicity and humility.

— *Ajit Kumar –Coordinator, Nepal Chapter, Bharatiya Janta Party*

"A brilliant and honest reportage of the spiritual journey of a 'lone seeker' who himself, in the process, metamorphosed and joined the celestial company of 'many masters'! A must read for everyone on the spiritual path."

— *Dr. Er. Uday Kanta Mishra former Vice-Chancellor of Aryabhatta Knowledge University Bihar, Patna*

"Lone Seeker Many Masters provides a powerful account of Swami Arun's meeting with Osho, who devoted all his life to raise the level of consciousness of humankind. If you read it with love, curiosity and an open heart, this book has a great transformative power.

— *Bhagirath Yogi, BBC, London*

"Lone Seeker, Many Masters is a beautiful garden, where different varieties of flowers are blooming. Swami Arun has nurtured this book with a great devotion and love. Thank you Swami jee for letting us see the Masters through your eyes."

— *Vijay Kumar, Senior Journalist and Author*

"Lone Seeker, Many Masters reveals a kaleidoscope of enlightened possibility. Always soul-enriching, the impact of these stories accumulates and whirls the reader into a strong current of truth.

His timeless words are rich with truth and love, and will be read and savoured time and time again."

— *Sally Handerson, American Author*

"Lone Seeker, Many Masters by Swami Anand Arun is a spiritual autobiography and a rare gift to humanity."

— *Dr Iftikhar Ahmed Javed, Member, Haj Committee of India*

"I have personally met Swami Anand Arun a number of times. His book Lone Seeker Many Masters inspires us to introspect ourselves and helps in improving our values for the benefit of the society by leveraging the power of meditation."

— *Dr. Omkar Rai, Director General, Software Technology Parks of India (STPI)*

"Lone Seeker Many Masters is a riveting read. It provides insight into the deeper problems of human psyche and fills us with inspiration. Everyone who is interested in spirituality must read this book."

— *Brahmarshi Shree Kumar Swami, Spiritual Leader*

LONE SEEKER MANY MASTERS

Bodhisattva
Swami Anand Arun

Osho Tapoban
Publication

First edition of this book was sponsored by Swami Amrit Sagar (Gyan KC), UK

Copyright © 2015 by Swami Anand Arun

First edition : September 2015
Second edition : October 2016

Published by:
Osho Tapoban Publication
Nagarjuna Hills, Kathmandu, Nepal
sales.tapoban@gmail.com, www.tapoban.com
+977 01 5112012/13 +977 9851124801

Editing by Deborah Sart (Ma Dyan Sampada)
Swami Anand Arhat, Swami Anand Suvam,
Ma Bodhi Mudita, Swami Aatmo Neerav

Design by Swami Dhyan Yatri, Ma Bodhi Mudita, Swami Aatmo Neerav, Swami Anand Suvam

Cover photo by Baabu Muthur

ISBN: 978-9937-686-12-9

All rights reserved. No part of this publication may be reproduced, distributed, or transmitted in any form or by any means, including photocopying, recording, or other electronic or mechanical methods, without the prior written permission of the publisher, except in the case of brief quotations embodied in critical reviews and certain other noncommercial uses permitted by copyright law.

MRP ₹ 250.00 / Nrs 400.00

To
MY BELOVED MASTER OSHO
WITHOUT WHOM THIS WAS NOT POSSIBLE

Although long overdue, this book was not taking final shape due to my regular traveling and hectic schedule.

I would like to thank Swami Dhyan Yatri, Swami Anand Arhat, Swami Anand Suvam, Ma Bodhi Mudita and Swami Aatmo Neerav, my co-travellers on the path of truth. They are the architects who have given shape to my dream.

Osho is going to bless them for their dedicated contribution. I give them my thanks and love.

- Swami Anand Arun

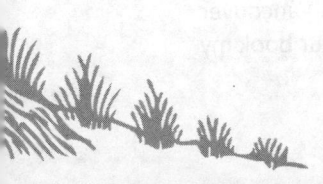

PREFACE TO THE SECOND EDITION

When I first wrote this book and it hit the stores, I did not know that the first edition for Nepal would be finished within 6 months. Edu Hub in India has published its own edition for India and the book is also being translated to Russian, Chinese and Hindi because of the growing demand from friends speaking the respective languages. Your response has humbled me and I am grateful to my readers who have acknowledged and received the stories of this lone seeker so well.

There were a few mistakes in the first book which have been rectified in this edition. Deborah Sart (Ma Dhyan Sampada) from Australia deserves my heart's sincerest thanks for her hard work in editing this second edition. Osho will bless her for her sincere efforts, I give her my love.

I just came back from my meditation events in the USA and Canada and while returning back a friend came all the way to Vancouver airport just to say, "After reading your book my life has changed forever." Those few phrases from that reader and the inspiration I saw in his eyes gave me a great sense of contentment and job satisfaction. The fact that it was able to inspire even one soul, that it could change even one life leaves me immensely grateful.

The book was not written by me, existence has authored it through me to share its beautiful gems. Every story in this book carries the blessings of the masters who make this book. I am grateful that I could be their messenger.

Bodhisattva Swami Anand Arun
Krishna Ashtami
August, 2016
Osho Tapoban

BEFORE YOU EMBARK

I have been blessed by many masters on my spiritual journey. After I met my master Osho, my relationship with those masters has attained new heights and reached unknown depths. Tapoban and all other meditation centers that have been initiated by me are blessed by all these masters and consecrated by their energy. This book has been long overdue to all those masters, who have ceaselessly illuminated my path.

It is my experience that if you really love and recognize one enlightened master you will immediately have the same reverence for all the others because the taste of enlightenment is the same. The taste of the ocean from any shore will be salty.

I am usually surprised that enlightened masters often share the same opinion, same expression and at times exactly the same words. In the beginning I thought perhaps they had read each other. But now I know, they speak from the same source. In fact, it is better to say that they allow existence itself to speak through them. Many times they also contradict each other. In accordance with time, space and context they might even criticize one another. But if you have a deep insight you will realize that all this is done with one simple purpose – to awaken us!

The enlightened masters' project is not a private limited company; it's a joint enterprise. And my experience is that all the masters work together in a team. Just like in a football game where the players pass the ball to whoever can make it swiftly reach its destination, the masters, too, pass their disciples to other Gurus, who can take them easily towards enlightenment. I have been passed on to different masters in my different lives, and so have you if you are a seeker.

This search is not new. The quest for truth is eternal. Many of us have been searching for the impossible for many of our lives. And we have been with many masters, sometimes consciously, but most of the time unconsciously. We were unconscious; the masters were not. So they have always tried to help us even if we are unconscious, arrogant and full of ourselves.

It is my understanding that if you really love and follow one enlightened master you follow all the enlightened masters of the past, present and future. Every year when I conduct meditation camps in the West, people recurrently ask me the same question, "I am a follower of Jesus or the Buddha or Ramakrishna or Gurdjieff, but I love Osho too, so if I get initiated into neo-sannyas from you will it not be a betrayal of my previous master?"

My answer is always the same. I tell them, "If you get initiated into neo-sannyas, your previous master will be the happiest. His soul will dance along with us in sheer ecstasy during your sannyas celebration."

And I do not merely say this to relieve them of guilt or to convince them to take sannyas. I say this from my first-hand experience, because the sole concern of the masters is to make sure that we become conscious and shed the skin of ignorance. It does not matter which technique is used: Zazen, Vipassana or Osho Dynamic Meditation. It is true that Osho meditation techniques are modern and powerful, yet they might not suit everybody. There are people who feel more comfortable with traditional techniques. Osho would be happy if a seeker is transformed through any of these methods.

As time passes, my love for and dedication to my master is increasing, and as my trust is growing for Osho, my understanding of all other masters is also deepening equally.

But I also want to caution you that spirituality is not like shopping, where you buy your shirt from one store and bargain for your coat in the second, and select the color of your tie from the third. You have to settle down and totally surrender to one master.

You cannot be treated by many doctors at one time. It will be very confusing and even dangerous. You have to find your personal physician and once you find him, trust him a hundred percent and follow his prescription to the word. If need be he will refer you to other experts. And once you are healthy, it is your physician who will feel the most rewarded.

And then there is the final question. Many seekers come to me and ask "I am attracted to many enlightened beings, but how can I know who is my real master?" My humble request is, be honest, be open and keep your quest burning. You cannot select your master because you are ignorant. Accept your ignorance. Let your heart wander freely in the open sky of spirituality. If your search is genuine, your real master will select you at the right time.

Bodhisattva Swami Anand Arun

September, 2015

Osho Tapoban

CONTENTS

ON THE PATH OF AWAKENING

1	THE SILENT MYSTIC	3
2	SWAMI VIVEKANANDA	13
3	OSHO	23
4	RAMAN MAHARSHI	35
5	PARAMHANSA YOGANANDA	49
6	RAMAKRISHNA PARAMHANSA	63
7	TOTAPURI BABA	77
8	SWAMI RAMTIRTHA	87
9	J. KRISHNAMURTI	105
10	SHIVAPURI BABA	119
11	SWAMI RAMA	133
12	DALAI LAMA	141
13	SRI AUROBINDO	153
14	GOKHLE BABA	163
15	INDIRA DEVI	177
16	MEERA BAI	189
17	NAGARJUNA	199

18	BUDDHA	209
19	YASHODHARA	219
20	SARIPUTRA & MAHAMODGALYAN	229
21	MASTARAM BABA	239
22	KRISHNA	251
23	KABIR	261
24	MAHARSHI PATANJALI	271
25	GURU NANAK	277
26	ASTABAKRA	285
27	MA ANAND MADHU	291

IN SEARCH OF TRUTH

28	MAHATMA GANDHI	300
29	SADHO SAHAJ SAMADHI BHALI	309
30	SUVADRA MATA	316
31	RAM BOMJON	320

GLOSSARY OF WORDS   326

On The Path of Awakening

THE SILENT MYSTIC

> "A yogi's past has no meaning and we don't usually talk about it. And since I wasn't initiated by anyone, I don't have a name either. Due to God's grace, I am usually blissed out, so you can call me Mastaram."

For as long as I can remember, I was seized by a sense of discontentment, which sprung from a rather abstract source. I could not pinpoint the reason for it and yet it left me longing intensely for something I could not explain in words. This is what triggered my spiritual quest. I gradually discovered that this longing was pacified to an extent when I read literature about enlightened masters. That's when I started looking around for a master. Of course, finding a master is a rare fortune and it was a good many years before I finally met Osho, my master. But during this phase many mystics mysteriously came along my way and helped me. One such mystic who helped me immensely is Mastaram Baba.

I used to be a BSc student at Trichandra College in Kathmandu. I had gone to Janakpur, my hometown, for some familial chore. By then, I had already been initiated by a few Gurus in India. I had been trying many different techniques of meditation but wasn't able to meditate at all. I was looking for someone to guide me towards the right path. Countless times I had prayed to God to bring this guide to me.

One morning, I woke up to find a yogi standing silently at our gate begging for alms. Such a sight is not that uncommon in Janakpur, one of the ancient buddhafields of Nepal. Janakpur used to be the capital of the Kingdom of Mithila and the centre of Mithila culture. According to the ancient Hindu scripture of Ramayana, Ram, the eldest son of King Dashrath of Ayodhya, himself had come here to woo Sita, his consort. Sita was the daughter of King Sirdhwaj Janak of Mithila. Later, the four sons of Dashrath married the four princesses of Janakpur.

The Kingdom of Mithila was at the peak of its glory during King Sirdhwaj Janak's time. The ancient texts talk about the ashrams of great saints such as Yagyabalkya, Bishwamitra, Balmiki, Astabakra, and Lomas, who added new dimensions to eastern mysticism. It is said that during the reign of Sirdhwaj, even dancers and courtesans of the city had attained enlightenment.

I noticed that this yogi had an exceptionally bright countenance as though he was dripping with radiance. I went inside the kitchen and filled a handkerchief with rice and came outside to give the pouch to the yogi. The yogi was in silence so instead of speaking he took out a slate from his bag and wrote down, "I don't have anything to carry the rice in, so it would be better if you could give me some money."

Back then, many people still used Indian coins in the southern plains of Nepal. I fished into my pocket and found a quarter, which I gave to the yogi. He accepted the offering gratefully. Since it is considered inauspicious to take an offering back from yogis, I requested he keep the pouch of rice for his journey. He accepted that as well.

We did not exchange words. He was about to leave when he suddenly turned back and started scribbling on his slate again. His English was notably good, as was his handwriting.

"What kind of meditation do you practice?"

I was taken off guard by this rather strange exchange and told him that I didn't practice any meditation. But he insisted, "Your vibrations tell me that you are trying hard to meditate."

Stupefied by his clairvoyance I told him how I had been trying different techniques of meditation without much success. "My meditation is not going well at all. Although I have learnt many things from many Gurus, I am not able to practice something that is meaningful," I told him with utmost honesty.

He again wrote on the slate, "If you are ready, I am willing to help you."

After hearing that, I cordially invited him into my house, made him comfortably seated, and started sharing my queries. He started writing the answers in perfect English and Hindi on his slate. After a while it was time for lunch and I asked him what I could serve him. He said, "Anything vegetarian which has been made in the house is good for me."

We had a tradition of eating all our meals together so my family members joined us too. Thanks to a strong political inclination of my parents, more often than not political discussions predominated our meal conversations. Personally I didn't enjoy those conversations all that much, and was a little worried for the yogi. But to my pleasant surprise, he partook in the conversation with natural ease. He knew a great deal about the political scenario of Nepal and India. At the end of the meal, everyone was thoroughly impressed by his clear understanding of politics.

After lunch, I invited him to my room. He shared some of the most insightful analyses of Aurobindo's *purnayoga*, Vivekananda's *karmayoga* and *gyanyoga* as well as Raman Maharshi's silence. The depth of his wisdom astonished me. His presence was so pleasurable that I lost all track of time. My family always knew of my fascination with yogis but this friendship only added to their worry. The yogi sensed this and wrote on his slate, "You have all my blessings. Now I shall leave," and prepared to leave.

Despite knowing each other for such a small period of time, I had already developed a deep intimacy with him. As he mentioned departure I started growing impatient. He looked at me lovingly and wrote on his slate, "Don't be sad, I will return tomorrow morning." I felt so rejuvenated by the meeting that I could barely sleep that night.

The next morning, the yogi arrived as he had promised. After a light breakfast, we again sat together. As I mentioned earlier, I was struggling with my meditation and asked a great deal of questions. His answers reflected the depth of his own meditation, inspiring fresh reverence in me.

I was intrigued by his answers and insisted on knowing more about him. He wrote that before taking sannyas he used to be a professor in South India. Gradually it dawned upon him that no outward excellence or accomplishment could satiate his deepest longing. When this realization crystallized within him, he took the jump and became an ascetic. Initially he had taken a vow of silence for twelve years. Those twelve years gave him the taste of solitude and beatitude. By the time his vow was over he had immersed himself too deeply in the blissful world of silence to ever utter another word again. Whenever necessary he communicated through his slate.

Soon, it was time for lunch again. My family gathered around the yogi with a rather fond curiosity. I knew that they felt threatened by his influence upon me and yet they themselves weren't immune to his charm. They were worried that I might follow his footsteps and renounce the "secure" future they were trying to build for me.

Of course, their fear wasn't entirely baseless. I have always had a strong fascination for yogis, and many times I had tried to go to the Himalayas to meditate in solitude.

After lunch was over, he gave me a short *mantra* and a beautiful technique of Rajyoga. I pleaded with him to be my Guru but he refused.

"I am not your Guru. You will find your Guru at the right time. I had come to inaugurate a yoga school in Siligudi. There I heard your cry for help and came to Janakpur to help you. I am happy with your thirst and inquiry. Your thirst is what will take you to your Guru one day," he said.

I got the *darshan* of Osho three years later.

On the third day, the yogi arrived at my house as usual. That meeting was to be our last one. With a cryptic precision he told me to fetch a diary, and wrote his answers on it. Later he told me that his answers were going to guide me in the future and he wanted me to document them properly.

I brought a small notebook and started asking him questions. His answers remain safely with me to date.

Q. Which sect are you from and who is your Guru?

I don't belong to any sect and I haven't been initiated by anyone. God himself is my Guru and humanity is what I believe in.

Q. How can I meet you?

I don't have an ashram. I am a wandering monk. I go wherever God takes me.

Q. What shall I call you?

A yogi's past has no meaning and we don't usually talk about it. And since I wasn't initiated by anyone, I don't have a name either. Due to God's grace, I am usually blissed out, so you can call me Mastaram (the divinely intoxicated one).

Q. Is it true that yogis have various miraculous powers? Do you also possess such powers?

Mind starts to become pure and sharp once meditation takes hold of you. A silent mind becomes very powerful. A lot of miracles start happening. These miracles are not necessary on the path of samadhi, rather they are hindrances. I do experience such powers but discussing them will not help you in any way. You are very inquisitive about such spiritual powers. Begin practicing meditation as I have taught you and soon you will experience these powers by yourself. But it is not good to think and inquire about them. A lot of meditators go astray this way.

Q. There are many yogis such as you who have a lot of spiritual power but misery and injustice is only growing in this world. Why don't the yogis make this world a better place to live? Why do they escape from the world?

The world has always been like this. There was injustice and misery even in the time of Ram, Krishna or Buddha. Ram himself had to live in the forest for fourteen years in exile. Sita was also kidnapped. Buddha had to bear a lot of humiliation. During his own lifetime he saw the end of the Shakya clan and Kapilvastu. Krishna couldn't stop the Mahabharata war or the demise of his Yadav clan. The war between good and evil has been going on since eternity and will go on for eternity. The desire for freedom from this world arises only after you understand that absolute justice, peace or system is not possible here. This world is a school. Learn your lesson and be free of it. This is not a place where you live forever. I see a strong wish in you to change the world. This is a good wish but you will not be able to change the world. We come here with limited time and energy which should be used for self transformation. First realize God, then whatever the divine wishes for you will be the best for you and the world at large. After enlightenment, God made Buddha roam around villages for forty-five years while he made Raman Maharshi sit silently below the Arunachal hill.

Q. It is said that not even a leaf on a tree can move without divine will. If this is true then why do you tell me to make constant effort in my meditation? Will my meditation not happen naturally if he wishes? It is probably not happening now because he doesn't wish it to be so.

On the surface, your question looks like the ultimate philosophical query but underneath it shows the lethargic tendency of the mind. It is <u>my</u> understanding that even a leaf doesn't move without God's wish. I am telling you to make effort in meditation so that you realize this by yourself. Through constant meditation when your ego melts and you realize that you are not the doer but just the watcher, only then will you see that this whole world is a divine play and runs exactly according to his wish. When you say this now, it only aids your laziness.

TO DISRESPECT A YOGI IS TO DISRESPECT GOD

My family members were disappointed at my lack of interest in family affairs and my obsession with Mastaram. It so happened that I had to leave for the town of Malangwa the next morning. In those days one could reach Malangwa only via Sitamadhi in India. I told Mastaram about my obligation. He said, "I will accompany you to Sitamadhi, after which I will catch the train to my destination."

When I told my family members that I would like to take Mastaram with me, they created a big scene. Just to avoid having him accompany us, they invited a few extra friends to join us on the trip. There was only so much space in the car and they used this as an excuse to exclude him. If I had been courageous enough to say no to their nonsense I would have been able to take him with us, but unfortunately I wasn't courageous enough. As much as I had wanted

Mastaram to accompany me, I couldn't rebel against this foolish move by my family. A stream of guilt ran through my blood as I caught a glimpse of his luggage that he had carried along for the departure. I told him what had transpired between my parents and apologetically offered him a five rupee note. We both wanted to spend some more time with each other as was evident from our faces. But destiny had desired otherwise.

As soon as we rode off for Malangwa we were greeted by a series of mishaps. I intuitively realized that those mishaps were the punishment for insulting a yogi. As soon as we crossed the Nepali border, the axle of our jeep broke and we suffered a bad accident. Since it was necessary for us to go to Malangwa, we got on a bus to Sitamadhi. In Sitamadhi we rented a rickety jeep and left for Malangwa in the evening. The road was bumpy beyond description and we lost our way in the night. The jeep was stuck there the whole night. We heard that the area was infested by bandits. We had to spend that cold and fearful night shivering in a field. None of us could make use of the jeep that had been refused a yogi. Those who were placed in the jeep instead of him suffered for no reason. When a person who has totally surrendered to the will of existence is insulted we violate the subtle law of nature and it doesn't go unpunished. I have experienced this many times in my life and in the lives of others. As we shivered and waited impatiently for the morning to arrive, Mastaram's face sailed gently through my memory like a luminous star. That night and for the next three years before I met my master, his words became my pathfinder, always challenging and assuring me at the same time.

SWAMI VIVEKANANDA

" Swami Vivekananda was a true manifestation of the heights that human consciousness can attain. His exterior burnt with the brilliance that arose from his passion to serve for the upliftment of humankind while his interior was drenched in the sublimity of the vast matchless wisdom of the Self. "

Puberty and spirituality struck me simultaneously. When I was in eighth grade, sexuality hit me as an unknown and powerful force. I was overwhelmed by this sudden emotional upheaval that paralyzed my rationality and turned me into a helpless apparatus designed to bear the whims of hormones. Of course, I had no intention to let this force win over me. So it was rather predictable that Swami Vivekananda, the charismatic young celibate, would become my idol.

Back then, I was a student at the Mujaffarpur District School. I was quite popular in school and had remarkable diplomatic skills for a young boy. We used to have the students elections where students could chose the Head Prefect of our hostel. Being Head Prefect was a matter of pride and one could enjoy certain privileges. But I was cut out for a different game; I wanted to become a student librarian. So despite receiving favourable votes for the post of the Head Prefect, I chose to become the librarian. I had puzzled quite a few people by this choice, but that was just the beginning. My whole life was to become a series of unpredictable adventures. And just as becoming the librarian enriched my life in ways I hadn't imagined, each of these adventures left me more blessed, more fulfilled.

Puberty filled me with desires and anxiety, and I had not the slightest clue as how to deal with them. It was in that state of turmoil I stumbled upon the books by Swami Vivekananda. His words helped me a lot. Although Swamiji never initiated me, I considered him my first Guru. I learnt yoga and Vedic mysticism from his books. I used to read his biographies and gaze at his bewitching pictures for hours.

Clad in yellow and orange with large eyes and a striking figure, he stood like the sun. He carried the exquisite beauty of the ancient heritage of spiritual truth, the heart and life of India.

When the clairvoyant seer Annie Besant first saw him in Chicago at the Parliament of Religions in 1893, she saw a warrior more than a sannyasin, every part of whose body was radiating divinity. She reminisces, "A lion head, piercing eyes, mobile lips, movements swift and abrupt – such was my first impression of Swami Vivekananda, as I met him in one of the rooms set apart for the use of the delegates to the Parliament of Religions. Off the platform, his figure was imbued with pride of country, pride of race – the representative of the oldest of living religions, surrounded by curious gazers of nearly the youngest religion. India was not to be shamed before the hurrying arrogant West by this, her envoy and her son. He brought her message, he spoke in her name, and the herald remembered the dignity of the royal land whence he came. Purposeful, virile, strong, he stood out, a man among men, able to hold his own."

Such was the glory of Swamiji. Just gazing at his pictures filled my being with blessings. I remember, those days I used to spend all my pocket money in buying his books. I read almost all literature on Swami Vivekananda when I was still in school. I used to keep his pictures on my reading desk. In fact, they adorn my desk even today.

Yoga helped me a lot to instill inner and outer discipline in my life. But I was aware that my meditation was not sufficient since my deepest longing remained unfulfilled. Being in the library helped me immensely. Apart from Swami Vivekananda's books, I used to read a lot on spirituality. In fact, I was so thrilled to own the key of the library that I eventually moved my bed over there. In solitude, I used to devour one book after another. One fine day I chanced on Mahatma Gandhi's *My Experiments with Truth*. The book had a lasting impact on me. I started practicing arduous food discipline, taking total abstinence from tea, sugar and salt. By the time I was in high school I had started eating only raw food. Gandhi used to say that raw food helped celibacy. Following in his footsteps, I used to fill a bucket with cold water and leave it outside. By morning the water would be twice as cold as tap water. I bathed every morning with this chilled water for three years. I felt I had won over that tumultuous force but I would learn many years later after I met my master Osho that at most, I had only succeeded in desensitizing myself.

Although Swami Vivekananda opened the door of spirituality for me, it would be years before he could reveal much deeper insights to me. I loved Swamiji very much but I wasn't mature enough for his guidance.

When I started my engineering course at Patna University in India, my relationship with him became even deeper. I was more interested in spirituality than structural mathematics. My interest and obligation were in serious conflict. If it wasn't for Swami Vivekananda I wouldn't have passed many examinations.

His guidance didn't come to me directly. In the Department

of Electrical Engineering at the University there was a student who received direct guidance from Swami Vivekananda because of his past life association with him. By that time I had already met Osho, who was known then as Acharya Rajneesh, and had accepted him as my master. The young man from the Department of Electrical Engineering had also visited Osho. As we were both spiritually inclined, our mutual friends used to mention our names to each other, but since we were in different departments (I was a student in the Department of Civil Engineering), we didn't know each other personally.

One summer afternoon, our paths crossed at the hostel gate, and we were introduced to each other. I was overjoyed to meet him. We bonded in a very short period of time. He gradually revealed to me how he received direct guidance from Swami Vivekananda. He once asked Swamiji if he could tell me about his relationship with him. To his surprise, Swamiji responded positively. Swamiji told him that he could tell everything in detail to me but not to anyone else and started guiding me through him. He has saved me countless times. Interestingly, Swami Vivekananda used to tell him, "Arun will initiate a great spiritual movement in Nepal."

I was baffled at what he meant by that. At the time, I was enmeshed in a lot of petty problems and couldn't imagine what Swamiji could possibly be hinting at.

I asked my friend to convey to Swamiji the message that I wanted to get his guidance directly, to which he replied, "Time is not ripe yet. When time will mature, his own master will guide him."

I had a rather serious disposition then. Time and time again Swamiji relayed me the message, "Always remain happy and do not worry too much. Everything will be all right in due course."

These exchanges were my first experiences of how a master can continue guiding his devotees even after leaving his physical body. For two years during my studies I received regular guidance from Swamiji through my friend, and I always did as he told me. Of course, my friend could have been telling me lies; it could have been all his mind-game, and the whole thing nothing but a fallacy. But I have the uncanny ability to trust the unknown. There was no way to prove whether or not Swamiji's guidance was genuine, but I never had a hint of doubt in my heart. Forty years since his prophesy, every word he uttered has come true one hundred percent; existence has indeed chosen me as its medium for the spiritual movement in Nepal and the world at large.

Before Swamiji went to America, Americans perceived India as a backward and uncivilized nation of elephants, snake charmers and black magicians. The hidden purpose of the Chicago convention was to bring together the representatives of all religions and boast about the enormity and success of Christianity. Under the shine of the materialistic success of America the Christians wanted to prove Christianity as the most scientific and supreme religion in the world. Because of Swamiji's presence, not only did the organizers failed to fulfill their purpose, instead the scientific abundance and vastness of Hinduism got honoured on American land for the first time. Even before Swamiji, Hindu saints had tried to preach Hinduism in America but white people were not ready to listen to anything about religion from a coloured person.

Swami Vivekananda was a saint whose heart was enraptured by the glory of eastern heritage. He had immense love for his nation and its countrymen, but his heart was always troubled by a great pain seeing the backwardness, poverty and adversity of India. In America, he used to sit alone and cry, remembering the hardship endured by the citizens of his country. When the Americans asked him why he cried so much, he said, "When will my country attain to material affluence? I can't bear the thought of my countrymen living in such utter poverty."

He brought a new version of sannyas into the world. "Service of the poor and needy is the path of spiritual development," he would say confidently. "A hungry stomach cannot be religious. Preaching religion to the poor is humiliating them. First we should make arrangement for their meals." These were the thoughts that became the heart and soul of the Ramakrishna Mission which he established.

In 1902 Swami Vivekananda had a vision that clearly showed the coming five hundred years in India. He said:

- The future of India will be greater than its glorious past.

- India will be independent in the coming 50 years and the independence movement will not be violent like that of other countries.

- There will be a world war in the next 20 years and if the West doesn't give up its materialistic ways, war will only continue.

- Independent India will adopt the materialistic ways of the West.

- Countries like America will slowly become spiritual. By reaching the peak of materialism they will find out that just material wealth and comfort is not enough for happiness and peace.

- Even after the British leave India, there will be territorial conflict between India and China. In time, the visionary words of the yogi came true, and even today his predictions are still manifesting.

One day the famed American industrialist, John D. Rockefeller, came to meet Swamiji. Swamiji told Rockefeller the events of his life which was only known to him. Rockefeller was stunned hearing that. Swamiji also said, "God has given you immense wealth. It is not just for you. Use the money for the betterment of the world."

Rockefeller didn't like this and left Swamiji's room feeling a little low. When he returned a few days later, he ran into Swamiji's room and showed him a newspaper clipping. It said that Rockefeller had donated a large sum to philanthropic causes. "You must be happy now, so thank me," Rockefeller said.

Swamiji calmly replied, "It is not I but you who has to thank me because I taught you the right way to use your wealth."

The Rockefeller Foundation has become famous in the world by doing philanthropic deeds.

While Swamiji was travelling in India as a monk, the Maharaja of Mysore was hugely impressed by him. The Maharaja was proud of his ministers. He wanted conformation of the greatness of his ministers from Swamiji and asked him, "What do you think about my ministers?"

"All ministers have the same ulterior motive. All of them flatter the king and earn as much money as they can," said Swamiji right in front of the ministers.

The Maharaja did not like what he heard and when alone with Swamiji told him, "Such honesty is not right, Swamiji. If you speak with such honesty elsewhere as well, you will be poisoned to death."

Swamiji answered, "I am a monk and I shouldn't be afraid of speaking truth. Even if it puts my life in danger, I will not change my ways. If your son comes and asks me about you, how can I only praise you when I know that you are not so rich in merit?"

Swamiji's ways were such that if he needed to criticize people, he would do it right in front of them, while he praised them behind their backs.

Swami Vivekananda was a true manifestation of the heights that human consciousness can attain. His exterior burnt with the brilliance that arose from his passion to serve for the upliftment of humankind while his interior was drenched in the sublimity of the vast matchless wisdom of the self. The richness of his personality left no soul unstirred of those who came into his presence. This can be well articulated in the words of Annie Besant, "The huge multitude hung upon his words; not a syllable must be lost, not a cadence missed! "That man, a heathen!" said one, as he came out of the great hall, "And we send missionaries to his people! It would be more fitting that they should send missionaries to us!""

OSHO

" Acharya Rajneesh walked into the garden. His long black beard and hair danced to the rhythm of the evening breeze, his radiant face blanched with the rays of the moon, emanated grace. I looked at him in disbelief. I couldn't believe a human body could be so beautiful. My heart was filled with the loftiest sentiments. He looked like a numinous being, who had just descended from the land of the rishis. "

The fateful evening of the 29th of March 1969 stands out vividly in my memory. That evening I had the *darshan* of my Guru, Acharya Rajneesh for the first time. The cool breeze rolled in waves from the banks of the Ganga. The air was spiced with the fragrance of flowers and fruits. Just when I thought the evening couldn't get any more beautiful there walked in Acharya Rajneesh – serene and otherworldly in his white *lungi* and a white shawl. My heart skipped a beat. I had never seen a mortal so beautiful, so sublime, so godlike.

Back then, I was doing my engineering course at Patna University. In my spare time, I frequented the Sinha Library in the city, which had a collection of rare books on spirituality. Engineering didn't intrigue me at all. If the truth be told, I was doing the course mostly on my parents' insistence. My real interest lay in spirituality.

At the slightest pretext, I used to abandon my classes and visit different religious Gurus and their ashrams.

One afternoon after spending a rather fruitful time at the Sinha Library, I was walking out of the hall when I noticed a poster for yet another religious talk in town. The poster announced that someone named Acharya Rajneesh was giving a discourse in the library garden that very evening. That was the first time I had heard the name Acharya Rajneesh.

My fascination with meditation and Gurus had survived the test of time. Since my childhood, I exhibited a great deal of interest in meditation, yoga and naturopathy, which often troubled my parents. They tried their best to discourage me from pursuing spirituality, chastising me every now and then for what they thought was a deplorable hobby for a young man. But I stood determined and continued my pursuit.

By then I had travelled to most of the ashrams of North India and met most of the popular Gurus of that time. Among them were Anandmurti, Maharshi Mahesh Yogi, Anukul Chand Thakur, Swami Shivananda of Rishikesh, Madhavrao Golwalker of the Rastrya Soyamsewak Sangh, and sannyasins of the Ramakrishna Ashram. They all were special in their own ways and I did learn something from each of these Gurus but I was not completely satisfied by them and I was still waiting for my own Guru.

The Sarvodaya Movement based on the philosophy of Gandhi and Vinowa Bhave had taken India by storm. Jayaprakash Narayanan had also recently left politics and joined the Sarvodaya Movement. I had met Jayaprakash Narayanan in Patna, and found in him a deep quest for truth and a heart that was open to the woes of the masses. This inspired me very much to do something to uplift society as well.

I was in a state of great turmoil and confusion when I first met Osho. I was searching for the balance between Krishna's devotion and celebration, Buddha's peace and meditation, Swami Vivekananda's fiery grace and Gandhi's truth and nonviolence. I felt betrayed by time. I used to think that, had I been born in their time and become their disciple, I wouldn't have been as lost.

Naturally, when I saw the poster I decided to give it a try. I was so excited that I was one of the earliest to reach the garden and took my seat in the first row. Right on 6pm, Acharya Rajneesh walked in. He had a very graceful way with his body. His hands had the beauty and precision of a classical dancer...Now he folds his hands in namaste, now he holds the seam of his *lungi* gently and now he strokes his beard...I turned around in my seat and watched him walk towards me. His long black beard and hair danced to the rhythm of the evening breeze, his radiant face, blanched with the rays of the moon, emanated grace. I looked at him in disbelief. I couldn't believe a human body could be so beautiful. My heart was filled with the loftiest sentiments. He looked like a luminous being who had just descended from the land of the *rishis*.

Acharya Rajneesh sat down on the podium and closed his eyes. I was still struck by his beauty and couldn't take my eyes off him. A woman started singing a verse by Kabir in a very melodious voice. I learnt later that Acharya loved the songs of Kabir and Meera and his discourses were usually preceded by their songs. Her voice filled the campus with calm. The evening was still except for the cool breeze of the Ganga. Beauty reigned everywhere.

"My beloved ones...." Acharya began his discourse.

My heart started to beat in violent spasms and tears rolled down my cheeks unchecked. A long forgotten chamber of my heart had opened, some long-lost beloved was remembered. Acharya continued the discourse in his deep hypnotic voice and I kept sinking into the core of my being. My handkerchief was already drenched in tears, and yet the sea that my heart had become was in no hurry to calm down. My tears alarmed a friend of mine who had accompanied me to the discourse.

"What's happening to you? Why are you crying so much?" He kept asking me. If only I knew why.

Every single word he uttered shook my being. Acharya was strongly denouncing celibacy, Gandhiism, and religious leaders. At that time, I was fascinated by all three and was trying to lead the very life Acharya was denouncing. His discourse went against my education and my conditioning. My rational mind was rejecting his ideas but deep down the truth in his words had already won me over. Somebody from the audience asked, "Gandhi was a saint and he always travelled in the third class compartment of trains but why you, a *sadhu* only travel first class?"

Acharya answered, "Gandhi used to say that he travelled third class because there was no fourth class on Indian trains, but I say that I travel first class because there is no air-conditioned carriage on Indian trains yet. The day they put air-conditioned carriages on Indian trains I will stop using first class. Unlike Gandhi, I do not consider poverty divine. For me poverty is a disease sprung out of stupidity and an unscientific outlook on life. Today due to the proper use of science and technology, the whole of Europe and America are travelling in air-conditioned carriages but what great sins have we committed that we always have to travel in third class?"

Acharya's logic was unparalleled. Even those who did not like his philosophy were stupefied by his analytical ability. He was destroying my borrowed beliefs and conditioning with his sharp logic. My mind was resisting with all its might and yet my heart had already recognized that the master I had always prayed for was sitting in front of me; graceful like a *rishi*, fearless like a warrior.

Acharya ended his talk with these words, "I am grateful that you listened to me with such patience and love. There is no reason to believe what I have said. Doubt my words, think about them, meditate on them. Accept only that which feels right to you. In the end I pay my respects to the divine residing within all of you. Please accept my *pranam*."

As soon as Acharya finished his discourse, a crowd surrounded him. People were frantically trying to hug him, touch his feet or wherever they could manage to touch. The crowd was impenetrable. I stood frozen in my place. Slowly I walked towards the bookstall instead. They were registering the name of annual subscribers for the Hindi magazine called *Yukrand* which propagated Acharya's philosophy. Annual subscription cost twelve rupees and half-yearly cost six rupees respectively. I only had three rupees in my pocket so I asked them could I make a quarterly subscription. They didn't have a provision for quarterly subscription so I came up with an idea.

"Take three rupees and make me a yearly subscription. I will send you the remaining nine rupees through money order," I said rather hesitantly.

To my surprise, the volunteer trusted me and handed me a bill that read, "Yearly subscription with nine rupees remaining."

That was the most important and intelligent investment of my life. It not only transformed my life but also became a catalyst in the transformation of thousands of lives all around the world. After some time it was announced that Acharya would give a discourse on Mahavir at Rabindra Bhawan in a programme organized by the Jain community and then he would return to Jabalpur in an express train that same night.

Mesmerized I decided to follow Acharya to the Rabindra Bhawan. Acharya left in an Ambassador car. I didn't have a single penny left in my pocket, so I covered the distance of four kilometers by running after the car. Since Acharya's car was slowed down by the evening traffic, I reach Rabindra Bhawan just in time for his discourse, although rather exhausted.

In those days Acharya's discourses used to be fiery, and he attacked all kinds of blind religious faiths and superstitions. That particular discourse was about Mahavir and he was saying how the Jains did not understand a word said by Mahavir and were only blind devotees. I could feel the tension brewing in the room as all the organizers were Jains. Acharya's talk stunned the audience as much as it disturbed the organizers. Honestly speaking, I was worried if Acharya's words were going to provoke a furore among the Jains, who sat down dignified in the first few rows of the audience. Despite the thick smoke of tension that filled the hall, the organizers exhibited no outward agitation on their faces. Since Acharya was from a Jain family, the organizers had not expected such criticism from a saint who they thought was one of their own.

Acharya's talk ended. It was announced that he would go directly to the railway station from the hall. I had a great wish to go to the railway station but neither did I have any money on me nor any strength left to run the distance. Instead I slowly walked the seven-kilometre distance to my hostel submerged in an indescribable bliss.

After that first meeting, I started corresponding with Acharya through the mail. My life was full of problems and questions. I started to write everything to Acharya. My letters were always answered in his beautiful handwriting. He used very few words but the words were full of meaning and they had the effect of a *mantra* on me. "The solution to all your problems is meditation. Meditation will provide you with spiritual energy and when the energy reaches its peak all problems will dissolve instantly. There is a meditation camp at Dwaraka this October. If you can make it to the camp then you will be able to meditate and we can also talk in detail," he wrote.

I couldn't conceive of travelling alone to Dwaraka so I asked my friends to join me for the trip. No one was interested. Disappointed, I returned to Kathmandu for the *Dasain* holidays with my heart and soul ever pulled by Acharya. I couldn't enjoy the festivities of *Dasain*, and all that merrymaking only made my sadness more pronounced. In the end I decided to make the journey from Kathmandu to Dwaraka alone. The resolution instantly pumped blood into my veins and I started making preparation with great enthusiasm. Although it was the festival season, I easily acquired railway tickets. Everybody seemed eager to help me. After a long trip I reached Dwaraka in faraway Gujarat.

I have a deep connection and attraction with the sea. Even today when I am close to the sea I am filled with a mysterious bliss and contentment. I feel enchanted by the vastness of the body of water, and my ego drops and my consciousness expands and feels peaceful. The loved *leelabhumi* of Krishna, the vastness of the Arabian Sea, and most importantly the joyous presence of Acharya took me to the peak of bliss. It was especially the meditations conducted on the beach at night that proved alchemical. Acharya's presence and his meditation instructions based on death revealed one mystery after another. Everyday was filled with silence, depth and deeper ecstasy.

The discourses he delivered during that meditation camp were transcribed and published under the name *Main Mrityu Sikata Hun* (I Teach the Art of Dying).

Most of the people attending the camp were Gujarati except for a few who were from Bombay. I was the only one who was from elsewhere. For the first time I met a group of young seekers who were blissful and loving and free from all conditioning. Although I was far away from home, I had never felt so much at home in my entire life.

In his first discourse itself, Acharya talked about the potential of spirituality. He said, "The Hindus say, 'the soul is eternal' but no one has experienced it. It is only a repetition of the scriptures. If there is even one self-realized soul in a village, he will be able to transform the whole village. Just as the presence of a graceful woman brings beauty to the whole atmosphere around her, just as a flower fills the whole area with fragrance, a realized soul lifts the consciousness of the whole society. The total number of sannyasins of all creeds in India adds up to more than ten million and they are all chanting, *Shivoham Shivom, Aham Brahmasmi* (I am Shiva, I am Brahma). Some remain naked while others walk around carrying a stick. Some sleep on a bed of nails while others smear ash all over their bodies and look like clowns. Some think it's spiritual to flog themselves and others stay in front of a bonfire in scorching hot afternoons. This is a spiritual circus, not penance. If there were ten million soulful people in our country then it would not be in such a miserable state. They are not saints, they are charlatans. It is because of them that young and educated people are losing interest in religion.

"The common folk are not responsible for this because their consciousness is always low. If there is anyone responsible for this it is the politicians, the priests and the so called saints. Today they are saying that they will improve the character of each individual and make them moral, but this is impossible. The world can only be changed if some people go through the process of intense spiritual transformation. They should become the light that guides society and become the ideals for humanity.

"I need only one hundred such courageous people. If they can be self realized then the whole face of society can be changed. Gurdjieff and Vivekananda also used to say that if they found one hundred dedicated seekers then they can change the map of the world. They couldn't find such one hundred dedicated seekers and had to die disappointed. I also need a hundred people but I am not going to die disappointed. I will travel to each village, I will gaze into each eye and when I see eyes that have the potential to become transformed, I will pull them out of all their problems and I am ready to put all my energy and ability towards their transformation. If you have the courage then come; I will show you the mystery beyond time and space."

These fiery words of Acharya shook me to my core. All night I remained in ecstatic energy. In the morning I wrote a note and gave it to Acharya. It read, "Acharyasri, now you only need to search for 99 people, one has arrived."

RAMAN MAHARSHI

"Raman was in silence most of his life and his silence was totally alive and powerful. It would take seekers to a deeper space and transform them more than did the discourses of many masters. Just one compassionate glance by him would bring deep peace and contentment to many of his devotees."

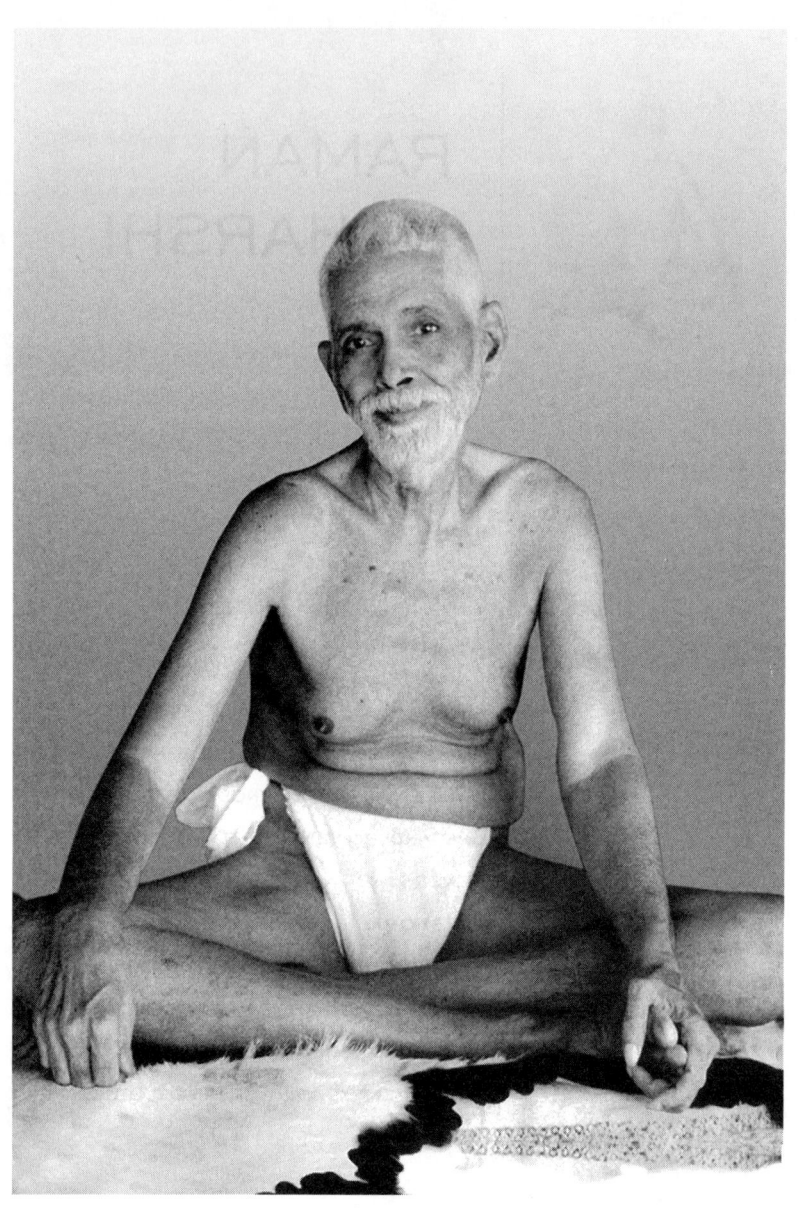

A rare saint lived in South India in the last century. His name was Raman Maharshi. Although fully enlightened, he lived the simplest of lives and remained mostly in silence. He was born at 1.00 am on December 30th 1879 in Tiruchuzhi, a small village in Tamil Nadu, thirty kilometres from Madurai, the famous Hindu pilgrimage in South India. He is considered the *anshavatar*, part manifestation of Shiva. Raman came to his abode, the Arunachal hill, two hundred kilometres east of Madras, at the age of seventeen and lived there for the next fifty-four years. Arunachal is thought to be the Kailash of South India and is considered the physical manifestation of Shiva.

Raman's father, Sundaram Ayyar, was a rural lawyer who was known for his honesty and purity. All the people in the area respected his honesty and truthfulness, even thieves. One day a group of thieves stole goods from a bullock cart. When they found out that the goods belonged to Sundaram, they promptly returned it. Even the thieves did not like robbing him. His mother Alagamma was also equally pure and saintly. When Raman was twelve, his father died and the family's difficult times started. Since they lived in a joint family, Raman's uncle, Subbier, took on the responsibility of Raman's family, and they moved to his house at Madurai. Subbier loved Raman dearly. He was admitted to Scott's Middleschool, but Raman had no interest in formal studies. He would rather spend his time playing, wandering around and meditating in the nearby temples.

Raman was known in his village as the boy with the miraculous touch. If someone had a stomach ache or a headache, they would be instantly cured if he touched them. When guests came to their house, his aunt would make sure that he touched all the food because she had experienced that if he touched it, the food would cook quickly, taste better and would be enough for everyone.

When just a child, Raman was fascinated by a book about the sixty-three famed Tamil Shiva devotees that he had found in his uncle's house. Raman also wanted to be a Shiva devotee and would spend hours meditating in the Shiva temples of the area. He would be completely mesmerized by the spiritual energy of the Meenakshi temple. He would not understand the spiritual phenomenon and would think that he was having a fever, but the experiences there would be utterly blissful and he started to frequently visit the Meenakshi temple to have those experiences.

One day an elderly relative came to visit Subbier's house. Raman asked him where he was from. When the relative said that he was from Arunachal, Raman was thrown into a sudden ecstasy. Raman had often heard of Arunachal but when he realized that the holy hill was a real tangible place on earth that men could visit, he felt a magnetic pull towards Arunachal.

An event that occurred when Raman was seventeen brought about the great turn in his life. One day in mid June 1896, he had the experience of death. In his own words, "The shock of the fear of death drove my mind inwards and I said to myself mentally without actually framing the words, 'Now death has come; what does it mean? What is it that is dying?'"

He felt his consciousness leave his body. His body lay dead but his consciousness felt fully alive. For the first time he experienced the eternal nature of the soul. This event made him absolutely introverted and he lost all interest in his studies and any other external work. Annoyed by his lack of interest in anything, his brother Nagaswami scolded him, "You don't know how to study and neither do you help out in household chores. It is better that you become a wandering monk."

Monkhood was not new to Raman's family. Once, a yogi had come to his ancestor's home begging for alms. When he did not receive anything, to teach them a lesson he forewarned, "May there be a monk in each of your generations." Maybe it was because of this incident that Raman's grandfather put on the ochre robes of a monk and left home with a staff and a water pot. His father's elder brother also became a monk while visiting some relatives and never returned home. But Raman was to become the most famous monk in the family.

One day Nagaswami asked Raman to go and pay his college fees and handed him five rupees. Instead of paying his brother's college fees, Raman used the money to go to Arunachal. When he found out that it cost just three rupees to reach Arunachal, he left two rupees in an envelope along with a note for his brother that became famous later. It said, "I am leaving home in search of my lord as it is his wish. This is a spiritual journey. None of you should be sad and don't waste money and energy trying to find me. I haven't paid your college fees. I have taken three rupees and the rest of the money is in the envelope."

When he reached Madurai station, it was already past the departure time of the train to Villupuram, but miraculously it only left once Raman got on it. A Muslim priest who suddenly appeared in the train saw that Raman was divinely possessed and asked him where he was heading. The priest then informed Raman that the train was going to Tiruvannamalai and disappeared as mysteriously as he had appeared. Raman reached Tiruvannamalai on the morning of September 1st 1896, where after the *darshan* of the Arunachal temple and hill, he went into a deep and blissful trance. After that he never left Arunachal till he left his body on April 14th, 1950.

When he reached Arunachal he had very few possessions with him. However, after the *darshan* of his beloved Arunachal he decided to get rid of whatever little was left with him. It included a little money, food and clothes. He tore a piece from one of his shirts and turned it into a loincloth, which became his only possession from then on. He started meditating inside the temple of the thousand pillars. When others of his age saw that he was entranced in deep meditation they started to play pranks on him. Some would come and shake him while others would throw pebbles at him. When the young Raman was fed up with their pranks he left his spot and started meditating in the basement of the temple where there was a Shivalinga, which was called the Patallingam. The youths stopped bothering him there but the Patallingam was heavily infested by insects since no sunlight reached there. The insects bit him all over his body but Raman, who was in deep *samadhi*, took no notice.

Seeing such deep *vairagya* (detachment) in a young boy, a local *sadhu* Shosadri Swami started to care for Raman. He started protecting Raman from the local boys as well as from the insects. He then shifted Raman to a safe place in a different temple. Slowly

Raman's *vairagya* and his ability to sit in one place, drowned in bliss for days, made him famous in the area. Curious folk started coming to have darshan of this silent young saint. Raman spent time in various temples of Tiruvannamalai and in the end he came to the Virupaksha cave in the Arunachal hill. Eventually Raman Maharshi and the Arunachal hill became synonymous with each other. Due to his presence Arunachal became famous around the world. If someone came and asked him a question, he would only gaze at the questioner with utmost compassion. After a while the questioner's questions would disappear and he would be filled with great peace and spiritual fulfillment.

The Superintendent of British Police in Vellore, F. H. Humphreys, came into contact with Raman Maharshi in the most interesting manner. Humphreys became the Superintendent of Police of Vellore at the age of twenty-one. Due to his past life *sanskars*, Humphreys was a clairvoyant seer and regularly had spiritual visions. While meditating, he started to frequently see the vision of a young saint clad only in a white loincloth sitting on a hill. He made a sketch of his recurrent vision and started showing it around. The locals said that it must be Raman Maharshi of Arunachal.

Humphreys came to Arunachal on his motorcycle all the way from Vellore, eighty-seven kilometres away. He parked his bike at the base of the hill and started scaling it in his heavy policeman's uniform. The extreme midday heat and the uphill climb left Humphreys exhausted and parched. Raman was sitting quietly under a tree as usual. When Humphreys came near him, Raman kept on looking at him without blinking. They were both of the same age. Humphreys couldn't take his eyes off Raman's gaze. After fifteen minutes Humphreys felt as refreshed as he had never been before. His exhaustion disappeared and he felt as if he was bathing under a fresh spring.

Humphreys had come there with countless spiritual questions

but in Raman's presence, his questions started to disappear. Neither did Humphreys ask any question, nor did Raman have to utter a word. Humphreys felt so light that he thought he could fly. Without saying anything to Raman, he started to climb down the hill. He was so elated that he spontaneously broke into a dance. While climbing up he was a serious police officer full of questions and queries; on returning he was happy and joyous like a little boy, without a tinge of worry on his face. Such was Raman Maharshi's magic.

Humphreys was Raman Maharshi's first western disciple and he visited him frequently. His love for Raman started to grow and he asked him if he could leave his profession and give up Christianity. Raman said, "No, you need not renounce anything at all. If the need to renounce is so great then why don't you renounce your assumption that you are this body? Search deeply within for your real self. To go into this search, there is no need to quit your profession or your religion."

Due to the past life *sanskars*, Humphreys had various spiritual powers and after walking on the path laid out by Raman, his powers only increased. He had an unconscious desire to display these powers but due to the continuous guidance of Raman Maharshi, these desires vanished as well. When his meditation ripened, he didn't have the will to continue his profession anymore and resigned from his job. He then started to live and meditate in an ashram in England.

Along with Humphreys, there were a few other seekers from the West who knew the value of Raman Maharshi and made him known to the world. Among them were Paul Brunton, Arthur Osborne, S. S. Cohen and Major A. W. Chadwick.

The English journalist Paul Brunton had come to the East to get answers to his spiritual queries. He travelled around the Indian subcontinent for years, meeting various yogis and visiting countless ashrams. He met many yogis with yogic powers and many others who were yogis just in name. But no one was able to pacify his quest. He then came to meet Raman Maharshi on the counsel of the Shankaracharya of South India. When he reached Arunachal, local pilgrims showed him the way to Raman Maharshi's ashram on top of the hill. Raman was sitting quietly among some devotees. When Brunton got there, Raman Maharshi didn't pay him any attention. Questions raced in his mind but since everyone was in silence, there was no way he would ask them. Raman didn't speak even after thirty minutes and kept staring out the window. Brunton, who carried the ego of a famous journalist, was hurt by this total disregard of his presence. But after another silent hour, Brunton started to feel that his questions were worthless. Their importance started to drop as he entered the world of silent bliss. In Raman Maharshi's presence, Paul Brunton's questions completely dropped. He felt peaceful and content.

Such was the power of Raman's silence. Raman was in silence most of his life and his silence was totally alive and powerful. It would take seekers to a deeper space and transform them more than did the discourses of many masters. Just one compassionate glance by him would bring deep peace and contentment to many of his devotees.

Another such example is that of the Tamil woman Echammal who was in a miserable condition when she came to Raman Maharshi. She had gone through a series of painful events that had devestated her. While she was mourning her husband's death, her daughter and son-in-law also died. Not being able to handle this, she lost her mental stability. Her relatives had taken her to various saints and holy places so that she might regain peace but it hadn't helped. When she arrived at Tiruvannamalai, she heard the name of Raman Maharshi and she climbed Arunachal to meet him. She found him sitting silently in front of the Virupaksha cave. She came in front of him and stared at him for an hour. Raman also poured his compassion on her. This silent *satsang* brought great change in her, and her sorrows started to drop one after another. As dusk approached, she left Raman's transforming presence reluctantly and climbed down the hill. The moment she reached the foothills of Arunachal she was no more the same person. Her heart finally found calmness and peace, and her sorrows left her forever.

After this incident Echammal bought a house at the foothills of Arunachal and started living there. For the next thirty years she made lunch for Raman Maharshi and fed him every day before she took her own meal. Her house became a free lodge for the devotees of Raman, who had started coming from all around the world. She spent her entire life and savings serving Raman Maharshi and his devotees who came to meet him.

Raman Maharshi was the epitome of simplicity. He lived what he preached. It so happened that the first President of independent India, Dr. Rajendra Prasad came to visit Raman Maharshi in his ashram, at the base of Arunachal. The ashramites started cleaning and decorating the ashram for the occasion. It was the tradition at Raman ashram to feed animals first, followed by the beggars and guests. Ashram residents would be the last to eat. This practice started by Raman is still in play in the ashram.

On that day the beggars and monks were told to stay under a tree a little further away from the ashram and that they would be fed there. The president came and went straight to Raman's hut to meet him. But he was not there. Everyone was perplexed because Raman never really left his hut. The president waited for him there and the ashramites started to search for Raman throughout the ashram but couldn't find him anywhere. After a long search, they found Raman sitting under the same tree designated for the beggars. The Ashram residents persuaded him to come back to his hut. Once he reached the hut, Rajendra Prasad touched Raman's feet in reverence and asked him why he was sitting with the beggars.

Raman answered, "It was repeatedly announced in the ashram that the beggars should go and wait for their meal under that tree. I also have been a begging monk my whole life. That's why I went and stayed with the other beggars."

Osho has said, "Raman and Ramakrishna are the manifestations of purity and detachment. Just remembering them can bring peace and serenity to one's heart."

Raman Maharshi used to say that silence is the most powerful and unending form of speech. For those who do not understand silence, the master uses words but with great difficulty. This is because truth is beyond words and words can never explain it.

Someone asked Raman Maharshi, "Why don't you give discourses?"

His answer was, "People don't change even after listening to hours of spiritual discourse. They return without any meaningful change in their being. But if they just sit silently in the presence of a saint a certain purity seeps into their being. Silence is the most powerful action and initiation."

As I have heard, a famous educationist of Nepal, Sri Rudraraj Pandey, reached Arunachal while on a pilgrimage. While performing *pooja* to the *Shivalanga* at the *garvagriha* of the Shiva temple there, he saw an image of Raman Maharshi sitting in the place of the Shivalinga. Being stunned by the mystifying experience, he went to the base of the Arunachal hill to have a *darshan* of Raman Maharshi. As far as I know, he was the first Nepali to have the darshan of Raman Maharshi. It has been more than half a century since Raman Maharshi left his body but such events still occur in the lives of many devotees.

In November 1989, I went on a spiritual tour to South India with a few of my friends. One of our destinations was Arunachal. The closer our bus came to Tiruvannamalai, the more blissful I felt.

We took a rickshaw from the bus station. I was so eager to reach the ashram and the pace of the rickshaw was so slow that I felt like getting off and pushing it so that it would gather some speed. When we had the first glimpse of Raman Ashram, my heart started beating violently. I was so touched by the sight that for a while I did not have awareness of my body.

It was difficult to find accommodation in the ashram during winter. Most of the visitors were staying in guesthouses near the ashram. I really wanted to stay in the ashram itself so I met the coordinator, V. Venkataraman, nephew of Raman Maharshi, and pleaded with him to let us stay there. He realized that we had traveled a long way from Nepal and saw the desperation in our request, so he took the trouble of moving people around to prepare two rooms for us. We found out that anyone who wanted to stay in the ashram had to make prior reservation. The reservation included free accommodation and food for a maximum of three days. Those who were lucky enough to find ashram accommodation did not have to pay, but they could donate according to their wish. We were very happy to get rooms there and I wanted to donate a thousand rupees immediately, but Venkataraman said that donations were only taken at the end of the stay. When I insisted he take the donation right away, he heeded my request.

The main attraction of Raman Maharshi Ashram is the room where he had stayed. My friends started to say that they wanted to go there immediately, but I persuaded them to have a shower and change into fresh clothes before visiting the sacred abode of Raman.

We spend as much time as possible in Raman Maharshi's room for the next three days sitting silently in his formless but intense presence. Apart from Raman's room, the place that attracted me the most in the ashram was their kitchen. While in his body, Raman Maharshi would wake up at three in the morning and go to the kitchen to prepare breakfast. He would always be the first one there. Other ashramites would join him later. Raman Maharshi breathed life into anything he cooked, and made the tastiest meals.

The kitchen rules of Raman Ashram might appear rather absurd to a visitor. Raman Maharshi believed that variety in cuisine distracts a seeker's mind. Thus the same recipe is prepared in the ashram 365 days a year: Idli, coconut chutney and coffee for breakfast; rice, sambar and salty buttermilk for lunch; one cup of coffee or milk in the afternoon; and again rice, sambar and buttermilk for dinner. If a devotee brings something special, it is distributed equally among everyone. Some of my friends were worried at the prospect of eating the same thing every day.

Osho has said, "Food in hotels might look good but it is usually dead. There is no life force in that food. Simple food cooked with love might not look attractive but it is alive and is full of *prana* energy."

This is why the food made in temples, *teerthas* and ashrams have a special taste and give a different kind of satisfaction. Simple vegetarian food is made in the Sujata kitchen at Tapoban, our ashram in Kathmandu, but most who eat there praise the food. They are actually praising the *prana* energy of the food.

It is because Raman Maharshi spent years cooking in the kitchen that the food there has a divine quality. I have not tasted such good food anywhere else in the world. I have always been hypnotized by the food in Raman Ashram. Day after day, the plain recipe of the ashram grew increasingly tastier. The food was so fulfilling that after finishing my meals I felt like eating the banana leaf as well on which the food was served. I realized that honesty and purity fills each mundane thing with divinity and bliss.

There is no daily program at Raman Ashram. Ashramites begin the day chanting Sanskrit *shlokas* at the Samadhi of Raman and his mother. Just as when he was in his body, Raman's room remains open for everyone today as well. Most of the seekers who come there spend their time sitting in silence in that room. Some who can climb the Arunachal hill also visit the Virupaksha cave and Skanda Ashram where Raman had stayed before he came down to the bigger ashram at the base of Arunachal.

Arunachal is a famous *teertha* for all Hindus but it has become famous around the world due to Raman Ashram. Seekers come here from around the world. During the winter months, the area around the ashram is teeming with international seekers and tourists. Many stay here for as long as their visa allows them. The whole area vibrates with strong spiritual energy. There is an otherworldly peace and beauty in this place. I realized here how one enlightened person can charge a place with the vibrations of truth that is helpful for seekers even years after he has left his body.

PARAMHANSA YOGANANDA

> "The night was silent and cool and the master's presence was very palpable. Suddenly, I was seized by this intense desire to look at the person who was wearing the robe. I looked up and what I saw left me dumbfounded! Paramhansa himself was looking at me and smiling. He stood that way for next few seconds and disappeared into thin air, just like that."

Steve Jobs, one of the greatest innovators of the century, in his last days, planned each detail of his own memorial service to be held at Stanford University in October 2011. Each attendee received a brown box as a farewell gift. This last souvenir, which Jobs believed could do justice to his extraordinary life was a book, the book that had inspired and shaped his spiritual journey - *Autobiography of A Yogi*.

The book has remained a close companion throughout my spiritual journey. I have read this book countless times. It has silenced my doubts when the path seemed precarious, reassured me when the inexplicable unfolded and meditation took me to the eclectic lands of mystery. The journey of spirituality is too mysterious and enigmatic for words. The relationship between a master and disciple is the greatest love affair possible. We can forgive the limitations of language for not being able to truly reflect its essence. And yet, whatever could be captured in words, *Autobiography of A Yogi* has expressed it all. We can never thank Swami Yogananda enough for giving this exceptional gift to the world. Paramhansa Yogananda was born on 5 January 1893 at Gorakhphur, a city near the border of Nepal. His father, Bhagwaticharan Ghosh, was a high-ranking officer in the Indian Railway. Yogananda's childhood name was Mukunda Lal Ghosh. In 1915, he took formal vows into the monastic Swami Order from Sri Yukteshwor Giri and became 'Swami Yogananda Giri'. Sri Yukteshwor Giri later decorated him with the title "Paramhansa". Paramahansa means "supreme swan" and is a title indicating the highest spiritual attainment. Swamiji's parents were the disciples of Lahari Mahashaya who was the direct disciple of Mahavatar Babaji, the primary Guru of the great tradition of Kriya Yoga. Mahavatar Babaji is believed to have been living in the Indian Himalayas near Badrinath in his physical body for thousands of years. It is said that Shankaracharya and Kabir were initiated by Mahavatar Babaji. Babaji is said to have defied the laws of time and is blessed with eternal youth. There is no trace of aging in his body. Babaji comes to Prayag in each Kumbha Mela, the largest gathering of Indian holy men that happens every 12 years. He still guides seekers who are very advanced in their path.

In the Kumbha Mela of January 1884, Mahavatar Babaji gave *darshan* to Sri Yukteshwor Giri and told him, "The future of the world is only possible if there is equal exchange between the East and the West. There has been great materialistic growth in the West, but no spiritual progress to match its proportion. I hear the cry of many Western souls who are seeking spiritual solace. Very soon I will send you a disciple whom you will have to train in the secrets of Kriya Yoga and send him to the West." Later, that inspired young man became Paramhansa Yogananda.

It must be the same spiritual call that inspired Swami Vivekananda, Shivapuri Baba, Prabhupad, Maharshi Mahesh Yogi and Osho to go to the West. And it is the same call for which my Guru wants me to travel around the West and conduct spiritual activities.

Yogananda was marked with unusual awareness and longing for spiritual experiences. Once, Yogananda's mother took her son to her Guru, Lahari Mahashaya, to be blessed by him. Lahari Mahashaya took the child in his lap, stroked his forehead affectionately and said, "This child will become a great Yogi. He will act like a spiritual engine and pull a lot of souls to the Kingdom of God."

Yogananda had a keen attraction towards saints and sannyasins since he was a young boy. The members of his family were surprised to see such spiritual ardour and divine faith in such a young child. He had a deep desire to go and meditate in the Himalayas. Once he even ran away from home to fulfill this purpose. He had reached Banaras and scouted around many ashrams there. In one such trip while he was walking the streets of Kashi, he saw an ochre-robed sannyasin with divine radiance. The sannyasin was looking at him, smiling. Yogananda realized that he was the same person he had seen in his visions many times.

"Oh my love, finally you have come to me. I have been waiting for you for years," said the sannyasin in a blissful voice. Yogananda also realized that this was none other than his enlightened Guru who would later guide *him* towards enlightenment too. As was the existential plan, after this meeting with his Guru, Yukteshwor Giri, Yogananda's life took a complete turn.

Yogananda moved to Serampore, a city close to Kolkata, where Yukteshwor Giri had a small ashram. Yogananda spent most of his time in his Guru's hermitage while pursuing his higher studies. Swamiji practiced his yoga and meditation with utmost devotion and patience for the next ten years. Although he had no interest in completing his studies, Swamiji's Guru insisted he complete them.

"You have to pass your BA examinations. A Yogi with a degree will be more effective in the West," he used to tell him.

Swamiji has beautifully described these years he spent in close proximity to his beloved Guru in *Autobiography of A Yogi*. He spent most of his time at the ashram and practiced meditation. One night when Swamiji was staying with Yukteshwor Giri and enjoying the beauty of the night, suddenly his master inquired about his BA final exams.

Yogananda was as though awakened from a spell, and realized the exams were just around the corner. He replied nervously, "The exams start in five days but I haven't prepared for them at all. It is sure that I will fail, so I had better not appear in the exams."

Yukteshwor Giri wouldn't listen to his disciple's plan and ordered him, "You have to appear in the exams. If you don't then your family will also be sad and it will also be a barrier in the divine plan. You appear in the exams and God will surely help you."

As ordered by his Guru, Yogananda went to his friend Ramesh and studied all night. Miraculously, whatever he studied in the night was to be be asked in the exams. But in the English exams, Yogananda calculated that he would get no more than 33 marks when the pass mark was 36. He went straight to his Guru's ashram and told him that he would surely fail in English.

"Don't worry, the sun and moon might change their course but you will certainly pass your BA exams," Shri Yukteshwor said to Yogananda.

When the results came out, Yogananda found out that in that particular year the Bengal University had reduced the pass marks of English from 36 to 33. Elated and perplexed he went straight to his Guru and prostrated at his feet. Sri Yukteshwor smiled and lovingly said to him, "God probably found it easier to pass you than to change the course of the sun and the moon."

Soon after Yogananada graduated from college in 1920, he received the invitation to participate in the International Conference of the Religious Liberals in Boston. Before he left for America, Mahavatar Babaji gave him a darshan and said, "Always remain fearless; you shall always be divinely protected."

Yukteshwor Giri also lifted his spirits by saying, "All doors are open to you now. Go to America. Spiritual energy will enter through the eyes of any person you gaze at and their spiritual journey will be kick started. Even if you are in the middle of a dense forest, you will find a friend."

His Guru's blessings came true. Wherever Yogananda went in America, he found a friend and through their help he established the headquarters of the Yogoda Satsang Society in Los Angeles in 1925.

In 1946, Yogananda published his book, *Autobiography of a Yogi*. The book is an enduring international best-seller. Over a thousand copies of the book are sold every day worldwide. It has been translated into all major languages of the world.

Yogananda took the United States of America by storm and had achieved much fame in a very short period. But when he returned from the United States in 1935 for a short period to meet his master for the last time, he was still longing to be praised verbally by him. One day when they were alone together he said, "Guru, when I came to you, I was only a kid. Today, my hair is already greying. Do you remember? You have expressed your love for me verbally only in your first meeting. I know that your love for me is immense but why are my ears so desperate to hear those words from you?"

Yukteshwor Giri smiled at Yogananda and said, "Be it as you wish. When I was a householder before I took sannyas, I had desired a son whom I wanted to grow up to become a great yogi. But my wife died before I had a son and the desire lay buried deep in my unconscious. When you came into my life, you fulfilled that desire too and liberated me from all desires."

Tears rolled down Sri Yukteshwor Giri's cheek. He embraced Swamiji and said, "Yogananda, I have loved you and will love you always."

A master always liberates his disciples. But sometimes, disciples like Yogananda can become a medium to release even their master from the bondage of desires.

After making arduous efforts to preach the spiritual significance of yoga in the West for thirty-two years, Yogananda left his body in California on March 7th 1952. On that day he was attending a dinner party for Binay Ranjan Sen, the visiting Indian Ambassador to the United States, at the Biltmore Hotel in Los Angeles. At the end of the feast Swamiji spoke about the possibility of a "United World" through the cohesion of the East and the West. According to Daya Mata, a direct disciple of Yogananda, who was head of the Self Realization Fellowship from 1955-2010, Swamiji concluded his speech with his poem *My India*.

> "...where Ganges, woods, Himalayan caves and men dream God
> I am hallowed my body touched that sod."

As soon as he finished the last verse of his poem he raised his eyes to his third eye and his body flopped on the floor.

His body is preserved in Forest Lawn Memorial Park Cemetery in Glendale, California.

Yogananda's death was also miraculous. His body was kept on display for twenty days before they interred it. During that time, it did not emit any foul odour nor show any visible sign of decay. The director of the Memorial Park, Harry T. Rowe, has described this event in a letter, "The absence of any visual signs of decay in the dead body of Paramahansa Yogananda offers the most extraordinary case in our experience... No physical disintegration was visible in his body even twenty days after death... No indication of mold was visible on his skin, and no visible drying up took place in the bodily tissues. This state of perfect preservation of a body is, so far as we know from mortuary annals, an unparalleled one... No odor of decay emanated from his body at any time."

THE UNEXPECTED MEETING

Between 2005 and 2010 I conducted several meditation retreats on a ferry in West Bengal through the Sundarban Delta and Ganga Sagar. I always visit the Belurmath and Dakshineswar temples whenever I am in Kolkata. During my stay in the city, I also visit Yogananda Ashram in Dakshineswar and Swami Yogananda's house at 4 Garpar Road, where he was born. I have met some of Swamiji's family members including his brother Sananda Lal Ghosh's son, Hare Krishna Ghosh. I also met the granddaughter of his younger brother, Ananta, at Serampore.

At the 4 Garpar Road House we were greeted by Mr Hare Krishna Ghosh, the son of Sananda and nephew of Swamiji. Mr Ghosh was taking care of the house in those days. He was a rather amicable person. We talked at length about Swamiji. I told him I was an admirer of Swamiji and had written several articles on him and spoken about him on national radio and television. He was kind enough to allow us to meditate in the small attic room where Swamiji attained enlightenment. It was empty except for a small altar with Swamiji's picture and a shelf with a few photos and relics. Swamiji has written in detail about his stay in that house in *Autobiography of A Yogi*. The room was still vibrating with his strong presence. Sitting in that tiny room for half an hour I was absorbed into deep meditation.

After the meditation, Mr Ghosh showed us around the place. Swamiji had presented a lot of things to him: a tea set, Swamiji's clothes and many of his rare pictures. Mr Ghosh was showing me a photo album and both of us were totally absorbed in the photos. He told me that Swamiji and Indian poet, Rabindranath Tagore, came from the same ancestral root. When we were busy peering at the family tree, from the corner of my eye I noticed a bright orange robe fluttering behind Mr Ghosh. I thought perhaps it was someone from the house. Mr Ghosh was talking in a deep sonorous Bengali accent. The night was silent and cool and the master's presence was very palpable. I was blissed out.

We spent a long time leafing through the pictures, and the robe kept fluttering in the background. Suddenly, I was seized by this intense desire to look at the person who was wearing the robe. I looked up and what I saw left me dumbfounded! Swami Yogananda himself was looking at me and smiling. He stood that way for the next few seconds and disappeared into thin air, just like that.

THE VISION OF HIS SAMADHI

In the eastern religions, there is a tradition of preserving the dead body of an enlightened being safely without cremating it. There are reasons for this. In the Hindu religion, the body of a normal person is cremated. After the body is cremated, the bioplasma of the body slowly diffuses into the sky. The body of a person is cremated so as to disrupt their attachment to their physical body after the death, and free their consciousness. The body of an enlightened master however, is preserved as it is, because it radiates very strong spiritual vibrations and creates a buddhafield around it. Prayers and meditation are natural in such places and the visitor receives spiritual blessings. The *samadhi* or burial spots of such enlightened masters are sacred spaces on this earth that can immensely help the transformation of seekers who come there.

In 2007, I visited the Self Realization Fellowship (SRF)

Hermitage at Encinitas, California. A very close and dedicated disciple of Swamiji, Rajarshi Janaknanda purchased this beautiful property for his beloved master. He was so much concerned about Swamiji's comfort that when Swamiji left for India in 1935, Rajarshi purchased a car and had it shipped on the same ship Swamiji was travelling in. Rajarshi had often heard Swamiji profess his love for the ocean. When Swamiji returned from India, Rajarshi decided to buy a beautiful cottage by the ocean for his master as a surprise gift. Swamiji instantly loved the place and spent a considerable part of his life there. Swamiji wrote *Autobiography of a Yogi* at the Hermitage.

The property overlooks the vast Pacific Ocean that silences the cacophony of the world behind and fills the place with blissful quietude. I walked through the neatly maintained garden dotted with fishponds, vines, cactuses and gnarled trees. The place is a work of art. Each vine, each tree, each flower was still fragrant with the memory of Swamiji, who must have walked down the path countless times. I could almost smell his fragrance.

There is an elegant cottage, where Swamiji lived. I wanted to visit the place and meditate, but was told the cottage is open briefly only on Sundays for visitors. Only special guests were allowed in non-scheduled time. I requested they allow me in as I had travelled a long way just to sit down in the cottage and meditate. Of course, my request was not entertained.

Because of the uncompromising schedule I had to give up my wish, and had to wait for one more year. In 2008 I visited the place again, making sure I arrived there on Sunday, and right on their schedule. There was a powerful energy-field around the place. The visitors are not allowed to enter his bedroom. One can only get the *darshan* of the room from the gate outside. I sat down in the porch and meditated. I have visited almost all places associated with Swamiji including his house in Kolkata, Sri Yukeshwor Giri's *samadhi* in Puri, his ashram at Serampore, his headquarters for the SRF at Beverly Hills, and Lake Shrine, Pacific Palisades and other ashrams and retreat centres in California. I have felt his strongest presence in his small attic room in Kolkata and in his cottage in the Hermitage garden at Encinitas.

As I sat down for meditation I had a vivid vision that Swamiji's body from the Forest Memorial Lawn should be brought here and a *samadhi* be built around it. The vision left me bewildered. I couldn't make head or tail of it. I had already visited the Forest Lawn Memorial Park. I saw that Swamiji's body was stacked among the bodies of non-meditators. In the beginning, I dismissed the vision as a mere projection. But soon, this idea started appearing regularly in my meditation. I tried to avoid the vision but it became increasingly difficult to do so. I tried to meet Daya Mata, who was the President of SRF then but I was told that she was in silent retreat and was only accessible to the senior disciples of Swamiji.

Every SRF temple has its own beauty. They are not just charged with spiritual energy but are also equally aesthetic and elegant. However, I realized that the retreat centres have become very rigid and mechanical. For instance, the SRF Hermitage at Encinitas and other centres in America open exactly at 10.00am and close at 5.00pm. The Californian summer afternoons are very hot, humid and uncomfortable. The sun sets late and the weather becomes pleasant after 7.00 in the evening, or in the early morning. If they could structure their schedule to make it more convenient for meditators who want to spend a longer time and soak the energy available there, it would be a welcomed feat.

Since I couldn't meet Daya Mata, I tried to explain the vision to some of the officials at Encinitas Hermitage and Lake Shrine Retreat. I was mocked, and they argued that if Swami Yogananda had desired such he certainly would have advised some of his senior disciples. To be honest, I do not have an answer to this. It sounds logical that he would have done so, but this idea keeps occurring in my meditation persistently. Many other enlightened masters, including Osho, have confirmed for me that the *samadhi* be built for the benefit of seekers and that's why I am inspired regularly in this regard.

When I told them that his body should either be brought to India or a *samadhi* should be built in America, one of the officials frowned upon my suggestion and said, "Do you know the cost of transporting the body from America to India? Who will bear the cost?"

It wasn't a call I could avoid, so I told him I would bear the cost. When I said that, they remarked, "But he was not born for India. He was born for America. Yukteshwor Giri sent him to America." I am not against building his *samadhi* in America. In fact, Swamiji has some of the most beautiful ashrams in the United States and his body should be consecrated in one of those ashrams. In California alone there are half a dozen beautiful SRF centres.

Even after the death of an enlightened master, seekers can still benefit from the energy emanating from the bodies of the masters. That's why there is a tradition of building *samadhis* of an enlightened being. There are certain rules and criteria that need to be maintained to preserve the energy and the sanctity of such places.

It is ironic that the body of a great yogi like Paramhansa Yogananda has been placed amongst the corpses of other non-spiritual, non-meditative people. The place where the body of Paramhansa is kept does not have any sanctity maintained. It fills me with sadness to see how his last treasure, his physical body that embodied the rare soul, is not given the due respect it deserves. There is not even any facility to sit in silence near his body.

It is a great loss to humanity that Swami Yogananda's body should be secluded in a mortuary, while millions of seekers could have easily benefitted if only his body had been interred in a proper *samadhi*.

Even today, the vision haunts me. Swamiji is not in his body anymore. It is up to us to allow ourselves to materialize this auspicious task. It is my humble request to all the devotees of Swami Yogananda and his lovers to think in this direction, and if this idea appeals to you, please extend your hands at materializing this long-cherished dream of mine.

RAMAKRISHNA PARAMHANSA

> " RAMAKRISHNA WAS BORN ON THIS EARTH TO ESTABLISH A CULTURE OF TOLERANCE AND INTEGRATION. THERE WAS A BEAUTY AND SPECIALTY IN HIS EXPRESSION OF GODLINESS AS HE WAS CONSTANTLY IN TUNE WITH DIVINE CONSCIOUSNESS. "

Ramakrishna Paramhansa

There is a small village called Kumarkupur seventy kilometres north-west of Kolkata. In that village, a divine child was born on February 18th 1836 in the house of a poor Brahmin couple, Khudiram Chatopadhya and Chandramani Devi.

Ramakrishna was not an ordinary child, he had his first experience of *samadhi* when he was around nine years old. Ramakrishna was walking by a paddy field. The sky was covered with black clouds, heavy with monsoon. Suddenly a flock of white cranes that were nesting nearby in the wetlands were roused and flew away. It looked as though lightning had flashed across the dark cloudy sky; the sight was breathtaking. Ramakrishna beheld this beautiful sight and went into a deep trance. He had no awareness of the outside world and fell on the field as if unconscious. His family members were worried and didn't realize that Ramakrishna was experiencing one of the highest states of meditation.

After this event, Ramakrishna had such experiences of *bhav samadhi* countless times throughout his life. When he turned seventeen Ramakrishna came to Kolkata with his brother. Since he didn't have much interest in either studying or having a vocation, he had been sent to Kolkata, but he had no interest in pursuing a vocation just to maintain his life-style.

There was a religious woman named Rani Rasmani, a low-caste woman who was married into an aristocratic family. She was preparing for a pilgrimage to Banaras with a hundred boats full of goods to donate there. The night before she left, she saw Goddess Kali in a dream.

"Instead of going to Banaras and making donations there, build a temple for me on the bank of the Ganga River. There I shall receive your offering daily," said Kali.

She built a beautiful Kali temple at Dakshineswar, Kolkata, which is known today simply as Dakshineswar Kali Temple. Traditionally a priest of any Hindu temple needs to be a Brahmin, but since the temple was built by a low-caste woman, no Brahmin was ready to be the priest at Dakshineswar. In the end, due to their poverty, Ramakrishna's older brother, Ramkumar became the priest of the temple. After the initial rituals of consecrating the Kali statue, he started living at Dakshineswar along with Ramakrishna. After some time Ramakrishna replaced his brother as the priest of the temple.

Rani Rasmani and her brother-in-law, Mathurababu, had profound love for and trust in Ramakrishna. Ramakrishna was a very intuitive person and didn't follow rituals mechanically. On certain days he would perform *pooja* all day long, and on other days he wouldn't even bother to open the gates of the temple.

Sometimes he would taste the food before offering it to the Goddess, and sometimes he would even be seen quarrelling with her. People were shocked by these seemingly bizarre activities of Ramakrishna and pressured Mathurababu to get rid of him. But Mathurababu had an unusual trust in Ramakrishna.

One day Rani Rasmani asked Ramakrishna to sing a *bhajan*, a devotional song. Ramakrishna started singing a hymn for Kali. While he was singing, Rasmani started to play with the flowers that were meant for the *pooja*. Ramakrishna couldn't tolerate this unconscious behaviour and slapped Rasmani. It was very outrageous to slap Rani and it could have cost Ramakrishna dearly. Everybody gathered around Rani and pressured her to punish Ramakrishna. They advised her that she should immediately fire him, but she said, "It wasn't Ramakrishna but Kali herself who punished me for my unawareness. His courage speaks for itself. He is a man of God, or else he would never have dared to do so."

After that event, Rani Rasmani's devotion towards Ramakrishna became more crystallized and she started to worship him as a saint, although she received lots of complaints about Ramakrishna's ways as they were very spontaneous and far from what was expected from a traditional priest.

A rebellious and authentic person doesn't care much for traditional norms. But ironically traditions begin once followers start emulating the ways of a rebel. The way a charismatic person talks and walks becomes the norm as other people copy it, and a new culture is born. There was a new culture after Buddha, which was known as the Buddhist culture. After Mahavir was the Jain culture, and after Krishna came the devotional culture. A new culture is born only after an enlightened master comes on Earth.

Such awakened ones don't care a bit about the old tradition. The old tradition is for people who don't want change and have no desire for self-transformation. For a normal person tradition might be necessary to maintain discipline, but when an extraordinary person is born, his consciousness cannot be bound by any outside discipline or rules because such consciousness is born to bring about a new revolution, new culture and to show the path towards a higher consciousness.

Ramakrishna was born on this earth to establish a culture of tolerance and integration. There was a beauty and specialty in his expression of godliness as he was constantly in tune with divine consciousness. He was the first saint to experience and announce that all religions lead to the same end: God. During his time there was a great divide between religions and there was lack of tolerance among people of different creeds. Each claimed that he was the only true representative of God. During such a time, Ramakrishna Paramhansa, who was born into a poor Brahmin family, also gave birth to the thought that all religions are true and equal in essence. A more modern version of this thought and its practical application can be seen in Osho. He didn't establish his own religion, but explained the divineness, greatness and religiousness hidden in all religions.

There are many instances of mystical events in the life of Ramakrishna Paramhansa. While worshipping Kali one day, he had a strong feeling that if Kali is real then she should show herself to him. He was overtaken by this feeling and started to cry. His prayer intensified. At one point the intensity was so much that he took a sword that was hung on the wall of the temple and said to the statue of Kali, "If you don't show yourself today then I will slash my own throat." And when he actually was about to do it, Kali appeared and stopped him from doing so. This is how he got the first *darshan* of Kali. That mysterious event changed Ramakrishna's life, as the statue of Kali that was just stone for everyone else came alive to

Ramakrishna. It was no more a statue but the Goddess herself. After that day, Kali and Ramakrishna had a relationship like that of a mother and son. Whenever in trouble, Ramakrishna would go into the temple and would ask for direction from Kali, just like a son would from his mother.

The temple still exists and millions come and pay homage to the Goddess. When we see, we only see a beautiful statue, but for Ramakrishna, she was Durga Bhawani fully manifested.

Ramakrishna didn't have to go anywhere to look for a master. Masters would arrive looking for him. When he was twenty-five, one day Brahmani Bhairavi Saadhvi came to Dakshineswar looking for him. She said, "You have been hiding so I came here looking for you."

Bhairavi was a master on the path of tantra. She initiated him into it, and with her help Ramakrishna learned the sixty-four difficult techniques of tantra, and mastered them. By practicing them he was able to see every woman as *devi*, or Goddess, and realized that the feminine force was the original creative force in existence. Subsequently he regarded every female of this existence as the mother divine.

After this, Ramakrishna learned the various devotional states from Baishnav saint and devotee of Ram, Jatadhari. Jatadhari carried with him a statue of Lord Ram as a child, and called it Ramlala. Ramlala talked with Jatadhari and also quarrelled with him like a little child. After meeting Ramakrishna, Ramlala did not want to leave him. For others it was just a statue but for Ramakrishna it was Ram himself. To be able to have *darshan* of a God or Goddess through a statue is the climax of devotion or *bhakti*. Only the purest devotees can have such experiences.

One day Ramakrishna was overpowered by the devotional feeling of Hanuman, the monkey devotee of Ram. All day and all night he chanted the various names of Ram. He also began to live like a monkey, spending most of the time in trees. He would put on a tail and jump around like a monkey. He was in this trance-like state until he had the *darshan* of Ram and his consort Sita. Such mysterious happenings seem fantastic to us, but for a pure, devoted heart nothing is impossible. After these events, a Vedanti *naga* swami, or naked saint, called Totapuri Baba came to meet him. He told Ramakrishna he should be initiated into Vedanta. Ramakrishna replied he would go and ask mother Kali if that was all right. When he asked her she said, "It's all right. It was I who called him here. He will give you the experience of *samadhi* through the path of Vedanta and you will teach him devotion. This mysterious event has been arranged by me. Go and learn what he has to teach you."

Totapuri Baba initiated Ramakrishna and taught him the way to meditate on the state of nothingness. Whenever Ramakrishna meditated on the third eye, he would see the image of Kali. Seeing that he couldn't go beyond the image of Kali, Totapuri Baba said, "When you see her image again, let me know and then I will do something about it." Ramakrishna sat in meditation. Immediately the image of Kali came to his third eye, and he indicated to Totapuri. Totapuri took a piece of sharp glass, and made a cut with it on Ramakrishna's forehead at the third eye. This made Kali disappear from Ramakrishna's meditation. He was then able to experience the ultimate state of *nirvikalpa samadhi*. It takes lives for yogis to reach this state, but Ramakrishna achieved it on the day of his initiation itself. After this, Ramakrishna was in a trance for three days, and he remained in uninterrupted meditation seated in one place. This surprised Totapuri. The rules of wandering monks, or *paribrajakas,* does not allow them to stay in one place for more than three nights, but due to the deep friendship between Totapuri and Ramakrishna, Totapuri couldn't leave Dakshineswar for eighteen months.

When Ramakrishna came out of his *samadhi*, he started

dancing like the most ardent devotee. Totapuri had never seen or heard of anyone else with such a combination of meditation and devotion. This is why he found Ramakrishna extremely unique. It was a divine plan that Totapuri stayed at Dakshineswar for such a long time. While he was there, he experienced a severe bout of cholera. He didn't recover even after medication. He was a yogi who had no attachment to his body. Now the body was weak, he thought it impossible to take care of it anymore, and felt it was time to leave his body. He decided he would leave his body by drowning in the Ganga that night.

When it was night-time, he went to the Ganga. He stepped in and walked around in the water, but couldn't find any place deeper than his waist. Tired and bemused, he met Ramakrishna in the morning and said, "What kind of mystery is this? I can't understand it. I was unable to find a place that could drown me in the Ganga that has the depth of two to three bamboos. Please go and ask mother Kali what is the mystery behind this event."

Ramakrishna went to Kali and asked her what was behind Totapuri's experience. Kali answered, "Totapuri has immense ego about his meditation. I had to show him that without my wish no one can even leave their body. Nothing is possible without my wish. Go and tell him that." When Totapuri Baba heard this, his ego shattered. He went into the Kali temple for the first time, and had the *darshan* of Kali there. After this event, his health recovered, and his spiritual journey ended. Having fulfilled the purpose of being at Dakshineswar, he left there the same day. Ramakrishna learned Vedanta from him, and he in turn learned devotion from Ramakrishna.

In 1866 when Ramakrishna was thirty, a Sufi saint by the name of Govinda Rai arrived in Dakshineswar. Govinda Rai initiated Ramakrishna into Islam, and Ramakrishna started to practice the ways of Islam. In those days he used to recite the Muslim prayer called *namaj* five times a day, and started to live like a devout Muslim. He didn't even look at a Hindu temple.

Ramakrishna's specialty was that whatever he did, he did it totally. This is also the philosophy of Osho. That whatever you do, you should do it with totality or not attempt it at all because transcendence is possible only through total effort. Ramakrishna achieved the ultimate state possible for a Muslim in just three days and he also had the darshan of Prophet Mohammad. This feat takes a Muslim seeker years of penance. He was able to have self-realization through the path of Islam as well.

In 1874 he had a vision of Christ and Madonna while he was sitting in the garden at Dakshineswar. After a few days he saw a person with divine grace and beautiful big eyes walking towards him. He realized that the person was Jesus himself. Jesus hugged Ramakrishna and became one with him. As Jesus disappeared, Ramakrishna experienced the peak of love.

Ramakrishna experienced God through many paths and through his life he established the fact that all paths lead to God but they all need true dedication. These were not mere words for Ramakrishna but the experience of his life. "There is no need to change your religion. What is necessary is to change your mind," he used to say, and this was the crux of his teaching. Having experienced God through all paths, and having no more desire left in him, Ramakrishna had the need to share his love. When desire ceases, the same desire becomes compassion. Desire has its own pain, and so does compassion. The first pain is that it wants to get something and the second is that it wants to share something. There is a pain that wants more happiness and there is another pain that wants to take away the pain of others. But both are pains. In this world, the worldly man is sad because he cannot fulfill his desire, and the saint is sad because he cannot find anyone with whom he can share his wealth.

One day while Ramakrishna was in a deep meditative trance, his consciousness entered the astral world. He saw many gods and goddesses on both sides of his path. After he went beyond even the astral world of thoughts, he saw the *Saptarishis* in their light form. He then realized, "These *rishis* are higher than the Gods of wisdom, detachment, purity and love."

Suddenly his consciousness took the form of a little boy, hugged one of the *rishis* from the back and said, "I am taking birth on Earth, you should come there too." The *rishi* opened his eyes and said, "You go, I will arrive soon." Even before his chief disciple, Narendra (Swami Vivekananda), came to him, Ramakrishna had told everyone about him. Whenever someone asked Ramakrishna to explain the Vedanta philosophy, he would be unable to explain it clearly, and he would say, "Wait, Narendra, a disciple of mine, is coming He will be able to explain this to you."

When Ramakrishna saw Vivekananda for the first time, and seeing his introverted, pure and detached eyes, he instantly realized he was one of the same *rishis* as those from the land of the Saptarishis. Vivekananda was a logician who did not believe in God. When he came to meet Ramakrishna, he didn't have any trust in him either. Whenever he met a saint, he would ask, "Have you seen God? And the God that you talk of, can you show him to me?"

He asked the same question of Ramakrishna who simply said, "I am seeing God more clearly than I am seeing you. I meet him every moment and converse with him. Do you want to meet him? I can arrange the meeting right now."

And suddenly, he touched Vivekananda's chest with his feet. Vivekananda fell into a trance. The friends that had come with Vivekananda were all worried. And Vivekananda was not the sort to fall easily into a trance. He was a skeptical intellectual and well-trained in logic and philosophy. The experience was so profound that it exceeded his rational mind. When Vivekananda came out of the trance, he was a totally different man.

In the beginning Vivekananda doubted Ramakrishna, but this experience made him realize that Ramakrishna was a man of truth. Still, Vivekananda did many tests on Ramakrishna. He didn't surrender easily. Vivekananda was the epitome of the doubting, intellectual and scientific mind, and Ramakrishna was the manifestation of religiousness, faith, devotion and simplicity. The meeting of Ramakrishna and Vivekananda is not an ordinary meeting, but the meeting of age differences, of doubt and trust, and of science and religion. Vivekananda came full of doubts and the doubting mind doesn't surrender easily. A Ramakrishna doesn't need to go searching for a Vivekananda; it is a Vivekananda who has to come searching for a Ramakrishna. It is the atheist who has to come and surrender to the one who is in love with God. The one who knows God never has to go and surrender to the atheist. Vivekananda's surrender to Ramakrishna was the surrender of Western science to Eastern mysticism, the surrender of the intellectual to the one with faith. Science has to test religion. If religion is tested scientifically, religion always wins. The so called religious people are afraid of atheists, but even the atheist is always afraid of the one who has actually experienced God. If there is a religious person like Ramakrishna then even today science will have to surrender to him. I have seen this in the life of Osho as well. When he went to the West, intellectuals including Nobel laureates joined his great movement of meditation and spirituality.

Ramakrishna was diagnosed with cancer of the throat eighteen months before he died. He was in great physical pain. The obvious question that arises is why such a pure and simple soul suffers so much Why did a compassionate person like Jesus get crucified at the young age of thirty-three? Why did Raman Maharshi, a person who was only compassionate to others and had no expectations whatsoever from anyone, die of cancer? Buddha died after suffering the pain of eating poisonous mushrooms in Kushinagar. Mahavir died after suffering immensely from cholera for two months in Pawapuri. Osho had to leave his body after suffering great pain at the age of fifty-nine due to thallium poisoning. The enlightened ones come to Earth out of compassion. Just their presence gives peace to the hearts of others; why do such extraordinary souls carry such diseases and pain in their bodies? Ramakrishna's last eighteen months were spent in utter pain. Ramakrishna also did not understand why he was suffering so much. He asked mother Kali for the reason behind his suffering. Kali said, "A lot of people come to visit you and most of them are in misery. They only remember saints and God when they are suffering. Seeing them, your heart is filled with immense compassion. Those who come and touch you to relieve themselves from their own pain have committed various sins. You bless them out of compassion but you have to take their pain in return. This is the reason for your suffering."

Ramakrishna left his body as a fully realized soul on the full moon night of August 16th, 1886.

THE TOUCH OF THE PARAMHANSA

I grew up listening to the stories of this innocent saint of Dakshineswar. For me he was the epitome of devotion, innocence and purity. Osho had great regard for Ramakrishna and his irrational ways of the heart to approach the divine. About Ramakrishna he has said, "He is mad, but he is superhumanly mad. His behaviour is irrational as far as our logic is concerned. But perhaps there is a higher logic, according to which his behaviour is not irrational. In India, such a man is called a "paramhansa".

It is not due to the relationship of just one lifetime that I feel so in tune with this mad mystic Ramakrishna and his disciple Swami Vivekananda; in my previous life I was born into an aristocratic family in Bengal, and had the privilege of visiting his ashram, and the opportunity of sitting in his presence. My heart always revered Ramakrishna Paramhansa, but many a times my logical mind could not understand the miracles that happened around him. I had a fascination to know how Ramakrishna could induce satori to Vivekananda just by touching his forehead. Satori is a great achievement for *sadhakas*; it is an outcome of great practice, meditation and self-discipline.

One night Ramakrishna appeared in my dream and he touched my forehead. I received a great *shaktipat,* and an ecstatic current of his energy ran over my whole being. This experience of ecstasy and joy lasted for many days, and even today its faint remembrance thrills me.

After this *swapna darshan* of Ramakrishna , I could understand how powerful and transforming a touch of an enlightened master can be. I bow down to the auspicious feet of Ramakrishna Paramhansa for giving me a spoonful of that oceanic experience.

TOTAPURI BABA

"Totapuri Baba was the Guru of Ramakrishna Paramhansa. He had the great realization of Adwait (oneness) and his life was the manifestation of Adwait. He left his body in a desolate forest in Puri, India at the age of 250 on August 28th, 1961."

The *teerthas* or holy places of all religions are beautiful, but the science that the Hindus have applied to their *teerthas* is astounding.

The Hindus have built their holy places in spectacularly beautiful places. There are four main *teerthas*; Jagannath Puri, Rameshwaram, Dwarka and Badrinath. The first two are on the Indian shoreline of the Bay of Bengal, the third is on the shore of the Arabian Sea and the fourth is in the high Himalayas. All four places are natural wonders. Just visiting these places is a blissful experience and makes one's mind turn within.

Water bodies are intrinsic to Hindu pilgrimage sites. Hindus understood the mysteries associated with water and built all their holy places either on riverbanks or on seashores. Where these were not available they created large artificial bodies of water and established a *teertha* there.

While on one of my trips to Russia, I watched a documentary called *Water*, which included the scientific findings of many Western scientists related to the mysterious behaviour of water. Their main finding was that water has the capacity to absorb information, thoughts and feelings. Different atmosphere can change the molecular composition of water in different ways. Each composition broadcasts a different vibration. Therefore, water-bodies can retain energy for a long time. Hindus understood this subtle science and built all their *teerthas* around waterways.

Among the four main holy places of the Hindus, Jagannath Puri is regarded as the supreme buddhafield and is called the heaven on earth. It is on the shoreline of the Bay of Bengal. The Baishnav sect of the Hindus has a special connection with this place. Enlightened masters such as Adi Sankaracharya, Ramanujacharya, Nimbakacharya, Chaitanya Mahaprabhu and Yuktshewor Giri spent large segments of their lives here.

Until a few years ago we used to organize a meditation camp there every year. The Holiday Resort at the beach is a three star hotel, but since the owner, Mr. Mahapatra, is religiously inclined, he provided us the space for the camp at a reasonable rate. The camp would get participants from India and Nepal, and other countries as well. One of the years when I was there for a camp, I stayed on for a few more days to visit some important places.

One day we were driving around a forest outside the city of Puri, and came across a small old temple called Loknath Shiva. There I heard about the Girinariwanta Ashram where a *naga* (naked) swami's body was preserved in his *samadhi*. Since the ashram was in the middle of the forest, we had a difficult time locating it. A dense forest and sand dunes surrounded the ashram. When I finally arrived there, I was amazed to find that the *naga* swami was no other than Ramakrishna Paramhansa's Guru, Totapuri Baba. He had

had the great realization of *adwait* (oneness) and his life was the manifestation of *adwait*. He had left his body in that desolate forest at the age of 250 on August 28th, 1961.

His name occupies a great significance in the life of Ramakrishna. Since Totapuri Baba was a *naga* swami of the Puri sect, Ramakrishna used to call him Nangta, the naked one. He was a wandering ascetic who ate only that which he himself cooked, and he didn't stay in one place for more than three days. He had taught Ramakrishna the philosophy of *adwait* and given him the experience of *nirvikalpa samadhi* (ultimate enlightenment). Likewise he had learned *sagun bhakti* (devotion) from Ramakrishna. He had spent eleven months in the Dakshineswar temple in Calcutta with Ramakrishna.

After leaving there, he travelled as a wandering ascetic until he decided to live alone in the secluded forest at Puri at the age of 210 in 1920.

When I reached the *samadhi* of Totapuri Baba by chance, a great joy filled me and I had the desire to learn more about him. However, there was nobody around. There was only a locked glass cupboard in the ashram. One *brahmachari* (celibate monk) lived there but he had gone to the city when we arrived. We spent the whole day waiting for him to return. He returned in the evening but he spoke very little, and I had great difficulty getting him to speak about Totapuri Baba. Later, when we were about to leave, he opened the glass cupboard and took out a book. He presented it to us; it was a book in English on Totapuri Baba written by his Bengali devotee, Monika Mitra. I came to know about Baba's life through this book.

Monika was a young girl who had come to Puri to recuperate from an ailment. She was pulled mysteriously towards Totapuri Baba's Ashram. Baba allowed her to spend time in the ashram as she had very good *sanskars*. Baba spent most of his time in solitude and silence. He used to meditate naked on a deerskin mat, and didn't entertain casual visitors; no seeker was allowed to stay in his ashram for any length of time.

Monika's memoir remains the prime source of information on Totapuri Baba's life. There are some anecdotes from the memoir which are worth sharing here:

THE MISCHIEVOUS COW

There was a cow in the ashram but Baba never drank its milk. Rather he preferred milk brought from outside. The cow used to eat the crops from a nearby farm. When the owner of the farm came to complain, Baba gave the cow to the farmer saying that since it has eaten your crops, the cow is yours. The cow was not willing to go with the farmer. Baba scolded the cow and said, "You had a habit of stealing in your past two lives. That is why you had to be born as an animal in this life. It is because of your habit of stealing which you developed in your past two lives that you eat crops that belong to someone else. Change your ways in time! Go with this farmer and serve him by giving him your milk, and wash your past sins. You were able to spend some time with me in this life. Now repay your debt by giving milk and be free of this animal life."

When the cow heard this, it shed tears and went with the farmer.

THE AGE OF A BANYAN TREE

A lot of visitors would ask Baba, "Are you Ramakrishna's Guru? Ramakrishna left his body many years ago but how come you are still alive? What is your age?"

Baba did not answer such questions to those who were only inquisitive. He would continue sitting silently in meditation. If a genuine seeker would ask the same questions he would say, "Go and ask this banyan tree how old it is. What will you gain by knowing its age? If you can sit in its shade when it's hot, isn't that enough?"

But once when Monika had asked him he had answered, "One day I was returning from Gangasagar after having a bath there. When I reached Dakshineswar, I saw tremendous spiritual potential in the poor Brahman Ramakrishna, and because of his love I stayed there for eleven months."

He never said anything more than that about himself.

THE BURNING LEG

Once Baba was meditating on the bank of the Ganga at a place called Bhagalpur. The villagers revered him and loved to serve him. This day the villagers smelt burning human flesh close to Baba's hut. The smell surprised them because there was no cremation spot anywhere around. They searched the area to find out what exactly was burning. The smell led them to Baba's hut itself. When they went inside they saw that a burning log from Baba's fire pit had accidentally fallen on Baba's leg and it was burning. But Baba was in the trance state of *nirvikalpa samadhi* and was not aware of what was happening to his body. The villagers put out the fire on Baba's leg and nursed his burn.

DIVINE INTERVENTION

Once there was a big flood of the Ganga. When it started to flood the whole village, all the villagers came to Baba crying for help. "If you don't have mercy on us, the whole village will be drowned. The flood has already taken our crops, please save our houses," they begged.

Baba did not say anything as usual. He listened to them quietly and closed his eyes, and started meditating. The next morning the Ganga changed her path, leaving a lot of silt on the villagers' fields.

The next year they had a bumper crop due to the silt deposit. After this miraculous event, Baba became even more famous in the area. People from far away started coming to meet him, bringing many gifts. When the crowd started to disturb him, Baba left Bhagalpur and went to Puri to live there in seclusion.

THE HEALING HANDS

Monika was weak and suffered from chronic headache. As no medicine was able to heal her, she had come to Puri to heal herself, and eventually arrived at Baba's ashram. One day, suffering from severe headache, she was sitting silently close to where Baba was meditating. Baba opened his eyes and asked her, "What is happening to you?"

Monika did not want to bother Baba by telling him her problems, but Baba knew what her problem was and called her towards him. He put his hand on her forehead and closed his eyes. When he opened his eyes after a while, he said, "This disease will not bother you again. You have been forever cured."

When Monika's parents heard that she had been cured, they started calling her back to Calcutta. She did not want to leave Baba, but when her parents started to pressure her heavily, she consulted Baba.

Consoling her, Baba said, "Now it is time to return home. You will be married very soon."

Monika didn't want to leave Baba's *satsang* to get married. What Baba said to her finally convinced her to go.

"A truthful and honest householder is far more pure than a so-called ascetic. A lot of frauds wear the garb of a monk, and for a young woman like you it is far safer and more enjoyable to lead a householder's life," said Baba.

Baba's words came literally true. When Monika returned to

Calcutta, she got married to a gentleman named Sachindrakumar Mitra who had a job in the United Nations. Because of his job, she was able to fulfill her wish to travel the world. After Baba left his body, Sachindrakumar also became his devotee.

SWAMI RAMTIRTHA

> Swami Ramtirtha is a relatively obscure name in the Indian spiritual sky. While his contemporaries, Swami Vivekananda and Sri Aurobindo rose to great fame, Swami Ramtirtha, the ecstatic mystic of peerless intelligence is unknown to many.

Only two enlightened masters have had their birthday, enlightenment day and their *mahaparinirvana* day (the day when enlightened people leave their body) on the same date. One was Gautam Buddha. He was born in *Baisakh Purnima* (full moon of April) under a Sal tree in Lumbini. He became enlightened at the age of thirty-five under a Bodhi Tree on the bank of the Niranjana River at Bodhgaya, which was also a *Baisakh Purnima*. And his *mahaparinirvana* happened at the age of eighty between two Sal trees in Kushinagar on a *Baisakh Purnima*.

The only other enlightened master whose life spelled out similar mysterious events was Swami Ramtirtha. He was born on the day of *dipawali* (the Hindu festival of lights) at Gujranwala, which now falls in Pakistan, on October 22nd 1873. He was enlightened on the *dipawali* of 1898 at a place called Brahmapuri, eight kilometres north of Rishikesh, and he left his body at the age of thirty-three at the confluence of the Ganga and Vilganga rivers at a place called Tehri in Garwhal. That was also the day of *dipawali*.

Swami Ramtirtha is a relatively obscure name in the Indian spiritual sky. While his contemporaries, Swami Vivekananda and Sri Aurobindo rose to great fame, Swami Ramtirtha, the ecstatic mystic of peerless intelligence, is unknown to many.

Swami Ramtirtha was born into a very poor family. Poverty seems to be the age-old friend of the saintly and honest folks. Poverty stayed with him throughout his life. Like many saints, Ramtirtha showed spiritual signs from an early age. As a child he was always attracted to the sound of a *sankha* (conch shell) and to temples. As a toddler, he was pacified only by the sound of a *sankha,* or if he was taken to a temple.

In school, Ramtirtha showed many signs of having the mind of a genius. He learnt Farsi from a Muslim priest, Mohammad Ali Shah in a very short time. His poor father wanted to offer the priest some money for teaching Farsi to Ramtirtha. Ramtirtha found out that the priest was in need of a buffalo. Ramtirtha's father had only one buffalo but Ramtirtha persuaded him to give it to the priest. The priest was amazed by the child's generosity.

Ramtirtha paid for his studies by giving tuition classes to his friends. There is an interesting anecdote about his MA examinations. In the mathematics test, the instruction was that the students could choose to answer nine out of the thirteen questions asked. Ramtirtha answered all the questions and wrote a little note for the examiner, "You can chose to examine the nine answers that you prefer."

He graduated from Punjab University with full marks in mathematics, becoming first in his department. Recognizing his talent, the government offered him a high post, but he declined as he did not like the servitude associated with being a government official. Rather, he preferred the position of Professor at Lahore Christian College. He soon became famous as a mathematical genius, and mathematicians from all around India started sending complex problems to him, which he would solve with ease.

Once he received an equation which was difficult for him as well. He tried hard but couldn't solve it. This gave him a lot of pain and humiliation, so one evening he brought a sword to his study and made a vow that if he couldn't solve the equation before dawn, he would cut his throat with it. He spent the entire night trying to solve the equation, but the solution seemed nowhere near. When the sun rose in the morning and the equation remained unsolved, Ramtirtha, true to his word, took the sword in his hand and was about to slash his throat. Right then he saw the solution written in golden letters on the dawn sky.

Modern intellectuals find it difficult to believe in such events, but there are many such instances that have happened in the lives of many men and women of science. For example, the Nobel Prize winning Danish physicist, Niels Bohr, tried hard to discover the structure of an atom, but only when he had given up in exhaustion, did he see in his dream the structure of an atom dance in front of him. Later he figured out that that's what an atom actually looked like. Similarly, the great Indian mathematician Ramanuj was given the answers to his complex equations in his dreams. Even Einstein had a dream where he was flying at the speed of light and he saw the stars and galaxies change their shape. He said later that this dream was crucial in proving his theory of relativity.

What parapsychologists say about such a phenomenon is that when the conscious mind gives up on the problem, it finally gets a deep rest, and the unconscious mind then solves the problem mysteriously, and projects the answer in various ways. There are countless such examples in the lives of people such as scientists, saints, writers and artists.

In 1902 Swami Vivekananda had returned to India from the United States after successfully having been the spokesperson of Hinduism there. Thus, he was very much respected in India and was being invited all over the country to give spiritual talks. It was Ramtirtha who organized Swami Vivekananda's talks in various cities and towns of Punjab.

Ramtirtha was immensely impressed by Swami Vivekananda's grace and wisdom. He became inspired to live a life just like Swamiji. While saying goodbye to Swamiji at Lahore train station, Ramtirtha wanted to give his whole life to him. But since all he had was a pocket watch, he offered that to Swamiji. Swamiji received the gift graciously, and then gave it back to him, saying, "Now think that the watch is with me, but on my other body. Never think that you are far away from me."

The watch showed one o'clock. Showing Ramtirtha the time, Swami Vivekananda said, "Look, even this watch is saying that we are one, and this is the crux of the Vedanta philosophy. The person I was looking for to spread Vedanta around the world is you."

Swamiji hugged Ramtirtha and added, "You will definitely be successful in spreading Vedanta around the world as this is what God has planned for you."

This emotional moment brought tears of love to the eyes of the two crusaders of Vedanta.

Swami Ramtirtha was an ardent devotee of Krishna, and the devotion was showing its magical colours on his life. He would wander, chanting the name of Krishna, in the forest on the bank of the Rabi River, just like Chaitanya Mahaprabhu did a few hundred years ago. Ramtirtha would search for Krishna like his lovelorn *gopi*. One night he dreamt that Krishna was playing with him. And then he suddenly disappeared. Ramktirtha started searching for him in desperation but couldn't find him anywhere. Feeling utterly lonely he started to cry, but after a while he saw Krishna peeping at him from behind a door. Ramtirtha became mad at Krishna for playing around with him, and pulled him by the ear and slapped him. He woke up from the dream in great pain and shock as he found out that he had slapped himself. His ear was also hurting. This dream made him realize that it is worthless to search for Krishna on the outside, and a great desire to search for God within himself arose in him.

Ramtirtha was very strongly attracted to the Ganga and the Himalayas. As soon as he had some leisure time, he would run to the serenity of the Ganga River. He travelled many times from the city of Haridwar to the source of the Ganga at Gomukh. He considered the Ganga his own mother, and would pray to her for self-realization. One day he was meditating on her bank at Brahmapuri, a little above Rishikesh, and was aching for the experience of self-realization. Again he made a vow that if he is not self-realized within twenty-four hours, he will jump into the Ganga and take his life. The twenty-four hours ended, and he was still not enlightened. As he had vowed, he jumped into the Ganga. In the beginning, the Ganga drowned her son, but when Ramtirtha became unconscious, she threw him onto a rock on her bank. When Ramtirtha regained consciousness, he had left unconsciousness forever; he was now a self-realized man. The effort of many lifetimes finally came to rest. Blissful and divinely content, he returned to Lahore to resume his work.

Ramtirtha found it very difficult to work, however, as his life had completely changed since his experience at Brahmapuri. While teaching mathematics he would prove the concepts of Vedanta using equations. He would prove the *sutras* of the Upanishads through mathematics. His colleagues from the Christian college did not like this.

Every dawn he would sit in meditation. Sometimes he would reach a timeless trance state and would lose time consciousness, making him very late for his classes. On July 14th 1900, Swami Ramtirtha's meditation only ended at 2.00 pm. He then remembered that he'd had a very important mathematics class at 12.00, which he had missed. He ran to the college, and when he searched for his attendance registry, he found that his name had already been signed. When he enquired with the clerk, he answered perplexed, "You came here and signed your name as soon as the college opened. You have also already taken your class."

Ramtirtha was surprised, and sat on a chair beside the clerk trying to figure out a plausible explanation for the mysterious happening. He said to himself, "I know who did this. It can only be Krishna himself who would care to carry out such a stunt."

He felt that because of his meditation, to save face, Krishna himself had to come in disguise and conduct his class. He said to himself that he couldn't continue his job anymore. He sat there silently for a while and then asked the clerk for an empty page. He immediately wrote a letter of resignation and handed it to the clerk, telling him to give it to the Principal. He then left the college without talking to anyone. The whole college was shocked to hear of Ramtirtha's resignation, and it became a topic of discussion. Not seeing any logical reason behind the event, the Principal even went ahead and declared Ramtirtha mad. The famed poet, Mohammad Ikbal, a colleague of Ramtirtha, was amongst those who defended him and said that if Ramtirtha is mad then no sane man is left in the world.

Ramtirtha, on the other hand, was getting ready to totally surrender his life to the will of God. "The God that made my mother's breast full of milk before I was even born will definitely take care of me and my family," he thought.

He then distributed all his belongings, and prepared to leave for Rishikesh as a renunciate. This made his wife, Parvatidevi, cry in despair, and she pleaded with him to take her with him.

"Life in the Himalayas is very unpredictable. There is no certainty of lodging and food supply there. I am leaving totally surrendered to God, so you should take the children and go to your mother's place," he said to his wife.

Parvatidevi didn't agree with her husband, and reasoned, "If Ram could take Sita along with him to the forest, then why do you leave me here?"

When Ramtirtha saw that Parvatidevi was adamant, he told her that he would only take her if she promised to fulfill three of his demands. His first one was that she had to give away all her belongings other than the clothes she was wearing, and come with him totally empty-handed. Secondly, she had to say loudly three times that her husband was dead and Ramtirtha is only a fellow traveller on the path of meditation. The third demand was the most difficult and heart-rending of the three. He told her that she had to leave her two sons on the main crossing of Lahore in the care of Lord Krishna. He himself was sure that the one who brought them to the world would also take care of them.

Since Ramtirtha's demands were dreadful and tragic, Parvatidevi started to cry.

"How can I abandon these children and leave them unaided? Please don't make such an impossible test," she pleaded with Ramtirtha.

Ramtirtha was harsh. "If you don't have total trust in God then go to your mother's place," he said.

Punjab is known as the land of the brave, and the women of Punjab are also courageous, brave and able to sacrifice. Parvatidevi was no less. She left the children on the main crossing of Lahore, and came to Ramtirtha weeping, having fulfilled all his demands. He told her she was now ready to travel on this path, and left with her for Lahore train station.

As Ramtirtha had already gained fame as a fine professor and an orator, many people came to the station to try to stop him. They told him they would make a very good ashram for him in Lahore where he could meditate, and that he had no reason to leave. Ramtirtha, however, had no doubt in his mind that he would find peace only on the banks of the Ganga and in the Himalayas. Seeing his *vairagya* (detachment from the world) and his absolute trust in the divine, some of his devotees decided to go with him.

Just as the train left, someone pushed Ramtirtha's two children into the compartment where Ramtirtha's troupe was seated. All were shocked to see them there. Parvatidevi hugged the children and started crying.

"What shall I do next? Shall I push them from the running train?" She said in utter despair.

"It wasn't you who brought them here. It was Lord Krishna himself who pushed them into this compartment. If he wished them to be with us, then he will take care of them; we need not worry," Ramtirtha told his wife.

When hearing this, Parvatidevi cuddled her children, and finally the torment of her mind subsided.

Ramtirtha arrived in Rishikesh with his small group of disciples. During their journey across the Ganga, when the ferry had reached the middle of the river, he said, "Those who walk with me have to be totally surrendered to existence. So throw all your possessions in the Ganga, apart from the clothes you are wearing. Those who don't have the courage to do so can go back on the same ferry."

His demand was straightforward and the authority in his voice indicated that he was not going to compromise. Seeing that

Ramtirtha was divinely possessed, some of them gathered enough courage to throw away their belongings, while the others thought the demand was too extreme, and decided to return.

Ramtirtha saw a little pouch hanging from his wife's sari and yelled, "What is this?"

"I have thrown everything else but I saved these two gold bangles in case you get sick," she answered.

"You have more trust on the gold than on the God that has made your own body? He will take care of us. Don't try to be a hindrance in his plans by carrying these bangles." Saying this, he made her throw the bangles in the river. This way, being totally devoid of any possessions and with all their trust on God, the little troupe started walking up the hills towards a place called Tehri.

In Tehri, Seth Muralidhar had created an ashram to serve yogis and sannyasins. Ramtirtha decided to rest there. It was already midday when they arrived, so the whole group was very hungry. Just then Baba Ramnath, the manager of the Kalikamliwala ashram of Rishikesh, which provided basic necessities to sannyasins in the area, arrived there by chance. When he heard the whole story of professor Ramtirtha's troupe, he asked him if he could take care of the basic needs of his whole group during their stay in Tehri. This incident proved to the group what Swami Ramtirtha had been insisting upon the whole time: that God is compelled to help those who surrender totally to his will.

While in Tehri, the Maharaja of Tehri Garhwal heard of Ramtirtha's repute and came to meet him. The Maharaja was an intelligent man, but due to the influence of the Western way of life, he had no belief whatsoever in Hinduism. He was a convinced atheist. The countless yogis who came to Uttarakhand and had met the Maharaja could not rouse the love of God in him. But most of his doubts vanished in his first meeting with Swami Ramtirtha. As he was hugely impressed by Swamiji, he asked him not to leave the state of Tehri so that he could receive his *satsang* and guidance on a regular basis. Thanks to the time that Maharaja Keerti Shah spent in Swamiji's presence, a great love arose in him for the Hindu faith and he became a strong supporter and promoter of Hinduism.

Seeing the change in the king and the respect that he bestowed on Swami Ramtirtha, a big crowd of locals started to gather around Swamiji. Such a crowd is full of inquisitive folk, and real seekers among them are almost nonexistent. It is a matter of great pain for saints and yogis to live among people with no spiritual thirst. Due to this, Ramtirtha left Tehri and started living in a silent barren cave in the Himalayas. The nearest village to his cave was three kilometres away. A happy-go-lucky farmer discovered that a yogi had started living in the cave, and would bring him a meal every day at noon. Ramtirtha felt that this arrangement was also due to Krishna's grace, and while eating his food and drinking *Gangajal* (water of the Ganga) he thanked Krishna countless times. Hearing this, the farmer's ego would get hurt, and one day he gathered enough courage and asked, "I bring you lunch every day exactly on time, but you have never thanked me. Why do you only thank Krishna and not me?"

Ramthirtha answered, "Because I am sure this is his arrangement. Wherever I go, he never lets me sleep hungry and never lets things be uncomfortable for me."

This statement hurt the farmer even more and he said, "I have some important work to do so I cannot bring your lunch tomorrow."

While leaving the cave, he thought to himself, "Let's see who will feed him tomorrow."

As he was leaving, Ramtirtha said, "You don't worry at all. The one who feeds an ant to an elephant will also feed Ram."

Not believing a word Ramtirtha said, the farmer decided to see what would happen when nobody brought him lunch the next day. When it was time for lunch, the farmer hid behind a bush and kept vigil over the cave. To his surprise he saw an old woman walking towards the cave with a clay pot in her hand. When she reached the cave he heard her say, "*Sadhubaba! Sadhubaba!*"

When Ramtirtha came out hearing her, she added, "Our family bought a new cow which gives a lot of milk. I felt that I should offer the first day's milk to a yogi. That's why I have brought this milk for you. If you could kindly accept this milk, I would be very grateful to you."

Ramtirtha accepted and drank as much milk as he could. Some milk was still left in the pot so the old woman asked him to keep it for later. Ramtirtha told her that it was his rule that he did not keep anything for the future.

"Whatever Krishna wishes and whenever he wishes is what I am satisfied with," he said. Hearing this, the old woman was filled with reverence for Ramtirtha.

She said, "I will come with some food for you tomorrow as well, please accept it."

When the farmer heard this from behind the bush, he got extremely ashamed and came forth and prostrated in front of Ramtirtha and started to cry.

"Dear lord of the forest, please forgive me that I wanted to test you. I will not leave your feet unless you forgive me. I did not see your Krishna but I am astonished to see his arrangement for you. Please bless me so that I also have unfaltering faith towards him just as you do," pleaded the farmer.

The farmer's ego melted and he started to bring lunch to Swamiji with great devotion. He now regarded Ramtirtha as his Guru and started taking spiritual counsel from him. He also changed his name to Ramsewak which means Ram's helper.

There are many such instances that prove the mystic's total trust with the divine.

Swami Ramtirtha was meditating in Gangotri one winter, near the source of the Ganga. A few businessmen from Mumbai had come there on a pilgrimage. It was freezing cold and when it started to become unbearable for the businessmen who were not used to such harsh weather, they started screaming in panic, "Oh lord! It seems that we will die here because of this cold."

To make matters worse it began snowing heavily which drove the pilgrims into a frenzy, and their screams were now beyond control. Swami Ramtirtha was listening to all this from another room. When it was too much he went to their room and shouted at them, "You think it's so easy to die in a holy place such as this! You need a lot of good karma to be able to die here. I have been trying to die on the bank of the Ganga for many years and I haven't succeeded yet. You men just got here yesterday, and you think you are going to be successful at it?"

This stunned the pilgrims who finally regained their minds and kept quiet.

THE JOURNEY TO AMERICA

It was due to Maharaja Keerti Shah's efforts and inspiration that Swami Rama went to Japan and America to preach Vedanta. In Japan he met Puran Singh who was to be his most loyal disciple. Puran Singh was a successful Seikh businessman in Japan who claimed he saw a great spark of energy and light come out of his mouth when Ramtirtha spoke at a function. He felt that it was God himself who came in the form of Ramtirtha to give him *darshan*. The experience was so strong that he left his business and surrendered his whole life to Ramtirtha, serving him throughout his life.

Swami Ramtirtha went to America alone by ship. When the

ship docked on the Seattle harbour, all the passengers were in a hurry to get off, but Swami Ramtirtha was just watching the whole clamour, resting on a chair on the deck. Seeing his disinterest in getting off, an American man was a bit taken aback and he asked Ramtirtha, "Where are you going?"

Ramtirtha answered, "America."

"Well, you seem to have arrived there. The ship will go no further. Pack your luggage and get ready to leave," said the man.

Swamiji answered, "Am I an ass to walk around carrying luggage with me? Only animals carry luggage. This body is the only thing that I have to carry."

Shocked at the reply, the man asked, "If you don't have any bags then where do you keep your money?"

Ramtirtha answered, "It's been years since I have touched money. All my needs are taken care of by God."

Hearing those strange words, the man said, "This country is run by dollars. Without dollars you will die hungry here. If you have the address of someone you know in Seattle, give it to me, and I will take you to him."

Putting his hand on the man's shoulder, Swami Ramtirtha answered most naturally, "Oh yes, I know a very good hearted American."

The man looked expectantly at Ramtirtha. After smiling at him lovingly, Swamiji caressed his shoulder and said, "It is you."

Swamiji's touch sent beautiful vibrations through the American's body, and he felt as though he had known Swamiji for a long time. The man's name was Dr. Albert Hiler. He cared for Ramtirtha with great respect, and kept him as his guest for one-and-a-half years.

During his stay in America, Swami Ramtirtha visited the Shasta Springs in Seattle. The beautiful sounds of the running water and the birds, as well as the silence of the forest and the mountains reminded him of his favourite place, the Himalayas. He refused to return to the city, and stayed there alone for months.

On May 20th 1903, American President, Theodore Roosevelt, was on a tour of the Shasta Springs. When he heard that a Himalayan yogi had been living alone in the forests there for months, he expressed his desire to see him. When they met, Roosevelt was impressed by Ramtirtha's intelligence and wisdom and said, "If you need anything please let me know, I shall manage it for you."

Swami Ram laughed at Roosevelt's words and said, "Ram is the emperor of this universe. It is because of my wish that the sun shines and the moon revolves around the earth. And it was I who made you president. I have no needs because all is taken care of by God. You need not worry about me at all."

Roosevelt didn't understand these words of Ramtirtha that were coming out of the ultimate realization of Vedanta, but the words of this quirky yogi fascinated him none the less.

Roosevelt said, "I want to spend more time with you but my schedule is packed, so I must leave."

Ramtirtha, with his usual wit, said, "I had thought that the most powerful man of the freest country in the world would be free but it seems you have no freedom. If the most powerful man of the country can't stay where he wants to even for a few more minutes then there is a problem with your system."

During his stay in America, he was called to speak at a religious conference. He used to call himself *Badshah* (emperor) Ram, and called his talks the decree of Ram. He had no qualms about calling himself the manifestation of God. Once he was asked, "How can you call yourself the emperor when you own nothing but a set of clothes?"

He answered in verse:

Hey desire, you are the lowest of the low
I was God himself if in the middle you wouldn't show
Now my desires have evaporated and worries defeated
I sail like a free bird
No less but Emperor have I become, freed from all shackles of the world

And then he said, "I call myself *Badshah* because I don't desire anything."

In another Christian conference he was asked, "Who made this universe and who runs it?"

Ramtirtha answered, "I made this universe and I make the sun shine and the planets revolve around it."

If he had made this purest expression of Vedanta in a gathering of fundamentalists, he would probably have been killed like Sarmad or Mansoor, but the Christians just made him leave the conference, calling him a madman.

Since Ramtirtha had immense love for the Ganga and the Himalayas, he couldn't stay away from there for long. He returned to Tehri, Garhwal, to continue his meditation. His need for seclusion was so great that he sent his disciples away, and started meditating alone in a hut on the bank of the Ganga. One morning he wrote his famous poem which says, "O Death, what can you do to me? You cannot kill me. If you free me from this body then I will be dissolved in each grain of sand on the bank of the Ganga, in each drop of water of the Ganga, in each leaf of every tree here."

The same afternoon he took *jal samadhi* (gave up his body) in the water of the Ganga. That day was also of *deepawali*.

When I am in the Utarakhand area to conduct meditation camps I feel the presence of many enlightened masters who have already left their bodies. If you remember the enlightened ones with love and reverence, you can feel their presence anywhere on earth. While I write this at Osho Upaban, Pokhara, Nepal, on the bank of the River Seti, I am feeling an intense presence of Swami Ramtirtha. I have a feeling that he himself is inspiring me to write this. My thousand salutations to the son of the Himalayas and the Ganga, Badshah Ram, who was totally surrendered to God, and whose love of God was the only purpose of his existence.

J. KRISHNAMURTI

> " Krishnamurti is one of the most beautiful men of the last century. My association with Krishnamurti is not a mere coincidence. I am naturally inclined towards enlightened masters, but my fascination with Krishnamurti goes deeper than just a mere attraction. "

Around twenty-five hundred years ago a girl named Krisha Gautami was born into a poor family in India. She grew up to become a very beautiful woman and was married to a man from an aristocratic family. However, since she came from a poor family, she was greatly disrespected and humiliated by her in-laws. When she gave birth to a beautiful boy though, her family started giving her due respect. She was greatly attached to her son. But her happiness was short-lived. Suddenly her son died, and this brought forth great despair in her. Utterly devastated, she went around the village begging everyone to breathe life back into the dead body of her child.

The villagers felt only Buddha could restore peace in Krisha's tormented soul. So a relative advised her to go and meet Gautam Buddha, who was on a retreat at Chetwan. Krisha rushed to meet

Buddha immediately. The grief had stolen all beauty from her and all that remained of her was a ghastly and bedraggled apparition. She knelt at Buddha's feet and started howling inconsolably. She begged him to make her child alive again. Seeing her tragic state, Buddha consoled her and said, "Don't cry. I can make your son alive again but you have to bring me some yellow mustard seeds first."

Hope glimmered on Krisha's eyes again. She gathered herself and was about to leave. The yellow mustard seeds, after all, were not all that difficult to find. Just then Buddha said, "But there is a condition - you have to bring the mustard seeds from a house where nobody has ever died."

Krisha went from house to house with her dead child. When she would reach a house, she would ask, "Nobody from this house has died, have they?"

But the answer would always be the same. She went around the city of Srawasti all day but couldn't find one house where nobody had died. As dusk approached, she realized that somebody had died in each household, and that death was inevitable. When she realized the inevitability of death, a certain calm gradually descended upon her. She then went to Buddha and surrendered to him, and became initiated into his *sangha*. Soon she achieved the state of *shrotapanna*, the state where one comes in contact with the source within oneself.

According to the famous mystic, Annie Besant, Krisha Gautami was born again in Andhra Pradesh, India, in a village called Madanpalle on May 11th 1895 into a simple Brahmin family, as Jiddu Krishnamurti.

In 1909, while Charles Webster Leadbeater was on an evening walk on a Tamilnadu beach, he spotted Krishnamurti and his brother Nitya. Leadbeater was a member of the Theosophist Society established in 1875 by Russian seer, Madam Blavatsky, and American transcedentalist, Colonel Olcott, to bring to Earth the consciousness of *Maitreya* Buddha. Leadbeater was adept in parapsychology. As Mary Lutyens has described in Krishnamurti's biography, Leadbeater saw the mesmerizing aura of the boy at once. She has related the description of his aura as "a radiant globe of flashing colours, its high vibrations sending ripples of changing hues over its surface – hues of which earth knows nothing – brilliant, soft and luminous."

Leadbeater felt that the search of thirty-four years for the medium of the *Maitreya* consciousness was over. Annie Besant, the president of the society, also received confirmation of this from her masters on the astral plane.

Leadbeater and Annie Besant started training Krishnamurti and Nitya to become the mediums of *Maitreya* Buddha under strict rules and discipline. They were especially trained in the mystical yogic science. It is said that they were brought in contact with the masters of the astral world who gave them esoteric training. During this phase, Krishnamurti wrote the book *At the Feet of the Master* when he was only fourteen. Osho regards this as the best book written by Krishnamurti, but Krishnamurti later refuted having written it.

Krishnamurti was sent to the best institutions of England. Since an early age, he travelled around the world and gave discourses as the future medium of Buddha. In 1922, he became enlightened under a large Pepper tree in Ojai, California. The Theosophists had established an organization called the *Order of the Star of the East* to propound a new world religion with Krishnamurti as its leader. The members of this organization included more than a hundred thousand intellectuals and wealthy people. The future world spiritual leader, Krishnamurti was kept under strict discipline and was prevented from building friendships, especially with women. On August 3rd 1929, during the Annual Star Camp of the *Order of the Star of the East* in Ommen, Holland, Krishnamurti was expected to address the audience as the world spiritual leader. But to everyone's shock, he dissolved the Order with his historical declaration, "I maintain that truth is a pathless land, and you cannot approach it by any path whatsoever, by any religion, by any sect." After this, he started travelling around the world as an independent thinker, and talked about the human being who is free from all conditioning and organized religion.

Krishnamurti was a very sensitive and compassionate person. The prevalence of violence and hatred around the world saddened him throughout his life. He had to see two world wars. In his view, nationalism created an artificial sense of division within humanity. He refused to align himself with any nationality. Krishnamurti was in St. Peter's Square when the Pope was being carried on a sedan chair. The Pope stopped the sedan to lean out and ask Krishnamurti, "Are you an Indian?" Krishnamurti replied, "I am supposed to be from India." Whether or not the Pope read his sarcasm between the lines remains unknown, but he studied Krishnamurti's face intently and said, "I like your face."

Krishnamurti had a very refined sense of aesthetics. His every gesture, every action reflected his deep-seated appreciation of beauty. He was very particular about his wardrobe. When in Europe, he used to dress in fitting trousers and shirts, and in India he wore starched linen *kurta-pajamas*. Once somebody asked him why he switched his wardrobes between Europe and India, to which he replied, "I don't want to offend anyone by trying to stand out among them. I don't want people to perceive me as someone other than themselves."

When I visited Pine Cottage in Ojai, California, where Krishnamurti spent most of his life, I met a rather amicable gentleman, Friederich Grohe, who shared some anecdotes from Krishnamurti's life with me. Mr. Grohe has beautifully recounted his memories with Krishnamurti in his book *The Beauty of The Mountain*.

According to him, Krishnamurti loved polishing his own shoes. Until his last days, he often polished his shoes himself. It once happened that Krishnamurti was out in the porch polishing his shoes when he noticed a pair of grubby shoes. Without any hesitation he started polishing them as well. The gentleman who owned the shoes came down to the porch only to find Krishnamurti busy polishing his shoes. He was embarrassed beyond description. Thereafter, all the visitors became careful not to leave their soiled shoes in Krishnamurti's sight.

Krishnamurti was oblivious of his position or his influence over people. His simplicity and his courtesy remained unsoiled by his growing popularity. Mr. Grohe recalled how during his usual morning walks in Rajghat, India, Krishnamurti used to hold hands with children who followed him in a curious caravan, and would impart occasional affectionate smiles at ice-cream vendors along the way. He never considered himself a leader or a teacher of any kind. He forged an unpretentious and close relationship with anyone who came his way.

His resistance to a master-disciple relationship was partly a reaction to the harsh training of the Theosophical Society. Osho has said that if he had been left to his own means, Krishnamurti would have taken two more lives to attain enlightenment. The arduous training hastened his spiritual growth, but left him embittered, grieving for lost childhood and adolescence. Krishnamurti's rebellion against the Theosophical Society is nothing but an expression of the same embitterment.

My understanding is that there are three main reasons why Krishnamurti left the Theosophical Society. The first one obviously is the death of Nitya. After Nitya left his body unexpectedly, Krishnamurti realized that the forced esoteric experiments could be disastrous, hence his lifelong insistence on natural living. The second reason was that when Krishnamurti was young he wasn't allowed to mix with women. This unnatural abstinence greatly scarred young Krishnamurti. Leadbeater was a declared misogynist. He saw women with contempt, and tried to influence his young pupil accordingly. Krishnamurti was far too sensitive to be corrupted. As we can often read in his journals, he had a very heightened sense of beauty. A single tree could move him to tears.

In his own words,

"Coming over the stile into the grove one felt immediately a great sense of peace and stillness. Not a thing was moving. It seemed sacrilegious to walk through it, to tread the ground; it was profane to talk, even to breathe. The great redwood trees were absolutely still. You stood still hardly daring to breathe; you felt you were an intruder, for you had been chatting and laughing, and to enter this grove not knowing what lay there was a surprise and a shock, the shock of an unexpected benediction."

- J Krishnamurti,
Brockwood Park 1st Entry 14th September 1973

Of course, if a single tree could instill such profundity in him, it was foolish to assume he would pass untouched by the beauty of a woman. Later, Krishnamurti had intimate affairs with many women, most of whom remained his close confidants throughout his life.

Osho has often commented on how sexuality is not a hindrance but a passage for a genuine seeker. He said, "It so happens that the more sexual a person is, the more inventive he or she can be. The more sexual a person is, the more intelligent he or she is. With less sex energy, less intelligence exists; with more sexual energy, more intelligence, because sex is a deep search to uncover, not only bodies, not only the body of the opposite sex, but everything that is hidden."

But it will be a long time before humanity grows wise enough to discern the wisdom in Osho's words.

The third reason Krishnamurti left the Theosophical Society was Leadbeater's rumoured homosexuality. Though Krishnamurti never validated the rumours, it is believed that Leadbeater's alleged affairs had also been one of the reasons for the rift.

After Krishnamurti abandoned the Theosophical Society, he travelled around the world giving spontaneous talks. Seventy books have been transcribed from his talks. The books are translated into forty-seven languages, millions of copies of which are sold each year. He has established modern schools running in accord with his philosophy in Ojai (California), Brokwood Park (England), Rajghat (Banaras), Rishi Valley (Andhrapradesh), Madras and Uttarkashi.

As Krishnamurti grew older he started practicing yoga again. He had been rigorously trained in yoga in the Theosophical Society, but when he left he abandoned all prescribed routine as well. When his health started to fail, he returned to yoga and *pranayama*, learning from the famous yoga Guru, BK Iyenger. Krishnamurti practiced yoga regularly until his last days, which helped him to retain his posture and agility.

Krishnamurti is one of the most beautiful men of the last century. His body was frail and delicate, and yet it emanated such grace and beauty. While many were touched by his penetrating discourses, his physical beauty had also stirred many. George Bernard Shaw made a famous statement: "He is the most beautiful person I have ever met." Khalil Jibran considered him the manifestation of "the God of Love". Aldous Huxley, who was very close to Krishnamurti said, "When you listen to him, it's like listening to Buddha himself."

Throughout his life, Krishnamurti denounced organized religion, priests and religious fundamentalism. He did not expound any philosophy or religion, but rather talked on the things that concern all of us in our everyday lives. He explained beautifully the subtle workings of the human mind, and pointed to the need for bringing to our daily lives a deeply meditative and spiritual quality.

THE MYSTERIOUS MEETINGS

I have always felt a deep admiration for Krishnamurti. When he was still alive, I had tried many times to meet him. But somehow the meeting never happened.

In 2009, two decades after Krishnamurti left his body, I was in California conducting an Osho meditation camp. We were about a five hour drive away from the Pepper Tree Retreat at Ojai, the place where Krishnamurti attained enlightenment and spent many years of his life. Ojai is to the lovers of Krishnamurti what Srawasti is to the Buddhists.

I had read a lot about the place. Krishnamurti has often described the beautiful nature that surrounded the retreat in his journals. He had attained enlightenment under a larger Pepper tree, after which the retreat is named. Krishnamurti has described the moment of enlightenment as follows:

"I sat under the pepper tree which is near the house cross legged in the meditation posture. When I had sat thus for some time, I felt myself going out of my body, I saw myself sitting down with the delicate tender leaves of the tree over me... The fountain of Truth has been revealed to me and the darkness has been dispersed. Love in all its glory has intoxicated my heart; my heart can never be closed. I have drunk at the fountain of Joy and eternal Beauty. I am God-intoxicated."

- Lutyens, Mary. "Krishnamurti: The Years of Awakening"

Krishnamurti's poetic description of Ojai had made a deep imprint on me. Naturally, I wanted to visit the Pepper Tree Retreat. We called the reception and booked four rooms. There was not much activity going on there, and the receptionist informed us over the phone that she only worked until 5.00 pm. She said that she would leave the keys in a basket in the reception desk. Since the Retreat only provided bed and breakfast, we had to arrange for dinner ourselves.

After a rather tiring drive, we arrived there at around nine in the evening. The nearest café was about a four kilometre walk from the retreat. Ramesh and Amritananda, my fellow sannyasins who had accompanied me, left for the café. I was so thrilled to be there that I much preferred to miss my dinner than miss the exhilarating presence of the place. So I stayed back giving up dinner. Chanda, another sannyasin from our group, stayed back with me. After my friends left for the café, I began my adventurous tour around the house. I had read so much about the place that every sight filled me with nostalgia.

The orange trees that spread all over the property left the air fragrant and tangy. The house was furnished tastefully in minimalist design. I walked through the corridor like an excited child on a treasure hunt. Each piece of furniture, each book, each tree spoke directly to me. I strolled joyfully and stumbled upon the main kitchen. I walked into the room and found some bread and eggs in the refrigerator. I made myself some toast and an omelette, and had a rather nice dinner. About an hour later, my friends returned back from the cafe, disappointed. Apparently, there wasn't much to choose from on the menu, since my friends were vegetarian and the cafe served mostly non-vegetarian food.

It was about midnight when they returned, so we called it a day and retired to our respective rooms. Although we had had a very tiring day, I didn't feel the least bit exhausted or sleepy. I also felt a presence. It was strange because the presence was so palpable I felt I was continuously being watched over or followed by someone. Of course, there was no-one around, but neither was I alone. I fell asleep briefly as morning approached. The entire night I browsed through the library in the adjacent room. There were a good many books on many different genres including Krishnmurti's favorite detective novels.

The next morning we had a very delicious organic breakfast. I also met Mr. Grohe for the first time that day. Ours was an instant bonding. He loved narrating the incidents from Krishnamurti's life, and I was an eager audience. He told me many anecdotes. He also fondly recalled one particular joke Krishnamurti often cracked:

Once God felt like knowing how humans lived in the world. He came to Earth with Saint Peter. People were toiling away and looked very busy just to sustain their lives. He asked Peter, "Why are people so busy?"

Peter replied, "Well, it's because you have told them to earn by making their own effort."

God smirked and said, "Well, that was just a joke."

During his tour, God reached the Vatican. He saw that the priests were seated in a dining hall, and lots of food, fruits, desserts and expensive wine was laid out on the table. "And who are they?" He asked Peter.

"These are the folk who have understood your joke very well," replied Peter.

He also showed me around Pine Cottage where Krishnamurti lived. The construction looked rather new so I enquired if Krishnamurti had lived there all his life. "No," he replied. "He spent thirty years of his life in the same room where you stayed overnight."

His reply left me speechless. I had many mystical experiences that night, all of which I cannot reveal here. What I can say is that I had always longed to meet him in person, but the meeting happened twenty-four years after he left his body in his private bedroom, in the bed where he slept for thirty years.

My association with Krishnamurti is not a mere coincidence. I am naturally inclined towards enlightened masters, but my fascination with Krishnamurti goes deeper than just a mere attraction. Truth is a complex phenomenon that cannot always be perceived rationally. On the spiritual path, seekers avoid revealing the truth because there is a great possibility of it being misunderstood. But I remember the lines of Indira Devi that truth doesn't need to be validated by the masses.

Today when I narrate the story of Krisha Gautami, it is as if no time has lapsed since then. I have had visions and indications from my master that I was a disciple of Buddha in one of my past lives. In that life, I was a *bhikku* of the Sravasti *sangha*. When Krisha Gautami had reached Buddha, maybe I, too, had witnessed her transformation. But one thing that is certain is that the intimacy and familiarity which I share with Krishnamurti extends beyond lives.

The same year that we visited the Pepper Tree Retreat we inaugurated Osho Niranjana, our commune at San Diego, California, which is only a six hour drive from Ojai. When I visited the commune again in 2014, the Pepper Tree Retreat drew me again. We made an online reservation and were almost ready to go when an unforeseen problem arose and we had to cancel the trip. Of course, I wasn't surprised because these unexpected interventions had become a rather regular phenomenon when it came to things associated with Krishnamurti. We had already made the payment so we called them and cancelled the booking. They explained that we could only receive 50% refund and that, too, couldn't be made in cash. The refund would be applied the next time we visited the place.

As the trip was cancelled, I remembered another joke Krishnamurti often cracked:

"There are three monks, who had been sitting in deep meditation for many years amidst the Himalayan snow peaks, never speaking a word, in utter silence. One morning, one of the three suddenly speaks up and says, 'What a lovely morning this is.' And he falls silent again. Five years of silence pass, when all at once the second monk speaks up and says, 'But we could do with some rain.'

There is silence among them for another five years, when suddenly the third monk says, 'Why can't you two stop chattering?"

I remembered the joke and laughed to myself. My meetings with Krishnamurti were just as sporadic. I was denied one more opportunity to go and visit him. I knew Krishnamurti was playing his usual pranks on me. But even as he denied me the meeting he made sure that I had to go and visit him again, if only for the $150 that was credited in my name at the Pepper Tree Retreat as the due refund.

SHIVAPURI BABA

> "Shivapuri baba accepted the royal invitation of Queen Victoria and lived in the Buckingham Palace for four years and had 18 private meetings with the Queen, in which she received direct teachings on yoga."

An unknown Indian mystic with deep penetrating eyes and a hypnotic presence arrived in Rome in the late eighteen hundreds. He had already travelled on foot through Afghanistan, Iran, Jerusalem and Turkey, and through the Balkans into Greece, before finally reaching the Italian capital. There he received an invitation from Queen Victoria herself to visit Buckingham Palace and stay there as a royal guest. Queen Victoria had developed an interest in Indian mysticism, and wanted to explore its deeper realms. After hearing that a mystic of divine countenance had come to Europe, she wanted to meet the yogi and learn the nuances of this esoteric science from him. He accepted this royal invitation and lived in Buckingham Palace for four years, and had eighteen private meetings with the queen, in which she received direct teachings on yoga from him.

Victoria had asked him not to leave England while she was alive, so he lived in the palace and became her spiritual guide and counsellor. After the queen left her body in 1901, the enlightened soul again continued his pilgrimage on foot. After spending three years in America, he went to Mexico and continued his journey on to South America, and then to New Zealand and Australia, and reached Japan in 1913. Then he went to China and Tibet, and finally reached Nepal in 1926 after crossing the great Himalayan range.

Shivapuri Baba was born in 1826 in a village near Kanyakumari, Kerala, India. He and his twin sister were born to a prosperous Nambodari Brahmin family. One of their forefathers used to be a minister in the palace of Tipu Sultan of Mysore. Having lost their parents at a young age, the twins were raised by their grandparents, Achyutam and his wife.

Achyutam was a prominent astrologer who would study the stars from his bed on the patio of his house. Once Shivapuri Baba placed a two-inch thick mattress on the bed and covered it with a bedsheet to make a more comfortable seat for his grandfather. Achyutam resumed his nightly routine of observing the stars and remarked, "How is it that the sky has come nearer today?"

Everyone was stupefied by the remark. Achyutam was so intuitively adept in the astrological calculations that he could measure the difference of an inch with his naked eyes without the use of an advanced telescope. It is due to the contribution of adepts like Achyutam that Vedic astrology evolved to become a highly developed and accurate science. Achyutam had predicted that his wife would die of snakebite on a certain date. Of that night Shivapuri Baba says, "My grandmother used to tell us all sorts of stories in the evening. One day, after storytelling, she went and slept near a serpent knowingly. She knew she was going to die that way." In the night she did, indeed, die of snakebite.

When Shivapuri Baba turned eighteen, his grandfather expressed his wish to hand over the domestic responsibilities to his grandson and leave as a renunciate to meditate in the forests of Amarkantak, the origin of the holy Narmada River. Hearing this, Shivapuri Baba handed over his property to his sister and went to Amarkantak with his grandfather. After seven years of meditating in the forest, his grandfather died; Baba was only twenty-five years old. Before dying, the grandfather predicted that Baba would be enlightened in this life, and made Baba promise that after enlightenment he would travel the world helping those in need of spiritual guidance. He also told Baba that no one had ever begged in their family and gave Baba a bag of precious stones to help take care of his expenses when he travelled to the West.

After performing the death rituals for his grandfather, Shivapuri Baba went deeper into the forest and started to meditate in utter solitude, sustaining his body on roots and wild fruits. After twenty-five years of arduous search for truth, he became enlightened at the age of fifty. He has described his enlightenment very poetically: "God appeared in a flash. All questions were answered and all problems were solved forever," he said.

It must have been extremely difficult to meditate alone in the forest, year after year, relying just on wild roots and fruits, waiting for the ultimate experience without anybody around to provide hope or consolation. After enlightenment, Shivapuri Baba, as he had promised his grandfather, travelled around the world mostly on foot for the next fifty years. During his world tour he met many heads of state and intellectuals including Aga Khan of Afghanistan, Leo Tolstoy, Madam Curie, Albert Einstein, George Bernard Shaw, Marconi, Ramakrishna Paramhansa, Sri Aurobindo, Sarwapali Radhakrishnan, Mahatma Gandhi, Balgangadhar Tilak, and Madanmohan Malwiya, along with the Shah Kings of Nepal, Mahendra, Birendra and Gyanendra. Renu

Lal Singh, who was a close disciple of Shivapuri Baba and a close friend of mine, has recounted to me several interesting anecdotes from Shivapuri Baba's world tour.

Shivapuri Baba met Albert Einstein when he was still a young mathematics student in Switzerland. Baba challenged the basic mathematical axiom $1 + 1 = 2$. Einstein, ever so humble and willing to learn, contemplated the proposition but couldn't follow it to its logical end. As Singh remembers, Baba told Einstein, "Absolutely speaking, only God exists, so the question of adding one thing to another cannot be entertained. Relatively speaking, no two things or beings are homogeneous. So, to say $1 + 1 = 2$ is convenient, definitely, but not correct."

Yet another time, Shivapuri Baba was late for a meeting with George Bernard Shaw. When he eventually arrived, Shaw remarked with sarcasm, "I don't like Hindu yogis because you people have no respect for time", to which Baba replied rather calmly, "You Westerners are slaves of time, but we dwell in the realm uncontaminated by the clutch of time, and are hence beyond its bondage."

Baba also spent a few days in Moscow with Leo Tolstoy. Singh told me how Tolstoy's housekeeper was overjoyed to learn Indian recipes from Baba. Completing his world tour, Baba eventually arrived in Nepal in 1926 at the ripe old age of one hundred. Shortly after he went back to Benaras in India. Madanmohan Malwiya was about to establish the Hindu University in Benaras. Malwiya was greatly impressed by Baba's wealth of knowledge and intellect, and offered him the first Vice-Chancellor position in the university. Baba rejected the offer, and instead donated Rs 50,000 to the university, then left for his hometown, Kerala, to inquire about his twin sister, the only surviving member of his family. After seventy years, the yogi had returned to his own home as a wandering sannyasin, to find that his sister had died a long time ago. Then he finalized a few family affairs, and retired to the Shivapuri forests of Nepal. He lived on the Shivapuri hill for thirty-seven years until he left his body at the age of one hundred and thirty-seven. The saint became synonymous with the Shivapuri hill, earning him the name of Shivapuri Baba.

Of all countries he visited, Shivapuri Baba loved Nepal the most. Renu Lal Singh told me how Baba loved watching the sun rise from the Shivapuri heights. Sometimes, when the sky was clear, the sun would gradually rise like a glorious orange disk, spilling a translucent orange blanket over Mount Everest. Baba used to remark, "Ah!" with great pleasure, and compare the sight to seeing God himself.

Shivapuri Baba always stayed away from social recognition and fame. While he was in Nepal, only a few people had the opportunity to meet him in person. When I was living with my master Osho at his ashram in Pune in 1974, he told me I should go back to Kathmandu and establish an ashram. He then advised me to visit the Shivapuri Baba *Samadhi* in Kathmandu, and said that Baba would be my local guardian, and whenever I needed support, energy and inspiration I should visit the *samadhi*, and I would receive it. I had grown up in Kathmandu, and many a time some unknown force would pull me to the Dhrubasthali forest, but I hadn't known anything about Shivapuri Baba until Osho told me about him. To my surprise, Osho even gave me the directions on how to reach there when he had never even visited Nepal before. He knew the intricate details of its location. He told me the ashram was behind the army barracks at the airport, and was fenced with barbed wire. When I came to Kathmandu I went to the Shivapuri Baba Samadhi Mandir in Dhrubasthali, a citadel near the Pashupatinath temple where Baba had spent his last days. To my surprise, I found it was exactly as Osho had described, and it seemed as if he had already been here. I experienced deep meditation at the *samadhi*, and felt the same bliss that I experienced when I was with Osho.

My visits to the *samadhi* became regular, and due to some good fortunes from my past lives, I was able to have deep friendship with two of Baba's close devotees – Professor Sri Renu Lal Singh and Sri Madhav Baje. I got to hear about Baba and his teachings regularly through them for years. I would like to narrate some of the stories they shared with me over the years.

BEYOND TIME AND SPACE

Once while living in the Shivapuri forest, Baba's rations ran out. Baba lit a fire and sat next to it to meditate, and told Madhav Baje to get supplies, before he closed his eyes and immersed himself in meditation. Madhav Baje went to the nearest market in Narayanthan, but couldn't go back to Baba's hut because he caught a severe bout of dysentery and was bedridden for a week. When he went back with the rations after a week, he found Baba's hut extremely quiet. He felt that Baba must have gone somewhere to find food, but when he went in he saw that Baba was seated in the exact position as when he had left him. When Baba heard Baje come in, he said, "Haven't you left for the market yet?" Baba had been in the trance state of *samadhi* for a whole week and had lost all sense of time and space.

THE FIRST MISTAKE

One night there was a big snowfall on the Shivapuri hill. Suddenly a yogi appeared at Baba's hut and asked if he could spend the night there. The yogis have a tradition of feeding and giving shelter if another yogi arrives in their hut or cave. Baba told Madhav Baje to prepare dinner for him but since there was nothing in the hut, Madhav Baje was a bit embarrassed and didn't know what to do. When Baba realized Baje's predicament, he told him, "Even if there is a grain of rice or a lentil left, bring it to me." Baje found a few grains of rice and lentils still left in the basket. Baba told him to put it in the cooking pot and place it on the fire. But since snow had soaked the firewood, he wasn't able to light a fire. Seeing this, Baba sat next to the fire, closed his eyes and blew on the wet firewood. The wet firewood started to burn as if it was dry. To Madhav Baje's surprise, after a while he saw that a full pot of *jaulo*, a mixture of lentil and rice, was boiling. Baje fed their guest till he was fully satisfied. Madhav Baje was amazed and happy to experience his Guru perform a miracle, but Shivapuri Baba looked a little sad. When the two of them were alone, Baba said to Baje, "Today, although it was out of compassion, I still broke a rule of nature. It was the first mistake of my life."

Although Shivapuri Baba had a lot of psychic powers, he refrained from using them, but sometimes compassion can overpower the determination of even the greatest among us.

THE SECOND MISTAKE

Baba, at over one hundred and fifteen years old, had already moved to the Dhruvasthali forest behind the Pashupatinath temple. His main source of food was milk that came from a cow which somebody had donated to him. The specialty of the cow was that she would give a quarter of a litre of milk whenever she was milked. The current international airport of Kathmandu used to be a common grazing ground for cattle in those days. The cow herders started talking about this special cow that gave milk any time she was milked. In those days, the aristocratic Rana family held power over the Nepali government. A cow herder of a powerful Rana family member found out about this special cow and told him about it. "That cow should belong to your palace; the yogi can make do with any cow," he told him.

The aristocrat told the herder to acquire the cow, and give three good quality cows in return. A few soldiers went to Shivapuri

Baba and announced the aristocrat's orders, but Baba refused it outright. The soldiers returned and told the aristocrat, "That yogi was extremely stubborn; he wouldn't agree to exchange his cow. How dare he live under your rule and disobey you? It is a great insult to us."

The aristocrat also became angry and said, "Tie the three cows in his cowshed, and get that cow here even if it is by force."

Following his order, the soldiers went back and forcefully took Baba's cow. Shivapuri Baba untied the three cows that they had left with him, and returned them back to the aristocrat. However a spark of anger came into Baba's mind towards the aristocrat. Just because he had the power, he had taken away the only source of food of a yogi who relied totally on existence. The same night, the aristocrat started vomiting blood, and the next morning he was dead. It is not that Baba hurt him or that his anger killed him, but when you disrespect a yogi who has become one with existence and is fully reliant on it, you disrespect the divine itself. The aristocrat had to bear the fruits of his own arrogance. When Baba heard this, he said that his anger of the other night was the second mistake of his life.

THE LAST TEST

Madhav Baje served Shivapuri Baba with utmost devotion throughout his life. A few days before Baba left his body, he said to Baje, "When I leave my body, you will be alone. You don't really have any property of your own. Because you were always taking care of me, you didn't get the time to study as well. You will need something to sustain your life. So I feel I need to make an arrangement for you. Why don't you bring that iron chair close to me. I will touch it and turn it into gold. That way you can live your life comfortably."

Hearing this Baje started to cry and fell at Baba's feet and said, "If my lord is not here with me, what will I do with a golden chair? I don't need it."

Baba smiled and said, "Good, this was your last test, and you have passed it. I will put you in the care of God himself. He will take care of all your needs and will make sure you have no problems."

A Guru tests his disciples till the last moments of his life. A disciple should have trust, patience and contentment just like Madhav Baje.

A few days before Baba had left his body, Renulalji had asked him, "Who will guide us when you leave your body?"

Baba answered, "Another enlightened master can also come and help you. And if you pray with total trust, I will come and guide you in your dreams."

It has been more than forty years since Baba left his body, but I have seen that even today trusting seekers receive personal guidance by Baba regularly.

DEPARTURE OF THE GREAT EMPEROR

Shivapuri Baba used to drink a glass of milk every night before going to bed, and he would leave one third of the milk in the glass as prasad for Mahdav Baje. The night before Baba left his body, Baje brought him the glass of milk as usual. Baba drank his share and handed over the glass to Baje. Seeing that Baba looked extremely week, Baje told him to drink all the milk. Baba smiled and said, "Shall I drink it all?" Baje answered, "Yes drink it all." That night Baba drank the full glass of milk. At midnight, Baba called Baje and told him to put a spoonful of water in his mouth. Baba swallowed the water and slept using his arm as a pillow as usual, and said to Baje, "Son, live Right Life. Now I am gone." Baba used to wake at three every morning, but since he was not out of bed even by six, Madhav Baje checked on him then, to find that the great emperor of a saint had already left his body, and was free from the circle of birth and death for ever.

Shivapuri Baba was born laughing, and he left his body in

peace. But for those who have trust in him, even today his presence remains available and will remain until eternity.

Osho remembered Shivapuri Baba with great respect. When he talked about the books he loved, he talked about *The Long Pilgrimage*, a book written by J. G. Bennett about Shivapuri Baba. In Osho's words Shivapuri Baba is a rare flowering, and to find a person like him is either out of great luck or the result of a tremendous search. Bennett was lucky. It was he who introduced Shivapuri Baba to the West. He also made George Gurdjieff well known to the world.

The essence of Baba's teaching is what he calls "Right Life." It has two parts – Discrimination and Devotion. He says that a seeker practicing 'Right Life' needs to have physical, moral and spiritual discipline. To understand his teachings further, I request that you read *The Long Pilgrimage* by John G. Bennett, *Right Life* by Professor Renu Lal Singh, and *Right Living* by Dr. Yogendra Bhakta Shrestha.

FAMOUS SAYINGS OF SHIVAPURI BABA

- One cannot turn towards God with sincerity unless he completely fails in life.

- The best place to live is the forest, next to that is a palace. All other places are hell.

- Orthodox people don't like me because I live like a modern man and modern people don't like me because I talk like an orthodox man.

- Nobody accepts me because if they could understand me they would understand God himself.

- As long as you are after material objects, there is no end to your misery. When this stops, you will become happy on your own.

- The Hindu trinity of Brahma, Bishnu and Maheshwor are also of no use. Before I used to run after them, now they run after me.

- Art should be idealistic, thinking should be realistic and life should be artistic.

- Until we realize God, everything we do will go against us.

- Relatively speaking everybody is right, absolutely speaking everyone is wrong.

SWAMI RAMA

> " Swami Rama was a handsome yogi from a Garhwali family. He spent years in various parts of the Himalayas and on the bank of the Narmada in central India. I met Swami Rama regularly, until he left his body in 1996 at the age of seventy-one. "

In 2007, during one of my annual visits to the United States of America to conduct meditation retreats, we were strolling leisurely along the busy Fifth Avenue in Manhattan. Fifth Avenue is always bustling with zealous cosmopolitans of New York City. The famous New York flagship stores scream loudly about exclusive items you only realize you need once you walk through this avenue. Quite unexpectedly, walking through the glitterati of the Fifth Avenue I ran into East West Living and Café.

East West Living and Café with its quiet and serene ambience came forth like an oasis in the middle of the chaos that Fifth Avenue was. This centre had a book shop and an organic vegetarian café. The faint waft of incense that filled the store immediately transported one into a meditative space. I walked leisurely around the shelves. To my great pleasure, they had a rare collection of books on eastern mysticism, holistic science and metaphysics. They also had other accessories related to meditation and holistic healing. I was very thrilled to spot certain rare books by Osho, Krishnamurti, Raman Maharshi and other eastern mystics that are difficult to come by even in Nepal and India. Books remain my ultimate indulgence. I was so overjoyed to find these books that eventually I ended up buying books that not only weighed on my wallet but on my luggage limit as well. Their massage chambers looked tempting too, but I spared those until my next visit. Unfortunately, when I visited the place again in 2014 it was shut down as the their lease had expired.

Jane Mathew, the owner of the store, is an initiated and close disciple of Swami Rama. She ran it out of her devotion for her master. Between 1982 and 1984 she had visited Swami Rama in his ashram in Banepa, a quaint place in the mountains just a few hours' drive from Kathmandu. Swami Rama had an ambitious master plan for a hospital and Ayurvedic institute at Banepa, and had chosen my firm, Building Design Authority (BDA), as its consulting bureau. Although Ms. Mathew frequented Nepal regularly during that period, we didn't met each other then. I loved Swami Rama dearly and we had a lot of common topics we both enjoyed talking about. She had also read many of Osho's works, and had great respect for him. Swami Rama himself spoke very highly of Osho. This meeting revitalized a great deal of cherished memories of Swami Rama, a mystic of rare brilliance and beauty, whose mysterious life, recounted in his biographical book *Living with the Himalayan Masters,* remains a source of inspiration for many seekers around the world.

Swami Rama was a handsome yogi from a Garhwali family. While he was still a child, his Guru, Madhavendra Saraswati, took him to live in the Himalayan forests for his spiritual training. He spent years in various parts of the Himalayas as well as on the bank of the Narmada in central India. From 1949 to 1952 he held the position of the Shankaracharya of Karvirpitham in South India. Shankaracharyas are the supreme Hindu leaders in India. But he realized in that short time that this position interfered with his meditation, and he resigned from the post and continued his meditation. When his meditation matured he had a calling to go to the United States. He opened his main ashram at Rolling Hills, Honesdale, Pennsylvania, which he called the Himalayan Institute.

Swami Rama had been of great help to Princess Shova, the sister of Late King Birendra, while she was delivering her twins in the United States of America. This earned him a close friendship with the royal family of Nepal. Queen Aishwarya invited him to Nepal, and offered him a property of about one hundred and twenty-five acres in Banepa, east of the Kathmandu valley. I first met Swami Rama then, when I was an engineering consultant.

Before this meeting, a few years earlier, I had spoken to him over the telephone. I was to travel to Rajneeshpuram, Oregon, to meet my master Osho. Swami Rama was then residing at Himalayan Institute in Pennsylvania. A friend of mine was a close disciple of his, and had asked me to deliver a letter to Swamiji. I posted the letter to Swamiji, and called him to inform him about it. After introducing myself and telling him about the letter, he talked very affectionately and invited me to his ashram. I was on a brief vacation so I could spare neither extra time nor money. I hesitantly stated my limitations. In the beginning I thought he was just being polite to invite me over, but he insisted several more times.

So a few years later, he had arrived in Nepal with a rather enterprising project. The word reached me that he was looking for an architectural firm for the project. The project was worth a million dollars, and naturally there were a lot of contenders for the position. Swami Rama was staying at Hotel Yak & Yeti. When I reached the hotel for the interview, I was intimidated by the long queue of contenders who had applied for the tender. I was received by Swami Rama in his hotel room. After my brief introduction, I reminded him of our telephone conversation. "Oh! So you are an Osho sannyasin?" he queried, and he inquired further about my spiritual journey. He expressed a very satisfied smile and said, "Okay. I have found my engineer. I needed someone who can understand the underlying spiritual aspect of this project as well. Because you are running a meditation centre, I can trust you on this." He also told me he had met Osho, and had a great respect for his revolutionary ideas.

When Osho was mistreated by the American government and jailed without warrant and for baseless charges, he had said, "It's always the same. I, too, left my ashram in Pennsylvania because I knew if I were to stay there longer and attract more white disciples from the Christian fold, the Christian fanatics would have treated me the same way they treated Osho." Maharshi Mahesh Yogi left America for the same reason.

Swami Rama's project was rolling in full swing in Nepal, when suddenly he had a rift with the queen. All the facilities that he had been receiving from the state were withdrawn. Swami Rama left the country abruptly. He took the whole project to India, and opened the Himalayan Medical College and Hospital in Dehradun. The college is recognized today as one of the oldest and finest medical colleges in India. I have visited almost all the ashrams of Swami Rama, including the ones in Pennsylvania, Rishikesh and Banepa. Like all his ashrams, the college, too, is very beautifully designed. It is nestled in the foothills of the Himalayas, and offers a spectacular view of the majestic mountains.

I went to Rishikesh to meet him after his abrupt departure from Nepal. He was very happy to see me. He always invited me for tea whenever I was in Rishikesh. That day, too, we sat down for breakfast. He didn't tell me exactly what had caused the rift, but whatever it was had really disheartened the yogi. Afterwards, he told me he wanted me to manage his property in Nepal. He wrote a Will that stated he wanted me to use the property for expanding Osho work in Nepal. Back then, Nepal was under the *panchayat* system where the king had supreme power, and since the Royal family looked after the property, I returned the Will and said I could not dare to do so. Later, the property was conferred upon Swami Bishudhadev. Time and again, Swami Rama insisted I go to Japan to manage his rather affluent ashram there. I told him I had made a commitment to my master, Osho, to spread his work in Nepal, and therefore couldn't oblige his affectionate summons.

Living with the Himalayan Masters is Swami Rama's autobiographical book, in which he has written about various mystical experiences with mysterious Himalayan yogis. For a logical mind, many of his experiences are hard to believe, and fall more in the realm of fantasy than reality. For example, once he was meditating at Tribenighat, Rishikesh, and became extremely hungry.

Suddenly a hand of a woman materialized out of the middle of the Ganga. It held a beautiful *kamandalu*, a handheld pot used by yogis to keep water and food. The hand was of mother Ganga herself. Ganga told Swami Rama the magical *kamandalu* was a gift to him, and whatever food he desired would appear inside it. Swami Rama writes further, that the food that he wanted to eat would always appear in it. He fulfilled his need for food through that magical *kamandalu* for quite a while. When his Guru found out about it he told him that it was not right to take help of miraculous objects while meditating, and told him to throw the *kamandalu* back into the Ganga.

There is a similar story in the life of the famous Avadhoot Ram of Banaras. Seeing his poverty, the Goddess of the Annapurna Temple, next to the Kashi Bishwonath Temple, appeared and blessed him saying, "To fulfill your needs, every night I will put a ten rupee note under your pillow." He received the money throughout his life.

Such stories are often very hard to believe unless one has experienced such moments oneself. Therefore, a few mystical experiences are ever shared in the public domain because most of the time the audience isn't mature enough for them.

I met Swami Rama regularly, until he left his body in 1996 at the age of seventy-one. He loved me dearly with paternal affection. A few months before he left his body, he composed a poem that forewarned his eternal journey:

> *Child am I of a sage of the mountains*
> *Free spirit am I; light walks by my side*
> *Fearless live I above glacial fountain*
> *In seclusion of Himalayan cavern reside*
>
> *With snowy weather beating around me*
> *Ascending the peaks of the mountains I go*
> *No one talks with me, no one walks with me*
> *As I cross streams and tramp glacial snow*
>
> *I roam in the mountains that hark to the skies*
> *And of silence have made me a friend*
> *My love whispers to me with silent replies*
>
> *And guided by thee I ascend.*

DALAI LAMA

> " I can attempt to describe the ineffable delight that overtook me when I first met the Dalai Lama but I am well aware that such mystical experiences are inexpressible. In his presence, just as it happens in the presence of Osho, all seriousness sublimated effortlessly. In its place, a deep ecstatic feeling filled my being. "

In Mongolian, *dalai* means ocean and *lama* is Tibetan for spiritual teacher. Dalai Lama, therefore, can be translated as the ocean of wisdom. Interestingly, this is also the meaning of the word Osho. During my two private meetings with the current Dalai Lama, Tenzing Gyatso, I realized the name was just one of the many similarities these two masters shared.

My first meeting with His Holiness was nothing if not a happy chance. After attending his first ever *Kumbha Mela* at Allahabaad, he was residing at Hotel Ashoka in Delhi as a guest of the Indian government. Long before I met him in person, I had been thoroughly inspired by his ever-joyous and light-hearted personality. That particular day though, I was quite excited by the prospect of meeting him, but I wasn't entirely sure if I could actually get an audience.

After waiting for about an hour it was announced that I had

made it to the list. A pleasant chill went down my spine. After a series of security checks, I was ushered into a rather spacious salon where His Holiness was seated along with his English translator and a few senior Buddhist monks. Dalai Lama noticed my mala with an Osho pendant and interjected joyously, "Ah! Rajneesh! Rajneesh!" He then turned around to the monks and said a few things in Tibetan about Osho. Throughout, a faint smile lit up on his face. He then turned around to me and shared his reflections from the recent Kumbha Mela. His Holiness seemed to have greatly enjoyed his visit. He told me how a few of his monks had advised him not to attend the festival as it had no relevance to Buddhism whatsoever but that had not changed his mind. One particular thing that seemed to have touched him most profoundly was the fact that in the gathering of twenty million people, not a single animal was slaughtered or harmed in anyway.

"During our seminars," he told me, "thousands of animals are slaughtered for food everyday. And we are the disciples of the Buddha, who preaches compassion and non-violence." I could see that his associates were clearly not happy with the remark.

I had attended his discourse the other day, where he had spoken about his Guru, Nagarjuna. As he gave his discourse I was so touched that I wept the whole time. Coincidentally our ashram at Kathmandu is situated in Nagarjuna Hills, where Nagarjuna had meditated for twenty-eight years, two thousand years ago. We had recently completed the construction of the Osho *Samadhi* at our ashram in the exact location where Nagarjuna attained enlightenment. I showed him the pictures of the *samadhi* and expressed my desire to have it inaugurated by His Holiness. He looked at the pictures eagerly and asked many questions about the place. For political reasons, he wasn't allowed to visit Nepal, so he asked me how else he could do it. I asked him to sign the picture and bless it, to which he complied happily. In this way, His Holiness inaugurated the Osho *Samadhi* at Nepal while sitting in a hotel room in Delhi. The picture remains in our archives, along with the gifts I received from Osho, as a cherished memento.

This brief meeting was followed by a photo session. There were around thirty rather influential personalities who had signed up for the session. To my pleasant surprise, the Dalai Lama took my hand and held it throughout the session. I can attempt to describe the ineffable delight that overtook me, but I am well aware that such mystical experiences are inexpressible. In his presence, just as it happens in the presence of Osho, all seriousness sublimated effortlessly. In its place, a deep ecstatic feeling filled my being.

The current Dalai Lama, Tenzing Gyatso, was born on July 6th 1935 in the north-eastern Tibetan village of Taktser. He is a monk of the Gelug, or the Yellow Hat, School of Tibetan Buddhism.

Tibetan Buddhism consists of four main schools. The oldest of them is the Ningma School. It is also known as the Red Cap Sect. It was started by Shantirakshit, the famous monk from Nalanda, and Padmasambhava, the Tantrik Guru from Kashmir. They carried the essence of Buddhism from India to Tibet in the eighth century. In 640 AD, Bhrikuti, the daughter of King Amshuverma of Nepal, was married to the Tibetan King, Tsrong Tsang Gompo. She had taken with her sandalwood statues of both Buddha and Tara. A temple was made in central Tibet to house those statues. But the credit for starting Lamaism in Tibet goes to Padmasambhava or Guru Rimpoche.

The second most famous sect is the Kagyu. It is also known as the Mahamudra School, or the Black Cap School. This was established by Tantrik Guru Tilopa in the tenth century. His lineage consists of famous tantric masters such as Naropa, Marpa, Milerapa and Gompopa. Its main monastery is in Churphu in central Tibet, but currently the Kagyu headquarters is at the Rumtek Monastery of

Sikkim. Its head is the seventeenth Karmapa, who currently lives near Dharmashala in Himmachal Pradesh, India. The sixteenth Karmapa, Rangjung Ringpe Dorje, was the first traditional spiritual leader to proclaim Osho as the Bodhisattva of this age in 1971. He had declared Osho as an avatar of a Tibetan master who would establish religion in this age through modern and rebellious methods, since the old methods have become redundant.

The third oldest school is the Shakya, or the Grey School. Its head monastery, the Tashikungpo, is in the south-western Tibetan region of Sigatse. Since the monastery is surrounded by an area that has grey clay, it is known as the Grey School. Its leader is the Panchen Lama who is thought to be the reincarnation of Amitabha Buddha. The tenth Panchen Lama died in 1989 at Sigatse. The two contenders for the eleventh Panchen Lama are both in Tibet.

The fourth and most important school is the Gelug School, or the Yellow Cap School. This is the mainstream Tibetan Buddhist school, and is headed by the Dalai Lama. This sect has teachings of all the other three schools, the Ningma, Kagyu and Shakya, and propounds the teachings of Tantra as well as Nagarjuna's middle path. The Dalai Lama is the spiritual and political leader of Tibet. The first Dalai Lama was Gedun Drub, who lived from 1391 to 1474. Tenzing Gyatso, the fourteenth Dalai Lama, has been living in exile since 1959. The Dalai Lama is considered the reincarnation of the Bodhisattva of Compassion, Avalokiteshvara.

The current Dalai Lama has touched the hearts of all sensitive people in the world, whether Buddhist or non-Buddhist. The simplicity of his personality, his light and humorous take on life, his compassion and open-mindedness towards all faiths and philosophies made a deep imprint upon my heart. You can't call him a skilled orator, but every word he utters is charged with the fragrance of truth and purity which hypnotizes his audience. Despite his skyrocketing fame, he is simple and innocent like a child. While I was listening to his discourse, somebody asked him, "What makes you happiest?"

He scratched his head like a child and repeated the question to himself and then said, "Perhaps good food and good sleep."

Once during his discourse, birds started to sing on a nearby roof. He stopped talking and started looking towards the roof. He then said, "I feel that the songs of the birds are sweeter than my discourse."

The Dalai Lama has a truly unique perspective, whereby he looks at each event of life in a very positive and hopeful way. He has tremendous love and belief in Tibet, and awaits the day he can return to his motherland, although he has no complaints against those who caused his exile and doesn't harbour any anger or animosity towards them. He says, "If I was still in Tibet, I would be on a completely different plane. I am now a refugee. This is also my good fortune. By being in exile, I have been able to see life in its reality. If I were still in Tibet, my whole life would have been spent in performing useless rituals. I am now free of it and thus I have had the opportunity to meet some of the most important and spiritual people of the world, and have learned tremendously from them. If I were still in Tibet, I would not have been able to visit the Buddhist holy places such as Bodhgaya, Sarnath and Kushinagar every year. It has only been possible because I am living as a refugee in India."

On the surface, the Dalai Lama's life appears to be full of misery and defeat. At the age of two, he was taken away from his family and placed under strict discipline at Potala Palace. Instead of being able to enjoy the joys and adventures of youth he became the King of Tibet when he was only fifteen, and was forced to engage in politics with one of the biggest and most rigid governments of his time. He also went to Beijing twice and tried to negotiate with Chinese leaders,

Mao Tse Tung and Chao En Lai. But despite being very flexible, all his efforts went down the drain and in the end he had to secretly flee from his country before the Chinese army invaded Potala Palace in Lhasa. He had to go through the agony of witnessing the execution of hundreds of thousands of monks, and arson on hundreds of monasteries that destroyed countless important religious texts and relics, all in the name of the Cultural Revolution. He saw his parents, teachers, siblings and relatives die before his eyes. Thousands of refugees come to him every morning, and shared their painful stories. The members of his own sect are often agitated by his non-violent approach to issues related to Tibetan politics. He is often questioned by young Tibetans, "Every day the culture of Tibet is being destroyed, What has your forgiveness and compassion given to the Tibetans?"

In the middle of all this he remains calm, hopeful and smiling. In fact, he even comes across as one of the happiest people on earth. Although the six million Tibetans revere him as an alive Buddha, he is not ready to consider himself more than a simple Buddhist monk. He appears to be blissfully oblivious to the effect he has on millions all over the world. In 2013 Harris Poll carried out a poll, across the five largest European countries and the United States of America, for the most popular world leader. He, along with Barack Obama, was voted as the most popular world leader.

His Holiness was presented with the Nobel Peace Prize in Oslo, Norway, on December 10 1989. While receiving the prize, he said, "I receive this prize with utmost gratitude in the name of all the oppressed people of the world, and for those who are struggling for freedom and peace around the world. I receive it as a token of respect for Mahatma Gandhi who established a culture of peace and non-violence in the world. His life has inspired me continuously. And I also accept this prize for the six million Tibetans who are living in great pain and sadness."

He concluded his speech by reciting his favourite prayer:

May I be a guard for those who need protection
A guide for those on the path
A boat, a raft, a bridge for those who wish to cross the flood
May I be a lamp in the darkness
A resting place for the weary
A healing medicine for all who are sick
A vase of plenty, a tree of miracles
And for the boundless multitudes of living beings
May I bring sustenance and awakening
Enduring like the earth and sky
Until all beings are freed from sorrow
And all are awakened

The Dalai Lama is not affected by either praise or condemnation but by accepting the Nobel Prize, he raised the glory of the prize itself. A large part of his prize money of $1.12 million was distributed the same day for victims of famine around the world, lepers in India, and for international organizations working for peace. The rest of the money was distributed to Tibetan organizations working for the welfare of Tibetans around the world.

The Dalai Lama starts his day at 4:00 in the morning with prayer. Like any other monk, he makes a commitment not to keep any property. In his bedroom he has a simple bed and a statue of the Buddha. After some exercise and a shower he meditates till 5:30, and after meditation he prays for the good of all creatures. After this he goes to the garden and tends his plants. In his own words he loves "listening to birds, and looking at the vastness of the open sky". After a light breakfast he reaches the meditation hall at 6:00, and meditates till 9:00. Between 9:00 and 12:30 he studies. Despite reading for three and a half hours every day, he says he doesn't get enough time to read. Apart from Buddhist texts, he likes reading

Western philosophy, quantum physics, astronomy and neurobiology, to name a few. He is famously quoted as having said that if he had not become a Buddhist monk, he would have been an engineer.

At 12:30 he has lunch. After that, he meets people and conducts meetings with his ministers regarding the management of the Tibetan Government in exile. Like all Buddhist monks, he doesn't have dinner, but only drinks a cup of tea in the evening. After that, he watches films on various cultures, or television programs on nature and wildlife. At 8:30 he prays and goes to sleep.

The Dalai Lama has equal respect for all religions and philosophies. He once said, "Osho is an enlightened master who is trying all that he can to raise human consciousness in this difficult time."

The critics of Dalai Lama call him an anti-revolutionary autocrat. However, those who know him from close encounters, and who try to understand him, have found him to be a reformist, a forward looking humanist as well as a tolerant religious leader. His universal values, relentless advocacy for world peace, and progressive views on religion and science, among other attributes, have rightfully earned him the status of an influential world leader. He has often said there is no need for any temple or any complex philosophy, as long as our life is motivated by compassion. He also has liberal views on sex. He has cast aside celibacy as a prerequisite for enlightenment. His teaching is based on the concept of natural and spontaneous living. It can be best summed up in his famous quote, "Be kind whenever possible. It is always possible."

Twenty years later in my second private audience with His Holiness I noticed the same grace, the same humour. This meeting too had come about unexpectedly. I was conducting an Osho meditation retreat in the United Kingdom in the same city where the Dalai Lama was giving a public talk. I tried to get a ticket for the talk, but unfortunately the tickets had sold out completely except for a few charity tickets, which were way beyond my budget. A few days before the talk, I received a random invitation from a Buddhist monastery in the city to give a talk on the Buddha. I was one of the four orators speaking at the event. Like every other orator, I was allowed forty-five minutes to present my ideas. However, the audience was so pleased with my talk that they requested an extra Question and Answer session. That session, too, was well received. Afterwards, each orator was offered a token of thanks. I, surprisingly, ended up with two free tickets for the Dalai Lama's talk. As luck would have it, soon after his talk, the Nepalese Buddhist Society was granted a private audience with the Dalai Lama. They wanted to build a Buddhist temple in London and had written a letter to His Holiness seeking his advice and support. Since some members from the Society had attended my talk the previous day, they asked me to accompany them. I was only too happy to oblige.

After hearing the plan, His Holiness remarked in good humor, "I am no more a king but a refugee. I cannot donate a lot, but I will donate a portion of the royalty from my books to the temple." With the Dalai Lama's support and guidance the Nepali Buddhist Temple has been built in London.

His Holiness then turned towards me and I reminded him of our meeting twenty years ago, to which he chuckled. I had carried a copy of my book, where I had devoted a chapter to him. I showed him the copy and told him it was rather unfortunate that the text was in Nepali and that he would not be able to understand it. He started leafing through the pages and told me, "I have a Nepali translator I will get him to translate it for me." I bowed down and touched his feet. I was overpowered by a strong sense of deja vu. The same ineffable joy ran through my nerves as it used to do when I had a meeting with Osho. For days after meeting with Osho, the intoxication would remain intact. I would enter the realm of the mysterious and ride on its ecstatic waves, totally liberated from all my thoughts, my past, and the idea of who I was. On several occasions I have tried to translate this into words, always unsuccessfully. Human words or languages are still premature and inadequate when it comes to the description of deep spiritual experience. I would be filled with a powerful euphoria interspersed with times of deep and nourishing silence. I had exactly the same feeling when I touched the feet of His Holiness. The communion was so vivid, so intense, that even as I write this, goose bumps break out on my body.

SRI AUROBINDO

> "A sadhaka is free from the traps of the worldly desires that the world runs after. The fulfillment of worldly desires dwells in the crowd while a free soul quenches its spiritual thirst away from the world immersed in the bliss of numinous solitude."

On August 15th 1947 India attained independence from the British Raj. Seventy-five years earlier on the same day it had given birth to Sri Aurobindo, a great yogi and a spiritual reformist, who was one of the pioneers of the Indian independence movement.

Aurobindo's father Dr. Krishnadhan Bose was a professional doctor in England. Aurobindo's father, Dr. Krishnadhan Bose was a doctor in England. Krishnadhan was so influenced by Western culture that he wanted to rear and educate his child according to Western standards. So Aurobindo's entire upbringing, including his education, happened in England. When he was five he was sent to Loreto School in Darjeeling, and when he was seven he was sent to England. He spent the next fourteen years studying at a school in Manchester, and later attended St. Paul's College, Cambridge.

Later, in 1892, he received the top marks for the main paper of the Indian Civil Service examinations. By then he had already become well acquainted with the freedom fighters of the Indian independence movement and an intense nationalistic fervor and patriotism had awakened in him.

He refused to become the administrator of the English establishment by deliberately skipping horse-riding competition, which was the final part of the test. Instead, he became an active member of Lotus and Sword, the revolutionary, semi-underground organization based in India. It was during this time that he met Maharaja Gaekwad of Baroda who urged him to return back to India for good and work for the government of Baroda while continuing to help the Indian independence movement.

In 1893, Sri Aurobindo received his degree and returned back to India. For the next nine years he served the Baroda government. During this time he also got acquainted with Indian culture, yoga and the Indian freedom movement.

While he was still stationed in Baroda, Aurobindo married fourteen-year-old Mrinalini Devi. During this time he also became close with the leaders of the Indian independence movement and was active in organizing armed rebellion against the British rule in India. As his political aspiration deepened, his interest in meditation and spirituality matured, too. Due to the *sanskars* of his past lives, in spite of his hectic schedule, he started managing time for inner exploration, and his search for a Guru led him to Bishnubhaskar Lele of Maharashtra. Lele could see great potential in Aurobindo. He urged him to spend some time with him and meditate together. It was very difficult for Aurobindo to arrange free time but he managed three days out of his busy schedule. He meditated in seclusion with Lele for three days and had deep experiences of meditation. He experienced the state of thoughtless consciousness and realized that he was a witness - a state that often takes years for a normal meditator to achieve. Lele was very much impressed by the progress and advised Aurobindo to leave his worldly affairs and devote full-time to meditation. Aurobindo felt that leaving India under the British rule to go and meditate would be escaping the need of the moment and didn't agree to do so. However, he continued meditating regularly. He started to get instructions and inspiration from within during his meditation. He shared his experiences with Lele who was very happy to hear them. Lele told him, "If you have full faith in your inner voice then you don't need any advice from outside."

In 1906, Aurobindo left Baroda for Kolkata, which was a fertile ground for the revolutionaries. He had accepted the post of principal at the Bengal National College but spent most of his time encouraging the revolutionaries, editing pamphlets and newspapers and supporting organizations. In 1908, the family of Kingsford, the British Governor of the area, was assassinated in a bomb blast. Aurobindo was one of the prime suspects. In May 5th he was arrested and put in Aligpur Jail. Initially, Aurobindo had been disheartened but when he started to meditate in the jail, his inner voice said, "Just wait and watch. " The message immediately restored his peace and calm.

Since his political and professional career had hindered him from exploring the deeper aspects of yoga and meditation, he found out that his arrest had been a blessing in disguise. He had had a lot of free time to devote to his spiritual quest now. He spent his days studying the Gita and the Upanishads and meditating.

In his books, Aurobindo has time and again expressed his gratitude to the English for keeping him in the jail for a year. Had it not been for his arrest, he would have never been able to immerse in deep meditation.

In Alipur Jail, among other things, Aurobindo experienced levitation of his body. He also heard instructions from Swami

Vivekananda continuously for fifteen days although it had already been six years since Swami Vivekananda had left his body. While meditating in the jail, a lot of his dormant *siddhis* also awakened.

There was a Kadamba tree right in front of his cell. Sri Aurobindo had the *darshan* of Lord Krishna, who, too, advised him to leave all other work and devote full-time to his meditation. Aurobindo was still worried about the Independence Movement.

Krishna assured him, "You just meditate in solitude; I will take the responsibility of India's freedom. The Independence of India will come as a gift on your birthday."

One year later, after Aurobindo was released from the jail, the talented revolutionary and fiery writer had transformed into a peaceful, content yogi.

After coming out of the jail, Aurobindo gave a very heartrending and historically significant speech in a spiritual conference in Utarpada, a town near Kolkata. It is now famously referred to as the Utarpada speech. In this speech, Aurobindo has clearly explained about the experiences and insights he gained during his stay in the jail. He said, "Going to the jail and coming out of it were both a part of an existential plan. The purpose of the jail life was to detach me from my strong attachment towards politics." His speech also related the vision he had of Lord Krishna in which Krishna had said, "India's main problem isn't political: it's spiritual. The prevailing foreign interference is simply a consequence of the spiritual cowardliness and lack of spiritual fervour. You'll have to revive and re-establish the authentic spiritual values of Hindu wisdom in the world."

Lord Krishna had indicated that a new leader was now ready to spearhead India's political independence, referring to Mahatma Gandhi. It was his prison experience that propelled Aurobindo to take the bold decision to abandon politics in order to continue his spiritual journey.

The chief disciple of Swami Vivekananda, Bhagini Nivedita, had become Aurobindo's political and spiritual assistant. She told him that the British were planning to re-arrest him and advised him to leave British India. I feel that it was Vivekananda's love for Aurobindo that manifested in Nivedita's words. Aurobindo got a similar guidance from his inner self as well. Immediately, he left Bengal for the French colony of Pondicherry in South India via Chandranagar and arrived there on April 4, 1910.

In ancient times, the mystic Agyasta Muni of North India had also made Pondicherry his last destination. It was from there that he had propounded Vedic culture in South India. In the ancient texts of the Ramayana, there is a beautiful description of how Ram had met Agyastamuni and received his blessings and spiritual power before winning the war with Lanka. To revive the same old Vedic culture, another North Indian yogi, Sri Aurobindo reached Pondicherry, where he established his ashram and spent the rest of his life there.

In its initial days the ashram was very poor and Aurobindo lived there with three other seekers. There was not even a bathroom in the ashram and the ashramites had to take a shower under the public tap and even had to share the same towel. There was only one lamp in the ashram under which all the activities were carried out once it got dark. Every evening, Aurobindo received a stick of candle to read by.

In 1912, Aurobindo wrote a very poignant letter to his friend, Motilal Roy which depicted the state of poverty in the ashram. The letter read, "There is only half a rupee left in the ashram fund while six-seven people are sheltered in it. Immediately, send us 50 rupees. All your physical, mental and spiritual energy can be used to attain this 50 rupees. I know that the divine shall take care of us but it has a very bad habit of making one wait till the end."

In 1914, French couple Paul and Mirra Richards, arrived in

Pondicherry. Later the same Mirra Richards became known as the Mother. As soon as she saw Aurobindo, she realized that he was the same yogi that she had been seeing in her visions throughout her life. Every Sunday, the Richards invited Aurobindo and his disciples for dinner. That was the only time in the week they would get to eat a full sumptuous meal and drink fine French wine. Despite his high yogic sate of consciousness, and unlike most Indian yogis, Aurobindo used to eat non-vegetarian food and drink alcohol. As he came from a Bengali family and grew up in the West, this was a normal practice for him. Ramakrishna and Vivekananda also came from Bengali families and used to eat fish regularly as a part of their diet. Even today, fish is accepted as a part of the daily meal in Ramakrishna Ashram.

A devotee of the South Indian enlightened master, Raman Maharshi, a contemporary of Sri Aurobindo, had complained to him about Aurobindo's consumption of meat and wine. Raman had instead praised Aurobindo, "He was born in a Bengali family and grew up in the West, that's why he has such eating habits. Don't evaluate a yogi through his habits. Aurobindo is in a very high state of yoga."

Later Aurobindo, seeing that non-vegetarian food and alcohol was hindering his spiritual practice, quit both and turned vegetarian. Today all the Aurobindo Ashrams are fully vegetarian.

In 1920, the Mother divorced her husband and started to live permanently in the ashram and took the full responsibility of running it. After this, Aurobindo confined himself in his room. 24 November is celebrated as the *siddhidiwas* of Sri Aurobindo. It was on this day of 1926 that the supramind consciousness descended on him.

Aurobindo left his body on December 5th, 1950. He was buried four days later in the ashram compound. Aurobindo had refused the post of the President of the Indian National Congress in 1907 and later refused to be the first President of Independent India. Aurobindo felt that the main reason for the misery of man was his spiritual unconsciousness and made efforts throughout his life to uplift human consciousness and to make arrangements to descend the supramind consciousness to the earth.

In the last twenty-four years of his life, Aurobindo came out of his room to give darshan to his disciples only four times a year. The time he spent alone in his room is steeped in mystery. He says, "Meditation is for those who can come out of the society and the world, and travel the lonely journey towards the unknown. Prince Siddhartha left his wife and palace at midnight, and also set out on his spiritual journey all alone, because this path is very personal and its destiny is also dependent on one's being. A *sadhaka* is free from the traps of those worldly desires that the world runs after. The fulfillment of worldly desires dwells in the crowd, while a free soul quenches its spiritual thirst away from the world, immersed in the bliss of numinous solitude."

GOKHLE BABA

"By the time I had heard of Gokhle Baba, he was already a hundred and teh years old. Baba was unusually gifted in music, and it was this very gift that earned him a stay in Nepal. The Ranas, then rulers of Nepal, were connoisseurs of music. When they heard Baba sing, they were very pleased by his song and succumbed to his wish to live in Nepal."

A mysterious yogi had made his home in Hetauda, a city in central Nepal. By the time I heard of him from a friend of mine, he was already a hundred and ten years old. Back then, I was supervising the construction of the Hetauda Leather Factory as a designer and resident engineer in the Hetauda industrial Estate, and I visited the city frequently. I had heard that the yogi lived in a tiny hut in a hill above Rapti River. He was said to have met many enlightened masters such as Ramakrishna, Vivekananda, Shivapuri Baba and Raman Maharshi. Every time, I heard about this yogi, I felt an unexplainable pull. The feeling, of course, was inexplicable and the only way to solve this mystery was by meeting him.

So, one fine day I set out on my motorbike from my quarter at the Industrial Estate to meet him. When I came close to the bridge, which was at the base of the hill where the yogi resided, I stopped my bike and looked at the pristine Rapti river. The wind blew gently over the river, drawing forth a number of shivering ripples on its surface. I was in my late thirties and my romance with rivers had remained intact since my childhood. Refreshed by the sight of the crystal blue Himalayan river, I parked my bike nearby the bridge and started climbing uphill.

Our first meeting is still vividly etched in my memory. After a short uphill climb, I found Gokhle Baba in a tiny hut. He wasn't wearing ochre as is customary with sannyasins. Later he told me that since he didn't have a Guru, and wasn't initiated formally into sannyas, he wore white colored clothes instead. That day he was wearing a white *dhoti* and *ganji* and a *janau* (ceremonial Hindu thread) across his shoulder. He looked old but robust. There were two simple huts facing each other, both didn't have any door or window. The yogi only possessed one clay pot to fetch water, a few cooking utensils, a few glasses, two beds, one umbrella, and three or four *dhotis* and a few pictures of Indian deities. On a tree nearby was a statue of Dattatreya, a Hindu deity considered to be an avatar of the three Hindu gods - Brahma, Vishnu, and Shiva - collectively known as Trimurti. A few puppies, monkeys and rabbits played around the hut.

Folding my hands in salutation, I offered him the fruits I had brought with me. As soon as he saw me, his face lit up and he smiled. He held my hand affectionately and asserted, "We have met before."

I felt that the old man had mistaken me for my friend, who had informed me about him. I told him, "You are mistaking me for my friend who also wears red clothes and an Osho *mala*. It was he, who told me about you. I am meeting you for the first time."

Disregarding my statement, he laughed and said, "No, we have already met before."

I did not debate further as I thought that his memory must have been impaired by old age. He asked me to sit on his own bed respectfully and started preparing tea. I requested he not worry about tea since I had come just for *satsang*.

He said, "People get thirsty when they climb this hill. The water of the stream here is not clear. It becomes fit to drink only once it is boiled and sieved. This is why I serve black tea to all those who come here."

I am not too fond of black tea. But the moment I took my first sip of the tea, I was addicted to it. We spent the entire day in spiritual discussion. His presence was very soothing and refreshing. I was so immersed in the discussion that when Baba pointed out to the sky and reminded me of the impending dusk, it was as though I was shaken out of a dream.

"It's difficult to climb down the hill when it gets dark so you better leave now," he said. The soft cotton candy-like clouds had scattered over the sky and were fringed with the frail, pink light. Unwillingly, I made up my mind to walk down the hill. Before I left, I made an offering of ten rupees to him. He accepted it with love.

A boy from the nearby village named Ram had come there. Baba told Ram to walk me till the road below the hill and handing over the ten rupee note to him said, "You said you needed an umbrella. Buy it with this money."

While climbing down, I inquired about Baba with Ram. He said, "Baba doesn't accept money from anyone. I don't understand how he accepted it from you." Along with Ram, Baba was supporting a few kids from the village. He gave them the money for stationery and in return, they sometimes helped him with household chores.

I returned to my quarter at Hetauda renewed and refreshed. I couldn't wait to go and meet him again. Under the slightest pretext, I would set out for Baba's hut on the hill. Although he did not prefer to discuss about his past, I gradually connected the dots and figured out a few things about his life.

He was from an educated Maharastran family, which was not only financially well-off but also shared a great love for music. He used to sing well since he was a child. As he was born in the Gokhle family of Maharastra, India, he was known as Gokhle Baba. He was a man of silence who liked to be by himself and during the eighty-five years he lived in Nepal, only a handful of people came in contact with him.

He left his house abruptly a few hours before his marriage. When the last minute preparation for the marriage was underway, he looked deeply through the apparent glitz and festivity and could trace the invisible chord of bondage, which would pin him down forever. The realization hit him so strongly that he left his home that very instance and became a wandering monk. He remained celibate throughout his life. He had often told me indirectly that his suppressed sexual desires had unnecessarily delayed his enlightenment. When I met him for the first time, I had recently separated with my wife. After learning about my separation, he told me over and again not to suppress my natural instincts, and to lead a natural and balanced life.

During his years as a wandering monk, he visited many spiritual places around India and met many saints. It was during this period that he met Raman Maharshi at Arunachal as well as Ramakrishna Paramhansa and Vivekananda at Dakshineshwor, Kolkata. He, then, came to Kathmandu, Nepal, to meet Shivapuri Baba at the Shivapuri hills and spent some days with him.

At that time, Indian yogis were allowed to stay within the Kathmandu valley only for a week during Shivaratri, Shiva's birthday, after which they had to return back to India. But he loved Nepal and continued living here.

Baba was unusually gifted in music and it was this very gift that earned him a stay in Nepal. The Ranas, the then rulers of Nepal, were the connoisseurs of music. When they heard Baba sing, they were very pleased by his singing and granted him his wish to live in Nepal.

Baba had carried a little money with him when he left his family and made some money along the way by singing. He lent this money to a grocery-store owner in the city. In return, the grocer had to supply ration for Baba regularly. This is how he managed his sustenance. He used to cook and eat once a day. He always offered tea to everyone, who came to visit him.

I always found Gokhle Baba in a peaceful and joyous mood. He neither enjoyed talking about his past nor about his meditation and spiritual powers. He used to behave with each person according to his/her nature and understanding. Whenever I went to meet him along with other people, he did not speak on spiritual topics; rather he would initiate a small talk on some socio-political issue, which was quite unlike him. Once he told me bluntly, "If you want to make a spiritual conversation, then come alone, don't bring anyone else with you. Because it is a pure violence to talk to people about those things that they do not understand."

I told him about my master Osho and gave him a few of his books. He returned the books to me and said, "It's been long since I stopped reading. My eyesight is also weak now. I want to hear about him from you."

And he listened with great interest.

He used to say that Osho had extra-ordinary brilliance and intelligence just like Buddha and Sankaracharya. The traditionalists cannot stand Osho's liberal views on love and sex but Gokhle Baba's understanding was astounding. He was fully supportive of Osho's fresh and rebellious teachings. He used to say that the society that tries to suppress natural human emotions will only be perverted.

I still remember him saying that it is easier to get married as well as to separate in Nepal than it is in India. This is why, he thought, Nepal was less sexually suppressed and perverted than India. This was truer during the time I met him than it is now.

Gokhle Baba was a devotee of Dattatreya and used to sit in meditation for hours every morning in front of the Dattatreya statue. His close disciples claimed that Gokhle Baba used to visit Baidhanathdham in India every year on a particular day where he had *darshan* of Dattatreya in his bodily form. Because he used to be a devotee of Dattatreya, he used to have puppies, rabbits and other animals around him. To feed them was a part of his daily penence. As far as I know, he had two Bengali devotees. One was the head of the English department of Bihar University and the other was the S.P of Bengal Police. They would come and stay with Baba whenever they could and served him. He hadn't initiated them but they were meditating under his guidance.

I remember a day when I saw that the Superintendent was meditating in Baba's ashram. He was meditating in front of the Dattatreya statue under the tree. I was talking with Baba. As our talks used to go on for hours, the Bengali devotee tried to draw attention by imitating sounds and expressions that are said to arise when one's *kundalini* awakens. Baba understood his intentions and told me to go a little away from where we were sitting. Then he went to the Bengali Superintendent and gave him a good verbal thrashing.

Baba never talked about himself but I learned a lot about him from these two Bengali devotees. They used to think that Baba was a fully realized enlightened master. They would always ask Baba to allow them to stay with him permanently but Baba would send them back to their respective places as soon as their holidays ended. Once, when Baba was sick, the S.P came to the ashram. He said to me, "Baba is now more than one hundred and fifteen years old. We don't know when he will leave his body. I will not leave him now, how much ever he tells me to. He has many spiritual powers. When he leaves his body those powers will be transferred to the one who is the closest to him. If I am not near him then someone else will get these powers."

After seeing such attraction towards *siddhis* even among advanced seekers, I felt tremendous gratitude towards my master who never allowed us to enter the complex and deluding world of *siddhis*.

Once, when we were alone, I asked Baba if he was fully enlightened and if his spiritual journey had ended.

"No, I still have some work left," he answered honestly.

I was dispirited to hear that and lamented, "If *you* haven't been able to free yourself completely even after eighty years of solitary reclusion, celibacy and meditation, then there isn't any hope for a worldly person like me."

Gokhle Baba said, "You will not need such a long time to finish your work because you have found a master. Those who don't find a master have to go astray and suffer a lot in this path."

I asked him, "You met enlightened beings such as Raman Maharshi, Ramakrishna and Shivapuri Baba but why didn't you make them your master?"

He said, "First thing, it is not so easy to find an enlightened master. And even if you find them, enlightened masters don't accept disciples so easily."

He clarified, "Raman, Ramakrishna and Shivapuri Baba did not initiate disciples when I met them. I didn't have enough good *karma* or *punya* to become a disciple of an enlightened master. I searched a lot but I didn't have the fortune to be initiated by a master. This is why I still have some work left despite an arduous and lonely penance of eighty years. You are extremely lucky that you found a master like Osho who accepts disciples with so little conditions."

When I met Osho, I related Gokhle Baba's story to him.

Osho said, "He is simple and honest but a man of great spiritual height. Meet him often and serve him as much as you can. This will help your own journey, as well. And through you I will also help him. The two of you have meditated together in your previous life. There is inherent love and friendship between the two of you that's why he gives you so much time and attention and can open up easily with you."

After hearing this from Osho, I understood why Gokhle Baba insisted during our first meeting that we had already met before. He was referring to our meetings in previous lives.

One day when I was in the middle of casting the concrete roof of the leather factory, I felt that Gokhle Baba was calling me. Resident engineers are supposed to remain at the site during critical casting work but the pull from Baba's ashram was so strong that I told Dwarika Shrestha, my subordinate to look after the construction for a while, and raced towards Baba's ashram on my motorbike. On the way, I bought some fruits and food for Baba. When I reached the ashram, I saw Baba sitting miserably in front of the statue of Dattatreya. I offered him what I had brought with me. His face lit up with joy and he said, "I always offer something to Dattatreya but today there was nothing with me to offer him, which is why I was so sad. This is the reason why God brought you here today."

Similarly, a few months later I again felt the same pull. That time, too, I went to the ashram and saw that he was in great difficulty. He had been suffering from diarrhea. When he had gone to the forest to relieve himself, somebody had broken into Baba's hut and stolen his cooking utensils and clothes. Baba's total asset was worth less than a thousand rupees. And yet, someone had been heartless enough to rob the basic necessities of a hermit, meditating alone in a jungle.

I have always had a strong fascination towards ascetics, and before I met Osho I often fantasized the life of a recluse. Time and again, I wanted to leave everything behind and go to the Himalayan caves and meditate alone. Osho had been very critical of such ideas. He used to tell me, "Even if you leave the whole world to meditate in the forest, problems won't leave you. Truth is not contradictory to the world. One has to fulfill his responsibilities and yet search for truth."

This particular incident reminded me of Osho again.

I was visiting the Garhwal Himalayas a few years ago. During my visit I was told how every year, thousands of monks are killed for petty goods or money inside their caves. Every time a monk is visited by a rich friend or a relative they are plagued by the fear of dacoits, who wear ochre robes and live under the guise of *sannyasins* along the range. Most of these dacoits are criminals who are in hideaway. They have even started a lucrative business of selling furnished caves for a few hundred thousand rupees. This just reminded me again how fleeing from the world is not really the answer.

Osho had once told me, "Arun, you will meet some of the best souls in the ochre robe. But beware, because some of the most crooked ones are also found in the same garb."

Osho never encouraged us to escape to the jungles. He says, "Meditation is not escaping from life: it is escaping into life."

Gokhle Baba would be aware of major world events even if he did not read any newspapers. Once when I had gone to meet him, he said, "I heard the cry of a lot of souls in the night. Has something happened in the world that has brought harm to a lot of lives?"

I was surprised to hear him because the night before thousands of people had lost their lives in an earthquake of 8.1 on the Richter scale in New Mexico City.

He further added, "Your Guru has been making indications of very difficult times ahead in his discourses. That time has begun. A lot of violence and destruction is about to happen in the world."

His statement reminded me of two things Osho had said: that a person who has achieved the state of no-mind can have realizations of world events in his meditation because these events create a lot of disturbance in the astral world. Those who are deep in their meditation will have great empathy towards these events. And he had also said that we are mistreating nature extremely and if we don't change our ways then the world will have to face great destruction. Osho spent his whole life creating this new consciousness in humans.

The last time I met Gokhle Baba was a few days before his death. I had completed my Hetauda project and was back to Kathmandu so our meetings were not as frequent as before. I was going to Birgunj with a group of engineers for a project's work. On the way, I had met Baba at Hetauda. That was my last *satsang* with him. I was meeting Baba after a long time, but I was enchanted as usual. Baba also received me joyously. Even if his body was frail, he looked happy and radiant.

"Baba, I am going to Birgunj and Raxoul. Do you need anything from the market?" I asked him.

"If you find good quality moong daal then please get some," he said.

I bought moong beans in Raxoul for Baba. But since I was travelling with other engineers, we left Raxoul very late and only reached Hetauda late in the night. I reached the road below the ashram. It was dark and quiet. Baba was already asleep. When I tried to go up to the ashram to give the moong beans to Baba, my friends didn't allow me to go there in the dark because the forest was infested with wild animals and it was not safe to climb in the dark. I asked them to spend the night in Hetauda and leave after meeting Baba early in the morning, but since my friends had already made plans to spend the night in Narayanghat, further up the highway, they did not agree to do so. I didn't have enough courage to leave the group and stay back in Hetauda. So I went with them to Narayanghat unhappily. The bag of moong beans stayed with me for a long time. Every time I saw the bag, a sudden sadness overtook me.

Soon after, I got occupied in my work and couldn't go to Hetauda for a while. After a few months I got an opportunity to go there. When I reached the road below the ashram, Baba's hut looked a bit dilapidated. A little walk away from Baba's hut, a woman used to crush stones on the side of the road. I walked down to her and asked her, "Baba is up there isn't he?"

What she said shocked me, "Baba died fifteen days ago. Nobody lives there now. The villagers have started scavenging the ashram."

I was stunned by the news. An image of his joyous and smiling countenance came in front of my eyes. I remembered the love and intimacy of Baba and the pain of this sudden separation brought tears to my eyes. I felt extremely guilty for not visiting him and giving him that bag of moong beans. I put the bag on the road, sat beside it and started crying. But howsoever I cried, I couldn't meet him now.

I realized then that the future is always uncertain and you should not miss the opportunity to meet, serve and spend time with saints. Later when I told this story to Osho, he consoled me and said, "Don't worry about him at all. He has left as a fully enlightened being. Now he doesn't need to return to earth again."

His words brought some solace to me. The arduous effort of this hundred and eighteen year old yogi who spent most of his lifetime in utter solitude in the forest did not go to waste.

We don't know how many unknown meditators are making their effort alone in seclusion. My heartfelt salutation goes to their effort and suffering they go through. I also express my deep gratitude towards Osho who helped people to attain the highest spiritual consciousness without renouncing anything.

Osho said, "I call a man a sannyasin who breaks out of these institutions and lives spontaneously. To be a sannyasin is the most courageous act possible. To be a sannyasin means to live without the mind, and the moment you live without mind you live without society. The mind has created society, and society has created the mind; they are interdependent. To be a sannyasin means to renounce all that is false but not to renounce the world, to renounce all that is unauthentic, to renounce all the answers, to be responsive, spontaneously responsive, and not to think about the reasons, but to be real."

INDIRA DEVI

> " Among the many spiritual experiences of Indira Devi, the most mysterious was her association with the 16th century mystic, Meera. She repeatedly had darshan of Meera in her physical form. "

During 1975-76, every evening after my workday was over, I used to sell Osho books under the Peepal tree in Newroad, Kathmandu. Much has become of the place now, but back then it was a lonesome affair in nonchalant company of leisurely cobblers and occasional idlers. One lazy evening, unexpectedly, Professor Renu Lal Singh, secretary of the then King Birendra, came to my stall to buy Osho books. As much as I was struck by the presence of this highbrow officer, what roused my curiosity was his grace and serenity that somehow set him apart from the rest of the mundane affair that Newroad was.

As I would discover later, Renu Lal Singh had been a close disciple of enlightened mystic Shivapuri Baba, and a seasoned meditator. This friendship that started unassumingly from the shade of the Peepal tree in Newroad would bring me close to spiritual luminaries such as Dilip Kumar Roy, Roy's disciple Indira Devi, Swami Krishna Prem, Ram Dass and many more. He also helped me to understand Shivapuri Baba deeply.

In no time, this friendship grew and we started meeting almost everyday. In those meetings, we used to share stories from the lives of enlightened masters. Renu Lal was a sincere seeker and had an extensive knowledge of Indian masters. I was also deeply interested in mysticism, so this friendship was destined to go a long way. Through him I got to know about the lives of Dilip Kumar Roy, Indira Devi and Sri Aurobindo, and I introduced him to Osho literature, which later became his literary staple.

It was Renu Lal from whom I heard amazing stories about these two close disciples of Sri Aurobindo – Dilip Kumar Roy and Indira Devi. He also gave me their autobiography, *Pilgrims of the Stars*, which he had borrowed from the palace library.

There was something ethereal about Indira Devi's pictures in that book. The more I looked at them, the more urgent became the desire to go and meet her. Indira Devi, ethereal, poised and fragile, entranced me with her beauty and compassion that oozed out of her pictures. Somehow it was very difficult for me to take my eyes off the picture. It had been a while since I had borrowed the book, and Renu Lal had to return it to the palace. So he started pressing me about it. Of course, I had already finished the book. But it was Indira Devi's picture I was reluctant to let go of. I went through several bookstores in Kathmandu to get a copy of the book, but to no avail. So, I just took off its jacket, which had a beautiful picture of Indira Devi. The hardbound had the same design, and I prayed that Renu Lal wouldn't notice it. If he did, he never told me about it anyway.

I was so fascinated by her that I used to carry her picture in my office bag and I used to gaze at her pictures, I felt as though she had been very close with me in some of my previous lives. I still have that jacket cover in my personal closet at my house in Tahachal.

I learnt from Renu Lal that after Sri Aurobindo's death, they were living in an ashram called Harikrishna Mandir in Pune. In those days I used to go to Pune at least thrice a year to meet my master, Osho. I was determined to meet her the next time I was there. Dilip Kumar Roy was born into a well-educated and wealthy Bengali family. While he was studying in England, the famed Indian revolutionary leader, Subashchandra Bose was his classmate. He was also a close friend of Radhakrishnan, the first president of independent India, who later appointed Roy and Indira Devi as the cultural ambassadors of India. Bose tried to involve Roy in the Indian Independence Movement, but his spiritual zeal took him to Pondicherry where he surrendered to Sri Aurobindo. He became Sri Aurobindo's close disciple, and Aurobindo considered Roy his spiritual son and friend. Roy wrote more than one hundred and twenty books and countless plays, and songs that he sang in his divinely gifted voice. His songs had a trance-like effect on the audience. Bertrand Russell, Roman Rolan, Herman Hesse, Nehru, Tagore, Radhakrishan and Gandhi were among the admirers of his singing.

Indira Devi was born into an upper class family in Quetta, present-day Pakistan. She was extremely beautiful and was a trained classical dancer. She had deep spiritual experiences from childhood. Her spiritual search brought her to Dilip Kumar Roy in Pondicherry. Sri Aurobindo regarded both of them to be true spiritual seers with very high consciousness. He had advised them to live together and had said that they would help each other in their spiritual growth, and considered them spiritual counterparts.

Among the many spiritual experiences of Indira Devi, the

most mysterious was her association with the 16th century mystic, Meera. She repeatedly had *darshan* of Meera in her physical form. Meera would appear in front of Indira Devi, and narrate the story of her life to her. Meera also dictated to her the songs that she had sung for her beloved Lord Krishna. Before this association, only around forty songs of Meera's were available, but she told Indira that she had sung more than eight hundred devotional songs in Rajasthani and Brij languages that were never recorded in any form. The songs that were available were also not in their original form. Indira Devi was born and brought up in a household greatly influenced by British culture. She could not read or write Hindi at all. But Meera sang all her songs to Indira Devi who transcribed the words through automatic writing. The Harikrishna Mandir has published the eight hundred devotional songs or *bhajans* in a series of six books, titled *Shrutanjali, Premanjali, Sudhanjali, Bhavanjali, Deepanjali* and *Ushanjali*. Mystics such as Sri Aurobindo, Mother, Osho, then President of India and renowned philosopher Radhakrishnan, famous saint Gopinath Kabiraj, Papa Ramdas and Krishnabai, among others, have authenticated these songs. These songs are being broadcast from the All India Radio and Doordarshan TV as Meera's *bhajans*. Acclaimed singers around India have started singing these songs as well.

Important spiritual texts that have been destroyed for some reason or the other have again come to life due to the efforts of some clairvoyant seers. Sri Aurobindo, Madam Blavatski, Machiavelli, Leadbeater and Anne Besant are some such seers who have brought back spiritual texts that were lost to the world. Two such ancient texts, *Seven Steps of Samadhi* rewritten by Blavatski, and *Sadhana Sutra* rewritten by Machiavelli, have been praised and explained by Osho in his books with the same titles.

Since I had a deep desire to meet Dilip Kumar Roy and Indira

Devi, with due permission from my master Osho, I went to the Harikrishna Ashram in Pune. Upon arriving there I found out that they had left the ashram that very day for a spiritual tour. For the next three years whenever I went to meet them, I would find out that my arrival and their departure would coincide every single time. It was rather uncanny how she always left the very day I arrived and would come back the day I left Pune. At times, I would stay in Pune for months, and even then I could never meet her.

Not understanding the mystery behind such recurring happenings, I asked Osho for the explanation. He told me the reasons in detail but since they are very personal and spiritual secrets, I cannot reveal them here.

I can never forget that balmy summer evening of 1978. I went to the Harikrishna Ashram and found out that Dilip Kumar Roy had already left his body, but I was surprised to hear that Indira Devi was in the ashram. Usually she didn't meet anyone other than the disciples of Aurobindo or herself, but as soon as I sent my name to her room, she called me up. She was enjoying the evening on the rooftop with a few of her disciples. She received me with great love and intimacy. After our first meeting we became very close to each other, as if we were fellow travelers of many lives, or perhaps, even the fellow pilgrims of the stars.

Whenever I went to Pune, I would spend time in her *satsang*. Although she did not like meeting anyone other than her own disciples, she showered her compassion on me ceaselessly. She would not deny me a meeting even when she was sick. She had tremendous respect for Osho, but she did not openly say that to others. As I had not been able to meet Dilip Kumar Roy, she would repeatedly tell me, "You missed a beautiful soul."

In one of our meetings, I invited her to come to Kathmandu.

Since my ashram in Tahachal was very basic, I was worried about her comfort. When I told her so, she said, "I will come to Kathmandu just for you, and I will not stay anywhere else but in your place."

When I told her that I was going to the Aurobindo Ashram in Pondicherry, she said, "You must go and meet the old residents who have lived with Sri Aurobindo. They are beautiful people."

In the large library of the Pondicherry ashram, I didn't find one book by Dilip Kumar Roy or Indira Devi. When I asked them the reason for this they replied harshly, "We don't have any regard for them here, and don't mention their names again."

I was very much inspired by the vision and concept of Auroville. It was designed to accommodate fifty thousand seekers from all over the world. At the top of it, the place was to be a totally secular space, inviting people of all nationalities and faiths. The Indian government immediately recognized the worth of the idea, and agreed to provide a basic stipend and non-tourist visa to any foreigner who is accepted at Auroville.

Auroville highly inspired me to build Tapoban. Tapoban is also a secular space open for seekers of any faith, any nationality or any creed. Every year we have visitors from at least eighty countries, whom come and meditate here. A lot of them often ask us to help them secure visas for longer periods of time. But its still a long way before the Nepalese government would secure the same status for Tapoban.

Although I was quite impressed by the master plan of Auroville, somehow I missed the presence of a master there. Development, too, was rather slow. The next time I met Indira Devi I told her, "You are a true devotee of Aurobindo with very high consciousness. You should be in Auroville materializing your Guru's dreams. What are you doing here alone?"

She looked at me mysteriously and said, "Your Guru is still alive so you will not understand me now. You will understand everything once your Guru leaves his body."

When Osho left his body in 1990, all his true devotees and those who wanted to spread his work around the world were banned from entering the Pune ashram one by one. The ashram management fell into the hands of rogues who desecrated the whole place. A holy ashram turned into a holiday resort. They slowly took out all of Osho's pictures from the Ashram and banned the celebration of his birthday, his enlightenment day and Guru Purnima. I then understood what Indira Devi had said to me years ago. Indeed saints like her had clairvoyant vision of the future.

To build an ashram is not an easy feat. It requires a lot of sacrifice, penance and hard work from dedicated disciples. This sacrifice and hard work in turn brings affluence to the ashram. Once the ashram grows affluent, people who are interested in everything else but meditation gather there, making it extremely difficult for the genuine seekers to continue their practices. The conspiracies and politics get so entangled that many real seekers have no choice but to leave. I have noticed that this has been the state of almost all ashrams after the Guru leaves his body.

All Gurus regularly test their disciples on how surrendered and accepting they have become. I have also been through such acid-tests. Between 1978 to 1981, whenever I lived in the Pune ashram, I would only get menial work such as sweeping, dish washing, cleaning the bathroom and doing laundry. By then, I was a certified engineer and there was a lot of clean work that I could do at the ashram. I had also finished all my money and the ashram did not provide me any food pass. Although I worked for 10 hours every day, I lived in the dormitory and paid for my own food and accommodation. Osho did not meet me and made sure that things were very difficult for me.

It would often sadden me and leave me helpless. When things got too heavy, I went to Indira Devi for consolation. I felt that if I could manage to get a room at her ashram, it would solve a lot of my problems. Since she had always been very loving towards me, naturally I was inclined to believe that she could easily arrange a room for me. When I hesitantly told her the real reason for my visit, for the first time I found her stern. She said, "*Sadhana* is not window shopping. You buy some from this shop and some from that shop. Whether you live or you die, it should be at your Guru's feet. It is because of immense compassion and great possibilities of the disciple that the master is sometimes very uncompromising and his ways severe. All this is arranged for your own good."

It took me twenty-five years to fully discern the truth of her words and Osho's compassion.

When Osho suddenly left his body in 1990, I was totally devastated by the news. I felt like an orphan. The world became dreary and meaningless. Unable to contain myself, I once again went to Indira Devi and asked her, "Under whose instructions do I work now? My Guru always pruned my ego. Who will melt my ego now?"

Indira Devi said with confidence, "Now you should go back to Nepal and you will find that your master has reached there before you. The responsibility of your spiritual growth is his and he knows how to do his work very well. He will use you as his medium in the future and do great work through you."

We had been struggling for years to acquire property to build a commune in Kathmandu. As Indira Devi had proclaimed, Osho indeed had reached Nepal before me. Miracles started unfolding themselves and within two months, Osho Tapoban, our ashram in Kathmandu, materialized.

With every passing year, this mystery school is only growing, making me realize the truth behind her divine prophecy.

Indira Devi was there to guide me in one of the most difficult times of my life - when Osho left his body. She not only gave me the faith that my master had not left me by leaving his body, but Indira Devi, who has already left her body, continues to guide and inspire me with the same loving compassion.

MEERA BAI

> "If only I knew that love brings such sorrow,
> I would beat the drum around town and tell everyone not to fall in love."

On a fine morning in 1950, Dilip Kumar Roy was singing morning *bhajans* in the Aurobindo Ashram in Pondicherry. Indira Devi, seated in the audience, caught a glimpse of an extremely beautiful woman in traditional colourful Rajasthani attire. Her eyes were closed, and yet the ethereal smile on her lips radiated the grace that only comes from the otherworld. This alluring woman was listening to the *bhajans* like hundreds of others in the audience, but her beauty shone through the crowd like the moon in the company of stars. All the women of the ashram wore white but strangely this woman wore a colourful Rajasthani dress.

Once the *bhajans* were over, people started leaving the auditorium. Just then Indira Devi caught sight of the same beautiful woman, who was walking out of the hall too. Indira Devi looked towards her and saw that she was walking as if afloat. Her feet did not touch the ground. After that day, Indira Devi started to see the mysterious woman recurrently, both in physical form and in her visions. One day while she was sitting in meditation, she had a vision of the woman again. Mustering courage, Indira Devi asked her who she was.

The woman said, "I am Meera. A devotee of Krishna, just like you. I am also a friend of yours from a past life."

The conversation was the beginning of a lifelong romance, which also remains one of the greatest spiritual mysteries of our age.

Since Indira Devi was brought up in a household greatly influenced by the West, she knew nothing of Meera. She told of the mysterious events that had recently unfolded in her life to her Guru, Dilip Kumar Roy, whom she called "Dada" affectionately. Dada wrote the whole thing to his Guru, Sri Aurobindo, who authenticated those events as true in letters dated May 7, June 2 and 11, 1950.

He wrote, "It is common for such events to occur in the lives of seekers of very high consciousness." Dada assured Indira of her good fortune and advised her to keep a spiritual diary. Indira Devi's diary has become an amazing and rare gift to seekers of the beyond. I would like to share some of those events in her own words:

8 August 1950: Yesterday night while I was praying, my room was suddenly engulfed by translucent blue light. When I raised my head from the ground I again saw Meera. Her eyes were extremely beautiful. She talked with me for a long time. She said, "In a past life I used to be a *gopini* of Krishna and my name was Lalita. Radha, you and I were all friends. Radha became enlightened in that life due to her pure love for Krishna but I had to be born as Meerabai in 1498 into a royal family in a village called Kurakhi (currently the name is not found on the map) in Rajasthan.

13 June 1951: Today Meera said, "I was the only child of my family. My mother died when I was only six years old. Chaitanya Mahaprabhu had given a statue of Balgopal, the baby Krishna, to his chief disciple, Sanatan Goswami. Goswami performed *pooja* to the statue daily. Once the statue came alive and instructed him, "The reason why Chaitanya handed me over to you is about to be revealed to you. A girl called Meera has been born into a royal family in Rajasthan. Find her and hand me over to her.

After hearing this from Krishna, Goswami went to many royal families in Rajasthan searching for me and finally came to my home. He recognized me instantly. On my seventh birthday he gave me the statue and left. A mysterious intense love sprung up in my heart after seeing the statue and I couldn't let go of it when I slept that night. In the night Krishna became alive and started talking and playing with me. This is how a seven-year-old girl fell in love with Krishna. The statue was no more a statue for me; it became my love and my friend for life. When I turned thirteen, my father started to prepare for my marriage as was the tradition in those times. I couldn't even imagine in my dreams that I could belong to any other man. I refused to marry but since my father said that he would commit suicide if I didn't marry, I succumbed to marriage. I got married to Raja Maharana, the King of Mewar. He was a humble and kind king. He also loved me dearly. In the beginning he gave me full freedom in my devotion to Krishna. He also built a Krishna temple in the palace garden. When I went in the temple, it would be very difficult for me to come out. In the middle of the night I would hear a tune of the flute from the temple calling me there. I would try to resist the temptation to heed the call of the flute and remain loyal to my husband and stop myself, but after a while the attraction would be too strong and it would break the thread between me and my husband. I would be compelled to break all worldly morals and go and stay close to my eternal beloved. It would cause me great pain when my husband touched me. I felt that my heart, my soul and my body belonged only to Krishna. Maharana accepted my behavior although he did not understand what was going on with me. In the nights when I went to the temple, he would follow me and wait for me outside. I felt great pain at not being able to fulfill my responsibility as a wife and would tell him, "What are you doing here? Why don't you go and sleep?"

He would reply, "You come here to worship your lord and I am here to worship my goddess."

Maharana's brother, Rana, and his sister, Uda, were very jealous of me. They would tell Maharana that I was a woman of bad character and all my devotion was only a drama. When he heard this, my husband would be very sad, but throughout his life he never raised his voice against me. Thirteen years after our marriage, he died in a war, after which I had to face a flood of miseries."

Meera said to Indira, "After the death of my husband, his brother, Rana, became the king, and he and his sister, Uda, started to torture me. In the end they decided to kill me, and brought a cup full of poison and said, "You have brought great shame to the royal family. The whole of Mewar is laughing at us. To save the dignity of the family you have to drink this and end your life."

I was so much in love with my lord that I drank the poison without thinking at all. The poison only wet my throat, which had become parched from hours of singing. Nothing happened to me. They were very surprised. They started to think that not only was I characterless, but also a witch. That event changed my life forever. I realized that the palace was not for me, I only belonged at the feet of Krishna. Krishna himself told me, "Sanatan Goswami is in Vrindavan; you go to him."

I left the palace and started the journey to Vrindavan with my *ektara* and the statue of Balgopal. All were happy to see me leave. They felt that they were now free from dealing with a mad woman.

After that, Krishna gave the most difficult test of my devotion for the next two years. He stopped giving *darshan* to me and I also stopped hearing the sound of his flute.

It's difficult to imagine how Meera, a twenty-six year old princess, must have passed this cruel test of time. How trying it must have been for a woman who was brought up in the luxuries of a palace to walk bare-footed in the extreme heat of the Rajasthani villages, begging for alms every day. How must she have survived eating what she got out of begging, sleeping in outdoor rest stops and saving herself from the predatory eyes of men? However, the most difficult of it all was Krishna's absence. Krishna had completely stopped giving her *darshan* even in her vision. His absence hung over Meera's grief like a dark cloud.

After two years of extreme struggle, Meera was waiting for her master under a tree on the bank of Jamuna River. Her only friend was the statue of Balgopal. Her clothes were tattered and she had developed a tumour in her calf, making it difficult for her to travel. Seeing a lone woman, many men would try to sexually assault her. The women who came to bathe in the river, instead of giving her support, would call her names and tell her, "Don't stay here alone like this. Our men come to bathe here. Your beauty will corrupt their minds. Go elsewhere."

Her beauty aroused jealousy in women, and sexuality in men.

One night Meera was sleeping under a tree embracing her Balgopal. Two thieves came to the ghat. Seeing her alone, one of them tried to assault her. Meera cried for help. Compassion arose in the other thief. He pushed his friend away from Meera. But while running away, he took Meera's Balgopal with him. When Balgopal's statue was stolen from her, she was also robbed of her last reason to keep living.

It was in such troubled moments that she sang,

If only I knew that love brings such sorrow,
I would beat the drum around town and tell everyone not to fall in love.

All spiritual seekers have to pass through difficult tests. Such moments in life dissolve the ego and make the seeker realize the depth of devotion and surrender.

When it became too impossible to bear anymore, Meera decided to drown in the Jamuna River. But as soon as she touched the cool water of the Jamuna, a strange transformation transpired. The pristine water of the Jamuna turned all her complaints and pain into a deep gratitude.

"Why am I complaining so much? For twenty-six years Krishna gave me all the comforts and luxury possible. He gave me darshan every day and loved me immensely. Why am I now being oblivious to his grace, and fretting over the agony of the last two years?" she said.

An intense feeling of gratitude towards Krishna was born in her heart. She cupped a handful of water from the river and offered it to Krishna and prayed, "May such devotion appear in my heart in my next life as well. May I never be disloyal or have doubts towards you," she said.

Suddenly Krishna appeared, hugged her and said, "Meera, you are blessed, you have passed your test. From today, you and I are one and will never be apart. You will meet your Guru, Sanatan, today. Spend the rest of your life serving him."

The tumor in Meera's calf had also healed. Suddenly, the friend of the thief who had stolen her Balgopal returned with the statue.

Each grain on the bank of the Jamuna and each leaf on every

tree there was shining with Krishna consciousness. Meera saw Krishna in the whole of existence.

While Meera was having her divine realization, Sanatan appeared at the ghat to bathe. He recognized Meera immediately. Sanatan lived in a hut in Vrindavan. Meera started living there as well, and served her Guru for the next seven years until he left his body. The hut was so small that Meera had to lay a mat under Sanatan's bed and sleep there.

When Meera arrived at Vrindavan's most famous temple, an attempt was made to stop her at the door because entry to the temple was forbidden to women. The high priest of the temple had never seen women. When they saw Meera trying to enter the temple, arrangements were made to stop her.

But those people who were standing by the door to stop her were dumbstruck. When Meera came dancing, holding her *ektara* in her hand, playing music with a crowd of devotees behind her, drunk with the divine, it stunned the guards as well. They forgot they were meant to stop her until Meera had entered.

The priest freaked out. He had been worshipping Krishna, but the tray fell from his hands. He had not seen a woman for years.

Once the ektara was playing inside and the crowd had gone in, then they became aware of what had happened. But the priest did not plunge in. Meera came dancing in front of Krishna, but the priest was not impressed. He said, "Hey woman, do you not know that women are not permitted in this temple?"

Meera listened and laughed. She said, "I was thinking there is only one man, and that is Krishna, and we are all his lovers; we are all women. I am glad to see that there is another man also in the world!"

The way she said it just penetrated the man's very heart. He fell at her feet to be forgiven. He said, "I have never thought about this — what I said is simply absurd. Only Krishna, only God, is a man

— we are all his lovers; naturally we are all women. You are right and I was wrong."

But trouble did not end for Meera after this event. Meera was unable to stay in Vrindavan. We have always given ill treatment to enlightened people. After their death we worship them; while they're alive we misbehave with them. Meera had to leave Vrindavan, after which she went to Dwarika and spent the rest of her life there.

NAGARJUNA

" MANY YEARS LATER, IT WAS REVEALED TO ME THAT IT WAS UNDER THE MOTHER TREE OF THE SAME TREE THAT EXISTS IN OSHO SAMADHI TODAY THAT NAGARJUNA ATTAINED ENLIGHTENMENT. EVERY MORNING, AS I DO THE ROUNDS AROUND THE SAMADHI, I AM REFRESHED BY THE SIGHT OF THIS LOVELY TREE, NOURISHED FOR CENTURIES BY THE FRAGRANCE OF NAGARJUNA'S ENLIGHTENMENT. "

In the beginning days of the Gregorian calendar, a child was born into a rich Brahmin family in South India. As soon as he was born, astrologers predicted that unless certain rituals were performed and a lot of wealth donated, the child wouldn't survive for more than seven days. The parents did as they were told, and the child lived past seven days. Despite this, the astrologers claimed that it was impossible for him to live for more than seven years. The parents didn't want to see their only child die in front of their eyes, so before his seventh birthday they sent him on a pilgrimage. The journey took him to Nalanda, the famous Buddhist holy site. The head of the Nalanda Buddha Bihar was Saraha, the eminent Buddhist tantrik Guru. Saraha was the disciple of Srikirti who was the direct disciple of Buddha's son Rahul Bhadra. The Buddhist sect of tantra was started by Sahara whose lineage was followed in Tibet by renowned masters such as Tilopa, Naropa, Marpa and Milarepa.

It is said that the child had an extraordinary memory. Saraha was very much impressed by him so he inquired about him. After learning about the astrological predictions, Sahara told the child's relatives, "Taking sannyas is also like a worldly death, so if he takes sannyas his death could be avoided."

He advised them to conduct a *puja* for the Amitabha Buddha and recite the Dharani *mantra*. Sahara initiated the child into the Buddha *sangha* as *bhikkhu* Srimanta. After being educated on the mysterious and hidden teachings, he became a *siddhayogi* of tantra, yoga and alchemy in no time.

As Srimanta's prominence grew, many people from far and wide started attending his discourses. One day, two young men arrived at the discourse. They had a mysterious aura about them. As soon as they entered the hall where Srimanta was giving his discourse, a dense perfume of sandalwood engulfed the atmosphere. Even Srimanta couldn't help being intoxicated. So he asked them about it. They told him that they were princes form Nagalok and that they covered their bodies in sandalwood paste in order to protect themselves from outside influence. They also told him that there was an abundance of sandalwood where they came from. Enchanted by the fragrance, Srimanta asked them if they could donate some sandalwood to build his monasteries. The princes asked him to come to their land to preach the Buddha Dharma, and also take as much sandalwood as he wanted. Srimanta's fascination with the sandalwood took him all the way to Nagalok. But the sandalwood was not the only gift that was waiting for him there.

He was received with great fanfare at Nagalok. The King told him that Ananda, Buddha's caretaker, had given the *Pragyaparamita Sutra* to his ancestors for safekeeping. Srimanta was elated at finding those texts that the Buddhist world had been searching for centuries. We can assume that Nagalok fell in the current South Indian state of Karnataka, as it is still full of Sandalwood forests. Even today people from Karnataka have surnames such as Nagaswami and Nagaraj. The Buddhist texts also refer to South India when they mention the *Pragyaparamita Sutra*. Osho has explained these sutras beautifully in his book *The Heart Sutra*, reinterpreting the relevance of these sutras to contemporary seekers.

The Nagas regarded Srimanta as their Guru and started calling him Nagarjuna.

It is said that nobody was able to understand and teach the philosophy of impermanence, the greatness of the middle path, and the philosophy of nothingness for four hundred years after Buddha left his body.

It was Nagarjuna, who, for the first time, studied, contemplated and explained these philosophies of Buddha. His *Mahamadhyakarika Sutra* is thought to be the most exquisite explanation of Buddha's philosophy. He was a great philosopher whose explanation of the Buddha Dharma is considered the clearest and most logical. In Buddhist scriptures, Nagarjuna is regarded second only to Buddha.

He was also responsible for starting Mahayana Buddhism, and was the inspiration behind the Nalanda University. Along with the Dalai Lama, most Buddhists regard Nagarjuna as their principal Guru.

Nagarjuna meditated for thirty years and became enlightened in the Nagarjuna hills of Kathmandu, but it is difficult to find certified historical facts about Nagarjuna's life in Nepal or elsewhere. Those that exist are also debatable. There are texts that say that he lived for six hundred years and that he was resurrected even after his death, and that his body and head were buried separately, and that he used to travel freely in various dimensions. Since Nagarjuna has often been portrayed as a miracle-churning wizard, it is extremely difficult to excavate the truths about his life buried deeply in the womb of history.

It is said that Nagarjuna was quite romantic when young. He learned the tantric *anima siddhi,* and thus could disappear at will. Using this, he and his friends would enter the pleasure gardens of queens and princesses and make love to them. Once while returning from a palace, two of his friends who hadn't yet mastered the *siddhi* got caught by the palace guards. Nagarjuna managed to escape but his friends were executed. He was very much saddened by the death of his friends, and blamed his own desires for it. The event was a big shock for Nagarjuna who made a vow not to be involved with women thereon.

Legend talks of a great famine of Nalanda that killed many people. The *bhikkhus* also stopped getting alms when they went begging. Seeing this, Naagarjuna's Guru ordered him to save the Buddha Sangha by using his psychic powers. Nagarjuna was adept in alchemy. Using alchemy he sustained the Nalanda monastery for twelve years by turning iron into gold. Later he became the head of the Nalanda Buddha Bihar. According to Buddhist texts, he evicted eight hundred undisciplined *bhikkhus* from the monastery.

In those days, Bodhgaya was the centre for Buddhist studies. Nagarjuna's role was pivotal in protecting the Buddha Bihar there. He built many temples and also constructed a wall around the Bodhi Tree to protect it from wild elephants. The ruins of the wall exist even today. He invited many Buddhist teachers of Bodhgaya to Nalanda, and developed it as the centre for Buddhist studies. It later became famous as the Nalanda University.

Buddhist folklore has another interesting incident about Nagarjuna's life. Once when Nagarjuna was travelling, he passed by a child, who for some unknown reason fascinated him. Nagarjuna approached the child and intently studied his palm and body structure, and prophesized that the child would become a king. Twelve years later, when he went back to the region, the child had indeed become King Udayabhadra. Udayabhadra recognized Nagarjuna, and took him to his palace with great respect. They became close friends. Udayabhadra gave Nagarjuna a large number of jewels to help him spread the Buddha Dharma. In return, Nagarjuna taught the king the essence of religion, and gave him the scrolls containing his teachings. The scripture is well known by the name of *Ratnavali*. Nagarjuna admired King Udayabhadra deeply, and gave him a blessing that nobody could kill him while Nagarjuna was alive.

One day Udayabhadra's wife presented her son, Shaktiman, with an exquisite robe. Shaktiman loved the robe and said he would wear the robe the day he became king. But his mother said, "You will never be king because Nagarjuna has blessed your father in such a way that he will live as long as him. And Nagarjuna is a tantric with the ability to live as long as he wants."

Hearing this, Shaktiman became miserable and started to think of ways to kill Nagarjuna. The queen told him that since Nagarjuna was a *siddhayogi*, it was not easy to kill him. Instead she advised him, "Nagarjuna is a Bodhisattva full of compassion. If you pray to him he may leave his body for you. "

It is said that Shaktiman went to Nagarjuna and expressed his predicament. Nagarjuna's heart melted to Shaktiman's honest appeal. He said, "In one of my past lives, I had killed a person by cutting his throat. I still have some seeds of karma left from that. So just go ahead and slash my throat and become king."

Shaktiman followed the advice and decapitated Nagarjuna. As soon as the sword halved the body of Nagarjuna, King Udayabhadra left his body as well. Shaktiman feared that Nagarjuna's head and body might attach again so he buried the two parts separately at a distance of four miles, and made separate stupas on the burial sites.

Nagarjuna's middle path is based on the concept of nothingness. Like quantum physics, the theory of nothingness propounds that matter actually doesn't exist. Nothingness is the primordial emptiness from where all matter came into existence, and to where it will perish. Manifestation and dissolution are only possible in nothingness, as it provides a backdrop for the existence of the material universe. Without nothingness, no creativity is possible in existence. It has been scientifically proven that matter is nothing but the condensed form of energy. Since everything in the universe is moving at an unimaginable speed, it creates an illusion of static objects. For instance, one can see the blades of a fan when it is moving slowly, but if the fan is moving at its optimum speed, one cannot see the blades separately, and the fan appears to be an opaque circle. Physicists have also found out that "nothingness" is the primary building block of an atom. They say, if you take out the space within and between the atoms, and therefore compress all solid particles, the whole earth can be contained in an object no bigger than a football.

Thus form is just an illusion created by condenced energy. According to the Mahayana philosophy, the experience of nothingness is extremely difficult to achieve, and requires intense meditation. A religious text or philosophy fills us with knowledge, but cannot make us realize nothingness. It is only in a state of *samadhi* that a thoughtless consciousness can experience nothingness and its beauty. This is the essence of Mahayana Buddhism.

Nagarjuna's whole life is a series of mysteries. Two thousand years after he left his physical body, his magic continues in Nepal. Nagarjuna Hills, where Osho Tapoban, our ashram in Kathmandu, is located, is named after him. Initially, we didn't realize the esoteric interconnectedness between the place and Nagarjuna. However, as my meditation deepened it was revealed to me that the dome-like hillock where the Osho *Samadhi* is built is actually the exact place where Nagarjuna attained enlightenment two thousand years ago.

When we purchased this land, the locals warned us against cutting down one particular tree that stood in the middle of the hillock. Since we had decided to make the Osho *Samadhi* in the same hillock, it became tricky to execute our design with the tree standing in the middle. My engineer friends had decided to chop the tree down. However, I intuitively felt the need to protect that tree. The locals, over and over again, had narrated stories of how misfortune was brought to those who tried to harm the tree in any way. It wasn't just a superstitious inclination but deep intuition that inspired me to preserve the tree and mould our design around it. Many years later, it was revealed to me that it was under the mother tree of the same tree that exists in Osho *Samadhi* today that Nagarjuna attained enlightenment. Every morning, as I do the rounds around the *samadhi*, I am refreshed by the sight of this lovely tree, nourished for centuries by the fragrance of Nagarjuna's enlightenment. Even today, in deep moments of silence, one can hear the ancient wisdom of nothingness in the rustling leaves of the Nagarjuna forest.

BUDDHA

"Buddha is such a pragmatist that even atheists find refuge in his teaching. His teaching is so scientific and accurate that it has withstood the test of time, and continues to illuminate the path of millions of seekers all over the world."

Twenty-five centuries ago, King Suddhodhan reigned over a fertile plain in the foothills of the Himalayas, which now falls in modern-day Nepal. The land, succulent with lush green vegetation, was inhabited mostly by the Shakyas. One beautiful summer afternoon, Queen Maya, the wife of Suddhodhan, retired to her chamber for her afternoon siesta. The fragrant air, spiced with sweet fruits and flowers, soon lulled her into sleep. The queen woke up to the vivid memory of a dream she had just had. In her dream, a white elephant with a blossoming white lotus in its trunk circumambulated her three times, struck her on the right side and vanished. The queen related the dream to her husband, who invited sixty-four Brahmins to interpret the dream. They all unanimously predicted the birth of an extraordinary child, who would either be a great emperor or an enlightened one.

As the birthing date neared, the queen expressed her desire to give birth in her childhood home at Devadaha. A royal procession left Kapilvastu, the capital city of the kingdom, for Devadaha. On the way they arrived at Lumbini grove. The grove was full of trees laden with beautiful flowers, and the joyous spring mood permeated the orchard. The queen alighted from her chair, and walked through the garden to touch a blossom. As she walked towards the flower, she was suddenly seized by the convulsions of labour pains, and gave birth to Siddhartha Gautam, the prophesized prince. On the same full-moon night, princess Yashodhara, his wife-to-be, was also born in a palace of the Koili dynasty at Devdaha. Thirty-five years later, Siddhartha Gautam attained enlightenment on the same full-moon night and became Buddha. He left his body at the age of eighty on that very day. This full moon of spring, known as *Baisakh Purnima*, is celebrated as *Buddha Jayanti* all over the world. Buddha heralded a new age. His teaching was based on understanding, logic and contemplation, and left little room for superstition. During his time, Hinduism was rife with traditions and superstitions, which had long lost their relevance. The prevalent priests used these rituals as a means to impose a false authority over people. With Buddha, religion matured. For the first time, religion became free from prayer, rituals and superstitions. His teaching awakened spiritual thirst in the hearts of many young men and women that followed his path.

Buddha is such a pragmatist that even atheists find refuge in his teaching. Nietzsche, who famously declared God is dead, couldn't deny the obvious truth in Buddha's word. He praised Buddhism for setting out to treat 'suffering' as opposed to 'sin' as the primary point of all religious quest.

Buddhism is best described in the words of Einstein, who was thoroughly inspired by Buddha. "Buddhism has the characteristics of what would be expected in a cosmic religion for the future: It transcends a personal God, avoids dogmas and theology; it covers both the natural and the spiritual, and it is based on a religious sense aspiring from the experience of all things, natural and spiritual, as a meaningful unity." Buddha said, "*Sabbe sankhara anichchati* – Nothing is permanent in this world, everything is in constant flux."

This includes relations, position, wealth, health and even life itself. This is why to be attached to anything here is to give birth to sorrow. If we can accept this philosophy of impermanence then we can be free from attachment and anxiety, opening up the path for peace and contentment. Buddha based his argument on impermanence, and refused the idea of an eternal God. He also refused the existence of the soul. According to Buddha, the soul does not reincarnate, rather it is desire that changes its form and is born again and again. When all desires cease, one achieves nirvana or ultimate emancipation. Buddha preached that this world is the manifestation of sorrow, and until and unless we are free from desire, we will keep getting entangled in various webs of grief. All have to go through the pain of disease, sorrow and death. Every love results in separation, each admiration in bitterness, and each victory in defeat.

During Buddha's time it was common belief that to attain success in anything, one had to appease the gods. Animal sacrifice was a common sight. Some even resorted to human sacrifice as a means of pleasing the gods. This sado-masochistic approach is not uncommon in many religions. Hindu scriptures are full of descriptions of netherworlds where the sinners are drowned for eternity in huge cauldrons bubbling with hot oil. Similarly, Jesus and Mohammad often speak of the Judgement Day, when the sinners will be weeded out and condemned to eternal suffering in hell. Buddha discarded these myths. He said, "No deity can either do good or bad to you. Your own actions lead to happiness or sorrow. *Ata hi atano natha, ata hi atano gati* - you are the creator of your destiny and you are the sole reason for your rise or fall."

Buddha preached the middle path - neither indulgence, nor renunciation, but a balanced and aware living. According to the eight-fold path, awareness and balance in all aspects of life is the key to meditation: right view, right intention, right speech, right action, right livelihood, right effort, right mindfulness and right enlightenment. The mind thrives on extremities. As soon as one refuses to relent to either extreme, one is released from the clutch of the mind, giving birth to a calmness and equanimity within. Buddha's teaching is so scientific and accurate that it has withstood the test of time, and continues to illuminate the path of millions of seekers all over the world.

THE TRANSFORMATION OF QUEEN CHHYAMA

The Magadh Emperor, Bimbasar, was married to Chhyama, the princess of Syalkot. (Syalkot today is in Pakistan). Chhyama was extremely beautiful and proud of her beauty.

Bimbasar was a devotee of Buddha. Whenever Buddha was in Rajgriha, the capital of Magadh, the whole royal family would come and pay their respects to him. Chhyama, however, was too proud of her beauty and youth and never joined the king on his visits. One day, Buddha was walking in the Benuvan forest, at Rajgriha. Queen Chhyama had also gone for a walk there. King Bimbasar sent her a message that she should not return to her palace without having the *darshan* of Buddha. Rather reluctantly, she went to see Buddha. Buddha greeted Chhyama tenderly and yet she saw no desire arise in his eyes. She could see that her beauty and charm did not affect Buddha in any way. He remained serene and equanimous. Chhyama was aware of her beauty and how it inspired lust and awe in each man she ever met. Buddha alone received her with equanimity.

This enraged the queen and she set out to leave angrily. Buddha read her mind and immediately created two beautiful women on either side of him using his *siddhi*. These women were by far more beautiful than Chhyama. This sight infuriated her still more. However, gradually those divine looking women started to age right in front of her. They became sickly and old, their beautiful teeth fell apart, the dark cascading tresses thinned and became grey wisps of hair, and their supple skin soon wrinkled into ugly flesh. Eventually, death came and both dropped dead by Buddha's side. The carcasses were a wretched and horrid sight to behold. Chhyama was horror-struck by the sight. She instantly realized the impermanence of the world and the transience of beauty. She fell at the feet of Buddha, begged for his forgiveness and asked if she could be initiated. Buddha transformed her without uttering a word. Chhyama achieved the state of *shrotapanna* and became an ideal *bhikkhuni*.

THE WOES OF PATACHARA

A rich merchant from Shrawasti had a very beautiful daughter named Patachara. Many young men were attracted to her beauty. Her parents used to lock her up in the upper chambers of their house so that no man may lay his eyes on her.

Patachara, however, fell in love with a servant of the household. The merchant had found a rich young fellow to be wed to Patachara, but on her wedding night she ran away with her lover. They fled from their village and made a simple living by doing menial labour. Patachara became pregnant and she left for her parents' house with her husband to deliver her child, as they did not have proper arrangements for the delivery of the baby. However, she gave birth to the child on the way, so they returned home.

Patachara became pregnant again. They again left for Patachara's parents' home to deliver her second child. They had to travel through a dense forest to reach her maternal home. On the way, a great storm broke out. Patachara started to have labour pains. Her husband went in search of firewood. While he was chopping firewood, a poisonous snake bit him and he died right there.

Patachara gave birth to another child in the desolate forest. She spent the whole night protecting her children and waiting for her husband. In the morning she searched for her husband and found him dead. Grief-stricken, she started walking towards her parents' home with her children. On the way there was a river that was swollen due to the monsoon rains, and it was impossible for her to cross the raging river carrying both her children. So she left her older child on the bank, and crossed the river with her newborn. Once she crossed the river, she left her infant there and went back to fetch her older child. When she was in the middle of the river, an eagle swooped down, grabbed Patachara's newborn and flew away. Seeing this she started to panic and scream. Hearing his mother scream, Patachara's older son thought that she was calling him, so he jumped into the river. The river took Patachara's older child and drowned him. Having lost both her children and husband on the same day, she lost her mental balance and started to cry in deep agony.

As she neared the home of her parents, she met a traveller from the village. Patachara introduced herself and asked about her relatives. The man was dumbstruck after he heard her story. After much pleading he told Patachara how the previous night's downpour had destroyed her parents' house. Her entire family had drowned in the flood. "They were being taken to the burning ghat when I was leaving. The smoke that you see coming from the west is probably from their funeral pyre," he told her.

This last tragedy totally broke her heart. She roamed naked around Srawasti wailing like a wounded animal. One day she arrived at Chetwan. The *bhikkhus* did not let her go near Buddha. Hearing her wailing, Buddha came out of the Gandhakuti, went near her and said, "Sister, come to your senses!"

As soon as she was in the peaceful presence of Buddha, she realized that she was naked. She sat down to cover herself. Buddha gave her one of his robes. She wore the robe, and lying prostrate at the feet of Buddha, narrated her tragic story. In the presence of Buddha, all her agony simply evaporated. A new calmness and peace descended upon her. Buddha said, "Just as you are shedding tears for your children and family now, you have shed tears in countless lives. The amount of tears humanity has shed for being separated from their loved ones is greater than the amount of water in the seven seas. Death and separation are the harsh rules of this world. Don't destroy your body in mourning; rather find out the way to be free from the bondage of sorrow."

Hearing these words of Buddha, Patachara achieved the state of *shrotapanna* right there. She then took initiation from Buddha and became a member of the Buddha *sangha,* and eventually became enlightened before she left her body.

YASHODHARA

> "YASHODHARA WAS A RARE FLOWERING BUT SHE HAS BEEN UNJUSTLY CONFINED TO THE OBLIVIOUS PAGES OF HISTORY. PUSHING HER INTO OBSCURITY, BUDDHISM HAS NOT ONLY UNDERMINED HER GLORY, BUT ALSO DEPRIVED MANY SEEKERS OF UNDERSTANDING AN INTEGRAL PART OF BUDDHA'S LIFE."

Lone Seeker Many Masters

Yashodhara

Around two thousand, five hundred and fifty years ago, on the beautiful full moon night of *Baisakh*, two beautiful souls descended on earth. Siddhartha Gautam was born in the forest of Lumbini and his wife-to-be was born in the royal palace of the Koili dynasty in Devdaha.

Yashodhara grew up in a very loving atmosphere in the palace of the Koilis, and enjoyed as much comfort as did Siddhartha. She grew up to be extremely beautiful. She was adept at playing the *veena* and was full of compassion. As she grew up, she started receiving marriage proposals from many princes. By then, Siddhartha had already earned the reputation of a sensitive prince who disappeared regularly and meditated under a tree for hours. Everyone thought that one day he would become a renunciate. Despite knowing all this and being warned by her family, she chose Siddhartha as her husband.

After Siddhartha left the palace to devote himself completely to self-realization, she brought up Rahul, their son, with great love and care. She also served King Suddhodhan and Prajapati Gautami, and supported them emotionally. The famous Vietnamese Buddhist scholar, Thich Nhat Hanh, and Osho both agree on the fact that Yashodhara constantly inspired Buddha to remain diligent on his path and not be lured by worldly desires. On the day he left the palace, she prepared his horse, Kanthak, and made sure that his charioteer, Chhandak, slept in the palace itself. Before he left, Buddha came to see his wife and newly-born son. According to traditional Buddhist literature, the gods came and covered Rahul's face with Yashodhara's shawl, but Osho and Thich Nhat Hanh say that Yashodhara had been awake and she knowingly covered the face of the child and her own self as well so that Siddhartha would not be distracted from the path of salvation.

There is a heartfelt instance of Buddha returning to Kapilvastu seven years after he left his palace in search of truth. When Suddhodhan heard that his son was residing in the Benuban forests of the nearby town of Rajgriha on the invitation of King Bimbisar, he sent Buddha's childhood friend, Channa, and his minister, Kaljayi, to invite him back home. When Channa and Kaljayi reached Benuban, they were received graciously.

Buddha asked about everybody in the palace, "How is Rahul? How is the health of father and mother? And how is Yashodhara?"

They said, "All are deeply grieved by your departure because they miss very much. We are here to bring to you their invitation to come to Kapilvastu."

Thus Buddha came to Kapilvastu after his monsoon retreat at Benuban, and stayed in a garden named Nyagrodha. Early in the morning, Buddha entered the town of Kapilvastu to beg for alms. When King Suddhodhan heard of this, he mounted his chariot and sped to welcome his son. Suddhodhan saw his son begging in front of a house. He stopped his chariot at a distance and watched a woman drop a potato into Buddha's begging bowl, after which he moved to the next house to beg. When he could no longer bear to watch his son begging, he got down from his chariot and called Buddha. "Siddhartha!" He said loudly.

Buddha graciously paid his respects to his father. Suddhodhan was overcome by the love for his son and wanted to hug him dearly, but he immediately realized that Siddhartha was not just his son, but had also become a great saint. Thus he gestured respectfully to the overwhelming presence of Buddha and said, "As you already know, no one in our lineage has ever begged for food. Why do you go begging from house to house? All facilities are available in the palace, let's go there."

Buddha listened to his father mindfully and said, "Revered king, I no more belong to the lineage of the Shakyas, but to the lineage of the Buddhas. And in the lineage of the Buddhas there has always been a tradition of begging for alms. There is no better method than this to melt the ego."

After this, Buddha went to the Kapilvastu palace with Suddhodhan. His presence brought great joy there. All the members of the royal family welcomed Buddha. Only Yashodhara was not there. When Buddha had met everyone, he asked, "Where is Yashodhara?"

Prajapati Gautami said, "Yashodhara feels that if she is virtuous enough then Siddhartha will go and meet her by himself."

When Buddha heard this, he went to meet Yashodhara with Sariputra, Mahamodgalyan and King Suddhodhan. On the way, he said to Sariputra, "I am free of attachments, but Yashodhara is still deeply attached to me. If she hugs me and starts crying, then please let her express her sorrow."

As soon as Yashodhara saw Siddhartha, her love for him

exploded and she grabbed his feet and started to cry. Seeing this, King Suddhodhan said, "This is not an expression of just this moment; it is the result of deep love for you. She had lived here the same way as you have in the forest. Hearing that you ate only one meal a day, she started doing the same. She started sleeping on the floor when she heard that you did not use a bed. And when she heard that you only wore a robe, she donated all her expensive clothes and started wearing simple clothes. When you left, she got marriage proposals from many princes, but she refused them outright and said, 'I have been born for Siddhartha, I will die for him. He will surely come to meet me one day.'"

After she had regained herself, she asked Buddha a very thoughtful question, "The truth that you experienced on the bank of the Niranjana River under the Bodhi Tree, is that truth not here? Could you not have realized that truth here?"

It is said that Buddha remained silent as he couldn't answer this question.

He then said, "You are my *punya salila*. I can never forget your help. We have been together for many lives."

After saying this, he gathered everyone around the Jamun tree where he had many experiences of meditation in his childhood, and told them a story:

Once upon a time, in the plains below the Himalayas, lived a poor but kind-hearted, hard-working and honest man named Megh. He was satisfied with whatever he earned by doing menial labour. Once he reached the capital city ruled by King Divapati, and he saw preparations being made for a grand event. There he also saw a beautiful young woman to whom he was immensely attracted. She was walking towards him with a lotus flower in her hand. Megh asked her what the celebrations were for and she answered, "The famous Acharya, Dipankara Buddha has come to town. This is the welcoming ceremony for him."

Megh said, "I also want to have *darshan* of Dipankara Buddha, but I don't want to go empty-handed to him. I have very little money. I will buy some flowers and come along with you."

Megh searched all around, but couldn't find any flowers for sale. The townsfolk had bought all the flowers to present to Dipankara Buddha. Giving up the quest, Megh asked of the young woman, "Please take this money and give me a few petals of your flower."

The woman said, "I cannot sell this because I have bought it to present it to the buddha. But *take* half of it so you can present it to the buddha as well."

Megh was an honest man, so he was not ready to take the flower without payment. He said, "You have to take something in return for the flower."

The woman was greatly impressed by Megh's honesty and so she said, "I am feeling a mysterious and strong attraction to you. I not only want to give you this flower but also my whole life. I am as pure and virgin as this flower and want to surrender myself at your feet."

Megh was also greatly attracted by the girl's simplicity and beauty and so he said, "We must have been related to each other in many past lives. Nothing else can explain this uncannily strong pull we feel towards each other."

Megh added, "But look, beautiful! I have already made up my mind to walk on the path of truth. I want to be a sannyasin of Dipankara Buddha. I am a very poor man. I cannot make you happy by marrying you."

The woman answered, "I feel that I have been born for you and I want to travel with you for lives. I will only help you on your path and will not be a hindrance. "

Megh's heart was also not ready to let her go, so he agreed to the woman's proposal with great joy. Both arrived at Dipankara

Buddha's *sangha* and paid respects to him by placing the lotus flower at his feet. Dipankara Buddha was very happy to see them and said, "May both your wishes come true. Megh, you will become enlightened in your next life, and thousands will seek solace in you."

He said to the woman, "Beautiful one, you will be Megh's beloved in this life and the next, and you will have to become an inspiration for his freedom rather than becoming the object of his attachment. This is my blessing. You two are beloveds of lives."

After telling this story, Siddhartha said, "I was Megh, and Yashodhara, you were his consort. We have been together for lives, and you have always helped me in my meditation and never hindered me in any way."

After hearing this, all of Yashodhara's sorrows melted away and her face radiated a divine aura.

Rahul was only seven when he decided to become a *bhikkhu*. Yeshodhara did not stop him, rather she herself expressed her desire to be initiated, but as Buddha did not initiate women in those days, she remained uninitiated. When Suddhodhan died, Buddha's aunt and stepmother, Prajapati Gautami, shaved her head, wore the ochre robe and went to Vaishali asking Buddha to initiate her. Anand, his caretaker, also spoke strongly in favor of initiating women into the *sangha*. Buddha reluctantly initiated Prajapati Gautami. This is when Yashodhara also became initiated as women could now enter the *sangha*.

Yashodhara never demanded to be known or respected as Buddha's wife, and lived the simplest of lives. She used to clean and take care of the sick in the *sangha*. Rahul, after his *arhattva*, had already become one of the ten chief *acharyas*. Although being the wife of Buddha and the mother of one of the chief *acharyas*, Yashodhara decided to keep a low profile. She dissolved herself completely in the Buddha *sangha*.

The conversation Yashodhara had with her beloved on the full moon day of Baisakh, when she was seventy-eight, in the Benuban forest of Rajgriha is very touching. She had said to Buddha, "Now I have become old and all my body parts are tired. I have fulfilled my innate duties as the princess of the Koilis, crown princess of the Shakyas and a *bhikkhuni* of the Buddha *sangha*. I have remembered my past lives. In many of them I have served you in some form or other with total devotion and love. In this life you accepted me as your wife, gave me a son, and as a master you guided me to enlightenment. I have no more desires left. With your permission, I want to leave my body. If I have made any mistake in my life, please forgive me."

She then went around Buddha three times, and went to her hut to light an oil lamp. Then she thanked Buddha, and left her body in a peaceful state.

After Yashodhara left her body, Buddha praised her while addressing his sangha, "Yashodhora was an exceptional *sadhika*. Although she was a beautiful princess, she did not have even a trace of ego. She fulfilled all her duties as a wife, mother and daughter-in-law honestly. She had the compassion to serve the sick and needy since childhood, and she served the sick of the Buddha sangha with the same compassionate heart. She felt blessed doing the simplest chores such as sweeping the floor and doing the dishes. Once she was initiated, she quietly performed her role as an ideal *bhikkhuni*."

Buddha himself was full of appreciation for her, and yet Buddhist scholars have forgotten Yashodhara. She has been unjustly confined to the oblivious pages of history. The renowned Buddhist scholar, Bhikkhu Amritananda, who has written rare Buddhist texts in Nepali, has only included Sujata, Bishakha, Shyamwati, Susuptawasa, Supriya, Uttaranandmata, Khajjutara, Kalyayeni, Nukulmata and

Kaliupasika as the ten main Buddhist bhikkhunis, totally disregarding Yashodhara. I am often moved to tears when I read the accounts of Yashodhara's selfless and unceasing devotion to Buddha. Pushing her into obscurity, Buddhism has not only undermined a woman who was a rare flowering, but also deprived many seekers from understanding an integral part of Buddha's life.

SARIPUTRA & MAHAMODGALYAN

" THE CONCEPT OF LEELA SAHACHARI IS UNIQUE TO EASTERN TRADITION. IT IS BELIEVED THAT EVERY ENLIGHTENED MASTER DESCENDS ON EARTH WITH A FEW HIGHLY EVOLVED SOULS, WHO COMPLETE THE CIRCLE AS HIS DISCIPLES. THESE DISCIPLES ARE REGARDED AS THE EXTENSIONS OF THE DIVINE CONSCIOUSNESS OF THE MASTER AND ARE INDISPENSABLE IN THE FULFILLMENT OF THE MISSION OF A MASTER. "

The two principal disciples of Buddha were born on the same day near Nalanda, towards the south of Rajgriha, the capital of the Kingdom of Magadh. Both were born into well-to-do Brahmin families who knew each other very well. At a very young age both were disenchanted with the world and became disciples of Acharya Sanjaya Bethaliputra, a well-known teacher in the area. Buddha was spending his second year on the Giddhakuti hill, and one of his first five disciples, Ashwajeet, came to Nalanda begging for alms. Sariputra saw Ashwajeet and felt a mysterious pull towards the serene monk. Seeing the peace and grace radiating from Ashwajeet, Sariputra aked him, "All your senses seem peaceful and joyous. For which master have you renounced the world, and what is your master's teaching?"

Ashwajeet said, "I am the disciple of Shakya prince Tathagata

Buddha. His teachings include the four noble truths, the five disciplines and the eightfold path. He is now in Giddhakuti. You can go and meet him by yourself."

Ashwajeet's words touched a deep chord in Sariputra's heart, and he felt as if he had finally found the key to the mysteries of life. He rushed to meet his friend, Mahamodgalyan. Seeing him, Mahamodgalyan said, "You look extremely blissful today, as though the rays of truth have descended upon you. Who is the source of this grace?"

Sariputra relayed how he had met Ashwajeet, and asked Mahamodgalyan to go with him to meet Buddha. Mahamodgalyan said, "Let's ask Acharya Sanjaya Bethaliputra to go with us as well."

They both went to meet Bethaliputra in his ashram where he lived with two hundred and fifty disciples. Bethaliputra became jealous after hearing from them about Buddha, and refused to go. He said, "Why are you leaving me now? You are young and I have become old. Stay here and look after the ashram. I will make you the heads of this ashram."

Sariputra and Mahamodgalyan did not like Bethaliputra's proposal, and they said, "We are going to meet Buddha; if anyone else also wants to come, they are welcome."

As they stood to leave, all of Bethaliputra's disciples stood up and followed Sariputra and Mahamodgalyan. When Buddha saw Sariputra and Mahamodgalyan coming towards him along with two hundred and fifty seekers, he said to his disciples who were present with him, "Look, the two pillars of my religion have arrived."

They came close to Buddha and sat down. The sermon of Buddha melted their hearts. Sariputra, Mahamodgalyan and all the others who had come along joined the Buddha *sangha*.

Sariputra and Mahamodgalyan had been meditating for many lives. In his Jataka Tales, Buddha has said that Sariputra had been meditating intensely for his past sixty lives. Due to the grace of Buddha and the virtues of their past lives, Mahamodgalyan attained the state of *arthattva* just in seven days and Sariputra in three weeks after they became initiated.

Sariputra was adept in understanding and explaining Buddha's message, and he was respected second only to Buddha. Well known for his humbleness and unceasing gratitude towards his master, he was the main *acharya* or teacher of the Buddha *sangha*, but his lifestyle was very simple. As said in the Buddhist scriptures, once the Buddha *sangha* was coming towards Srawasti and it became dark before the members arrived there. They had to spend the night on the road, and most of the *bhikkhus* occupied the best places to sleep. Sariputra, not finding a proper place, slept under a tree outside Buddha's cottage. In the night, Buddha heard someone cough, and came out of his hut and asked, "Who is there?"

Sariputra answered, "It is I, Sariputra."

When Buddha asked him why he was sleeping outside, Sariputra said there wasn't enough room indoors so he had to sleep there. The next morning Buddha scolded everyone and said that Sariputra should be treated second only to him, and that the best provisions should be made for him. Sariputra, on the other hand, had no complaints, and would have had none even if he had spent the night in the cold. When everyone would leave to beg for alms, Sariputra would clean and tend to the sick.

Since Ashwajeet had inspired Sariputra to meet Buddha, Sariputra felt a deep gratitude towards Ashwajeet throughout his life. Every morning he would bow down in the direction where Ashwajeet would be.

He had no special demands. He used to say, "Neither do I have the desire to live nor do I hanker to die. Whatever comes along the way, I accept it with gratitude."

Buddha himself used to praise Sariputra often. Since Buddha had meditated constantly for six years in extreme conditions at Bodhgaya, he had developed a back problem. Sometimes his back would start aching while he was giving discourse. At such times, Buddha would tell Sariputra to continue the discourse, and would go to rest. Once, Sariputra was giving a discourse as Buddha had fallen ill. When Buddha heard Sariputra talk about the Buddha Dharma, Buddha couldn't resist himself and came out of his hut and said, "Oh saint Sariputra! You have understood the core of the *dharma* and explained it better than I have."

Buddha's disciples took turns caring for him. When his health worsened, it was decided that one person who knew the habits and needs of Buddha very well should be given the responsibility of the job. The caretaker of Buddha had to walk like his shadow and serve him with full awareness twenty-four hours a day. All of them were scared by the demands of this work but Sariputra and Mahamodgalyan were the first to say they would love to do that work. Buddha said, "The two of them are my shadows. Where I cannot reach, they will have to go, so I cannot bind them to me."

After that Buddha chose Ananda, a very wise and compassionate monk, as his personal caretaker.

Mahamodgalyan was special in his own way. His continuous intense meditation had made him the master of many *siddhis,* but he would never show it in public. When the mind becomes still after continuous intense meditation, some *siddhis* develop naturally. In yoga they are called the *asthasiddhi* (eight *siddhis*) and Mahamodgalyan was adept in all of them. Buddha was against displaying such psychic powers in public, as such practice would lead to the fall of the meditator. While he was at Nalanda his disciples said, "If you allow Mahamodgalyan, a son of this land, to display some of his *siddhis* to the people here, the whole of Nalanda will join the Buddha *sangha.*"

Buddha refused this outright, and said, "People should join my religion by understanding its real value, and not by being impressed by some magic trick."

During Buddha's time it was the norm among yogis to show off their *siddhis* and earn wealth and respect from the common folk. Once, Mahamodgalyan and a fellow *bhikkhu,* Pindola Bhardwaj, were coming towards the city of Rajgriha. Seeing them, a rich merchant placed a golden bowl on a bamboo stick, and challenged them by saying, "You are *siddha bhikkhus*, aren't you? If you can take this bowl from the bamboo by using your *siddhi,* then I will donate the bowl to you filled with gold coins." Mahamodgalyan was not interested, but Pindola became excited and was able to extract the bowl that was stuck on the bamboo. From then on, Pindola Bhardwaj was hailed wherever he went. When Buddha heard this, he called him and scolded him harshly.

"You have committed a great crime. You made a cheap show of the divine *siddhi* that you gained out of your meditation, just as a prostitute tempts her clients for a little money by lifting her skirt and showing her undergarments. People who join the *sangha* by being tempted by siddhis can't walk on the path stably, and always hanker to achieve miraculous powers."

After saying this, Buddha banned the show of powers in his *sangha*. Both Mahamodgalyan and Sariputra were older than Buddha. When Sariputra's health worsened while he was in Magadh doing his master's work, he came to Srawasti and made a request of Buddha.

"My body wants to take rest forever; please give me the permission for *mahaparinirvana*."

When Buddha asked him where he would like to take *mahaparinirvana*, he answered, "I would like to go to Nalanda and take it in the presence of my mother."

Buddha said, "Sariputra! Do whatever you feel is right." And he bade him farewell.

Before leaving, Sariputra said, "In my past life I was able to meet a buddha named Anomdarshi, and had wished to be a disciple of such a buddha. My wish was fulfilled when I was able to be your disciple. I have had the good fortune of meditating in your presence and serving you in many lives. From here on I will not be able to have that fortune because this is your last life, and so is it of many of us here. Now we won't be able to be born again with you and take part in your *leela*, and that makes me very sad. If I have been of any harm to you or your *sangha* in this or in my past lives, then I ask you and the whole *sangha* for forgiveness. Buddha said, "Sariputra, you have never done anything that I haven't liked."

The whole Buddha *sangha* was filled with sentiments while saying goodbye to Sariputra. Buddha came to the main gate of Chetwan to bid him farewell. Sariputra went around Buddha three times, and making the whole *sangha* emotional, left for Nalanda with his youngest brother, Chunda.

Sariputra's mother had been extremely angry at Buddha because all her sons, Sariputra, Chunda, Upasen and Rewat, and all her daughters, Chala, Upachala and Shipuchala, had become *bhikkhus*. She was happy to see Sariputra come home, as she thought that he had left the *sangha,* and she felt that finally in old age some sense had come to him. But her happiness vanished and she became very sad when she heard from Sariputra that he had come there to leave his body.

Hearing that Sariputra had come home to leave his body, all the important people of Magadh came to have his *darshan* bearing gifts. Finally, when King Ajatsatru himself arrived to pay his respects to Sariputra, his mother realized the value of her son and Buddha. She also expressed her wish to join the Buddha *sangha,* and was initiated by Sariputra. In this way, Sariputra freed himself from his debt to his mother. To the *bhikkhus* who had come to have his last *darshan*, he said, "*Bhikkhus*, we are very fortunate that we had a great master like the *Tathagata*. Never be careless towards him."

Sariputra left his body in the morning of the full moon day of the month of November. Chunda performed the last rites, and went to Srawasti after fifteen days with Sariputra's robes, begging bowl and his holy remains. Buddha said, "*Bhikkhus*, the intelligent, composed and forgiving image of compassion, Sariputra, has achieved *mahaparinirvana*. Let's pray for him."

The whole Buddha *sangha* started to mourn. Hearing that his beloved friend had left his body, Mahamodgalyan didn't rise from where he was, and sitting there, left *his* body too. The two friends who were born on the same day achieved *mahaparinirvana* in an interval of fifteen days. Sariputra and Mahamodgalyan were *leela sahachari* of Buddha. The concept of *leela sahachari* is unique to eastern tradition. It is believed that every enlightened master descends on earth with a few highly evolved souls who complete the circle as his disciples. These disciples are regarded as the extensions of the divine consciousness of the master, and are indispensable in the fulfillment of the mission of a master.

The death of these two leela sahachari marked the end of an era in Buddhist history. Buddha himself said, "Just as a big tree looks frail and naked when its branches fall, so have I become alone after these two have attained *mahaparinirvana*."

MASTARAM BABA

> "In a cave nearby Hanumansheela lived a God-realized saint. His ever blissful countenance had won him the name Mastaram Baba, the blissful saint."

Mastaram Baba

On the bank of the Ganga between Ramjhula and Laxmanjhula in Rishikesh, there is a rock called the Hanumansheela. Legend has it when Hanuman was carrying the hill of Dronagiri towards Lanka, modern day Sri Lanka, a part of the hill had fallen in the Ganga. That fallen rock started to be called the Hanumansheela, the rock of Hanuman. In a cave near Hanumansheela lived a God-realized saint. He left his body on June 22, 1987. His ever blissful countenance had won him the name Mastaram Baba, the blissful saint. I had discovered this saint by chance. My love for the Himalayas and the Ganga took me on lonely voyages through those ancient peaks and the hallowed river countless times. And often these journeys granted me the good fortune of meeting rare saints. One such saint is Ma Nani.

Once, while travelling in Uttar Kashi, I was told of a highly evolved female sannyasin from the West living in Sainj on the way to Gangotri. I immediately decided to meet her. Nani Ma was living on a small patch of land on the bank of the Ganga, where she had built a few simple huts surrounded by a beautiful Himalayan garden that she had nurtured on her own.

In a thin white cotton sari, Nani carried a frail physique and wore a beatific appearance seasoned by age, experience and austerity. In our very first meeting, she told me of the glorious tales of her Guru, and I learned of the majestic Mastaram Baba for the first time. Every moment that I spent with her is imprinted in my heart.

After reading the Gita and the description of a *sthitpragya*, the one who is balanced and is in a constant state of mental and emotional equilibrium, as a young seeker in her twenties Nani prayed that she should also meet such a saint. The impact of Gita on her was such that she became a self-styled *sadhu,* and set off towards the Himalayas with just a small bag with a change of clothes and a *kamandalu.* Unaware of the language or the culture, fully surrendered to the divine without any money, Nani started to walk towards the Ganga because she had heard that many Gurus lived there. Except for a trusting innocent heart, she had nothing to support her search.

Soon her feet were in blisters and her bearings tattered. Seeing her crying in great pain, and listening to her story, a priest in a temple told her of his fully realized Guru who lived under a rock. She immediately knew that she had found the one she was looking for. Finally her prayers were answered on the white sandy bank of the Ganga, where she found her Master and a new meaning in life.

After meeting her Guru, she lived at Mastaram Baba's Ashram under his spiritual guidance, learning and meditating on the Vedanta. During these years she studied many ancient scriptures and also learnt Sanskrit. Seeing that she loved to read, Baba gave her many spiritual books on Vedanta and *bhakti*. One day he asked her to stop reading and to start meditating. This is how Nani spent sixteen years in Baba's ashram at Rishikesh until Baba left his body.

After Baba's *mahaparinirvana* in 1987, Nani moved higher into the mountains, living in Gangotri, and practised her *sadhana* and austerity for eight years before she descended to Sainj. Being a single woman and also a Westerner, it was not easy for Nani to live in the rather traditional ambience of the Hindu *sadhu* community, and she had to face all kinds of hardships and difficulties. But despite it all, Nani never left the laps of the Himalayas. It was her fervour for truth, her devotion to her Guru and her love for the Ganga that always kept her content and happy. Even today, regardless of the weather, Nani does not start her day without bathing in the freezing Ganga whom she considers her spiritual mother. She always said that there were two axes to her life, one was her Guru, Mastaram Baba, her spiritual father, and the other was the Ganga, her spiritual mother.

During our meeting, Nani also gave me a book that she had written about a rare account of Eric, another Western disciple of Baba. Eric was a young American who had discovered Mastaram Baba while wandering along the edges of the Ganga in Rishikesh. It was a deep love at first sight, it was the awakening of his dormant sanskaras of the past, it was the meeting of a devotee and the Master.

Eric's life took a leap and he became a full-time seeker and disciple of Baba, following everything that the hermit preached to the word. His devotion for Baba was like that of an innocent child. He was a true devotee with a heart of pure innocence and trust. With time this love deepened, and Eric was so inseparable from Baba that when his visa expired, he refused to leave the country. When the police came to deport him he ran away from them. At one time he jumped into the Ganga and swam across it, just so he could avoid them and stay longer with Baba. When Eric was forcefully sent back to America, he would count his days to come back, and would work very hard just so he could buy gifts for the people at the ashram.

The separation and the pain only brought Eric closer to Baba. Baba became Eric's lifeline, and without him, Eric was like a fish out of water. Every time he returned to Rishikesh, Eric would rush to Baba in tears and would prostrate himself at his feet. His love and reverence for Baba was always a unique sight. As his love grew, the rough edges of his being became polished, and he attained a great height in his devotion which transformed him into a humble being. He could no more tolerate the coming and going and the pain of separation from his Guru. Slowly, Eric's health started deteriorating, and it was as if by his own wish he developed different kinds of sickness in his body which never became cured. This became a blessing in disguise for Eric, as it helped him to stay longer in India on medical grounds.

As time passed, Eric became so weak that he could not even carry his frail body. The last moment of his life is very poignant. It was the climax of his devotion, and immortalized his pure love for his Guru. As the moment of death arrived, Eric struggled intensely, and rushed to his beloved Mastaram Baba, and peacefully left his body at the feet of his Guru.

Another disciple of Baba, Nepali Mai, shares a very beautiful story of Baba's love for his disciples. She is also the mother of the famous Nepali political leader, Pradip Gyawali. Nepali Mai was living in the mountains near the Badrinath temple which she had made her abode for spiritual penance. I met her several times during my trip to Badrinath. She never returned home after going on a pilgrimage to Badrinath, where she also met Baba when he was living there. When Baba was still in his body, one day a disciple of his came to her from Rishikesh with dry fruits and two shawls. He said that Baba had sent them, and had asked him to bring them to her. Nepali Mai burst into tears. Just few days ago, somebody had broken into her hut and had stolen all her possessions. Except for a blanket, she had nothing left. She was using it to cover herself in the freezing weather of the mountains. Although Baba was far from Nepali Mai, his love had no bounds, and he was fully aware of what his disciples were going through.

Mastaram Baba didn't speak much about his past. After persistent inquiries, I managed to extract a few details about his life from his disciples.

Again, not much is known of his childhood except a few details. His personality and manner of speech suggested that he was from a well-to-do family from North India. His disciples often narrate an incident that changed his life forever. Once, his schoolmate was severely beaten. Seeing the miserable state of his friend, Baba became infuriated, and cursed, "May that cruel one die!". Verily, the person was found dead the same day. This wasn't the first time his words had come true. In fact, many times the things that he would say out of the blue had materialized. However, after this incident, Baba became afraid of his own strange ability. He felt that the worldly life wasn't meant for him, and he left on a long pilgrimage around India.

During his pilgrimage, he reached the dacoit-infested region of Chambal Ke Ghati, and was spending the night on a riverbank. A group of dacoits approached him and asked from where he'd come. Baba was observing silence and did not speak a word. The dacoits grew suspicious, and took him for an undercover detective. They beat him till they thought he was dead, and threw him on the bank of the river. A few days later, a passer-by saw him and offered to take him to the hospital, but Baba refused and told the man that he did not take any help by way of medication. He told him that his wounds would heal in due time, and kept quiet. One of his cuts was very deep and became infested with insects. When an insect fell from his wound, he would place it back so that it wasn't robbed of its food. One night when he was in deep sleep, a wild animal came and vigorously licked his wound. Somehow, the chemicals in the animal's saliva healed the wound, and Baba continued his journey.

His only possessions were a wrap-around cloth or *dhoti* and a water pot that he carried with him. When he reached Uttaranchal in North India, and saw rivers, streams and waterfalls in abundance, he then felt it was superfluous to carry the water pot anymore, and now his only possession was his *dhoti*. He used to make it through the freezing Himalayan winter clad only in a *dhoti*. One morning when he had started living in Rishikesh, he was about to go out to beg when a stranger came to Baba and offered him food. Baba picked up the signals of existence diligently. That day, Baba realized he was totally provided for, and stopped begging completely.

After that incident, he started to rely totally on existence for his sustenance. If food came to him he would eat, otherwise he would drink the water from the Ganaga and go to sleep.

While Mastaram Baba was in Rishikesh, a Maharaja of a North Indian state came in contact with him. He told Baba that since his ancestor's time, there had been no birth in his household, and they had to always adopt children. Baba looked at them with compassion and said, "Your ancestors had killed a calf. Despite being the rulers of a Hindu kingdom, you people did not respect and protect cows. Go to the cows grazing in the ashram, hold their feet and ask for forgiveness for the act of your ancestors, and protect the cows in your state from now on. If the cows forgive you, then you will have children."

The Maharaja did as he was told, and in due course, had a son. The family came to Baba with presents, and offered to build a beautiful ashram for him, but Baba told them he didn't accept anything more than a meal from anyone, and thus refused them. He blessed them and sent them back home.

One day a princess form a North Indian state fled home after an argument with her family and arrived at Baba's ashram. By then a few women had already become devotees of Baba, and they were living in a room a little way away from the ashram. Madalsha, the princess, started living with the female devotees. No-one at Mastaram Baba ashram begged for alms. If somebody brought food, Baba distributed it among all the ashramites. One day, no-one brought any food, so Madalsha, unable to resist her hunger, went to beg and cooked what little rice and lentils she had collected. As it was the tradition in the ashram, she brought the food to her Guru first. Baba asked, "Who brought this?"

Madalsha said that she had begged for it.

"Whoever begged for it can also eat it. I don't beg and don't eat that which has been acquired by begging," he told her.

"But how can I eat without first feeding you?" She asked in desperation.

Baba took a grain of cooked rice and put it in his mouth and said, "Now that you have fed me, you can eat in peace."

The princess lived a simple devoted life with Baba for ten years under his strict rules. But once her relatives found out she was there, they came to collect her. Madalsha refused to leave the ashram, but Baba told her, "You still have some worldly desires left, you should get married and live a householder's life," and sent her home.

Mastaram Baba's state of unconditional bliss reminds one of Diogenes, whom Alexander regarded as his master. Diogenes walked around naked with a water pot as his only possession. It is said that once he saw a dog drink water from a river. He realized then that if an animal can rely totally on existence, why couldn't he? Immediately afterwards, he threw the water pot in the river and finally felt like the emperor of the world. Even Alexander was jealous of Diogenes, and felt belittled by his grandeur. When Alexander was about to begin his conquest, he had gone to Diogenes to receive blessings. It was a cold winter's day. Diogenes was lying down and sunbathing on a riverbank. Alexander said to him, "I am going to conquer the world, so I need your blessings."

Diogenes asked him, "What will you do after you conquer the world?"

"I will come back to Greece and relax," he answered.

Diogenes said, "If in the end you want to relax, then why do you want to commit so much bloodshed for it? There is so much space on this riverbank, lie down next to me and relax right now. I don't think that such a trouble-creating mind can ever relax."

Not being able to answer him, Alexander tried to change the topic, and said, "I want to do something for you before I leave. What can I do?"

"You are blocking the sunshine; I only ask you to move a little bit to the side. That's all I ask of you," said Diogenes.

After his conquest reached India, Alexander approached his death, but he wanted to die with his family in Greece. The day before he reached home, he had become very ill, and ordered his doctor, "Anyhow save me for one more day, I want to die in Athens. If you can extend my life just for one more day, then I will give you half of my empire."

The Doctor said it was not possible.

"I will give you the whole empire," said Alexander in desperation.

Even then it was not possible. It was then he realized the fruitlessness of the efforts of his whole life. He remembered Diogenes and his words. He then gave his soldiers his last command, "When I die, make sure that both my hands are hanging out of my coffin."

When the general of his army inquired why he should do such an absurd thing, he said, "I want the whole world to see and understand that Alexander was also not able to take anything with him, and had to die empty-handed. If I get the chance to be born again, I don't want to be another Alexander, rather I would like to be born as a Diogenes."

I have the feeling that the next life of Alexander must have been like that of Mastaram Baba.

KRISHNA

> Krishna does not shun love, he does not run away from women or renounce luxury. He is full of love and compassion, and yet he has the courage to accept and fight a war. His heart is utterly non-violent, yet he plunges into a war with the same equanimity. He dances, he battles.

Krishna seems to be a figment of a poet's imagination. He is quoted in the Gita as saying, "Among the seasons, I am spring; rich and vibrant. Among the gods, I am Kamdev, the God of amour and aesthetics. Among men, I am the King. I am everywhere where there is a manifestation of beauty, brilliance, bliss and creativity." He is depicted as the playful, flirtatious one, adorned in bright, flamboyant costumes, jewellery, and a peacock-feather crown. He enjoys playing the flute to his lovelorn gopinis, the celestial milkmaids, and hides behind trees to taunt them as they bathe in a pond, and dances and sings with them all day long. He is a prankster and a butter thief, but that's not all. It is also Krishna who encouraged Arjuna to fight the War of Mahabharata. Krishna does not shun love, he does not run away from women, or renounce luxury. He is full of love and compassion, and yet has the courage to accept and fight a war. His heart is utterly non-violent, yet he plunges into a war with the same equanimity. He dances, he battles.

As one can read in the Gita, Krishna embodied paradoxes. He wasn't bound to a personality. His response to life was spontaneous and unique. This is why among all the nine Hindu avatars, Krishna is hailed as the only purnaavatar, or the total manifestation of divine consciousness.

Most religions of the world are unnecessarily serious and dry. Jesus was crucified two thousand years ago, and Christians are still in mourning. Hazrat Imam Husain died in the Battle of Karbala in the seventh century, along with all his relatives, and Muslims still mourn his death. Buddha's teaching rests on the foundation of truth that proclaims life is misery. The disciples of Mahavir fast, destroy their bodies and pull out their hair. In a world of such joyless and miserable religions, Krishna's ecstatic and exuberant teaching is a breath of fresh air.

Krishna's religion is based on celebration. No other religious philosophy accepts all the facets of life. Krishna's religion is life-affirmative and multi-dimensional. It brings the teaching of detachment and love together, of wisdom and devotion, of celebration and death, all together. Krishna's religion is like a rainbow that embraces all the colours of life.

Krishna is also among the first spiritual psychologists. Long before modern psychology understood the nuances of the mind, he had declared the divided mind as the root of all malaise. The twentieth-century psychologist, Freud, gave a scientific explanation of the mind. With him, came the understanding that a suppressed and divided mind only brings perversion and anguish. After him came Jung, who talked about the collective consciousness and subconsciousness. He brought psychology closer to religion. Erich

Fromme and William Reich experienced the necessity of love in human life, and said that the biggest human problem was the lack of love. Against this backdrop, if we examine the religions of the world, they appear unscientific and inadequate, as all religions teach suppression in one form or another. Gradually, religion became more of a moral authority. It did not open avenues or channels to realize the deeper truths of life, or partake in the eternal celebration that exsistence is. It is not surprising, therefore, that Karl Marx thought of religion as, "...the sigh of the oppressed creature, the heart of a heartless world, and the soul of soulless conditions. It is the opium of the people". If anything, religion has only prevented us from enjoying the spontaneous joy of living an unprejudiced and wholesome life. In the beginning of the Gita, Arjuna's mind is in trouble. He is enmeshed in a moral dilemma. He cannot decide whether he should fight the battle for power, or abdicate the throne. Seated in the middle of the battlefield on his chariot, Arjuna surveyed the battlefront. He could foresee the bloodbath and corpses. He thought it much better to renounce it all and flee into the forest, than to partake in the battle.

Problems are the shadows of a split mind. A non-divisive mind has no problem. The Bhagavad Gita is an effort to bring Arjuna's mind into its undivided state again. Krishna speaks in the language of Freud and Jung - *sanshayatma binashyati* - a troubled mind leads to destruction. One can only attain this if one is deeply centred in his own being. In the Gita, Krishna talks about the importance of *Swadharma*, resting in one's authentic nature. Krishna says that unless one behaves according to his own nature, he is bound to live a troubled life. Modern psychology is on the same page as Krishna as far as the mind is concerned.

Krishna introduced laughter, love, music and playfulness into religion. Often, his behaviour appears absurd. He elopes with Rukmani from her wedding ceremony to another man, and encourages Arjuna to elope with Suvadra, Krishna's sister. He hypnotizes all the girls of Gokul with his flute. The gopinis, forgetting all social inhibitions, follow him and dance around him. He steals the clothes of young girls bathing naked in the Yamuna River, and tells them they will only get their clothes back if they come out of the river and ask for forgiveness from the River God.

He is playful, untroubled and calm even during a war. His response is spontaneous and unpredictable. One moment, he declares that although his army will fight in the war of Kurukshetra, he will only be Arjuna's charioteer and will not fight. But the next moment, when he sees that Arjuna is defeated, he attacks Bhishmapitamaha with the wheel of his own chariot. He doesn't reject the love request of Kubja, a crippled maid in the palace of his uncle, Kansha.

Krishna is also known as Banke Bihari – the twisted and the joyous one. Banke is a metaphor for a person whose behaviour is tangential, who cannot be morally defined or understood logically. This is the specialty of Krishna. He is neither connected to any conditioning of the past, nor are his actions a means for a particular purpose in the future. This is what Osho regards as being centred in one's own being. He who is not bound by any decision or idea from the past, and he who lives in the moment and decides according to the call of the moment, is centred in his being, or in Krishna's language, is a *sthitpragya*.

Although he is the source of romantic love for many women, he is completely free from attachment. None of his beloveds, Radha, Rukmanai or Lalita, can stop him as he leaves for the battle of Mathura or Dwarika when duty calls. While fighting on the side of truth, he is ready to become the charioteer of his disciple Arjuna, but when Arjuna is not on the path of truth, Krishna does not hesitate to put him straight, either. He is for justice. It is difficult to find a person like him in the world who is completely free from attachment.

It is because of this that he can love everyone equally. Hundreds of *gopinis* felt that Krishna was dancing with them. This must mean that a person who is not bound with anyone is available for all. This is why, despite all his romantic engagements, Krishna is considered to be a *brahmachari*.

It is a sad truth that all geniuses and enlightened masters are born before their time. The more gifted they are, the longer it takes to understand them. Personal transformation can happen quickly, but collective consciousness evolves very slowly. The message of peace, non-violence and forgiveness that Buddha preached two thousand, five hundred years ago, is becoming more and more relevant in this troubled atomic age. After the Second World War, the West has become intensely attracted to Buddha. This is why new Buddhist monasteries and meditation centres are mushrooming in every city in the West. The collective consciousness of the world is reaching towards the state Buddha reached two thousand, five hundred years ago. But Krishna, who was born five thousand years ago, still remains elusive.

Even among the devotees of Krishna, there are different sects because none of them are able to accept Krishna in his totality. Tilak only accepts the Karmayogi Krishna, while Surdas only loves Balgopal, the child Krishna. Gandhi and Vinova find it difficult to accept the Krishna of Mahabharata and Vrindavan.

In the last century, when the Bhagavad Gita was translated into English, the great philosophers of the twentieth century, Schopenhauer, Thoreau, Emerson, Einstein and Roman Rolan, hailed it as one of the most important books on spirituality. The day Schopenhauer read the Gita, he danced on the streets of Paris with the book on his head. He famously said, "Some books are worth reading, some books compel you to sing, but the Gita makes one dance."

Even Einstein, the greatest physicist of our time, was

mesmerized by the insights of the Gita. He said, "All our intellect put together is nothing compared to the Gita. This is the universal expression of wisdom."

Gandhi, a true devotee of the Gita, said, "Whenever I am surrounded by gloom, I go to the refuge of the Gita."

Schopenhauer, Einstein, Emerson and Thoreau, the intellectual giants of our age, sometimes delve into that space from which Krishna functioned five thosuand years ago. Krishna can only be understood when the collective human consciousness accepts love, romance, music and the attraction between male and female guiltlessly. In the coming days when we will gather the courage to understand the science of the body and the mind in totality, only then will Krishna be contemporary.

Albert Schweitzer has made an important critique of the religions of the Indian subcontinent. He has said that all the religions of India are life-negative. There is certainly some truth in his words, but he, too, has missed Krishna. Krishna is a thriving oasis in the unending desert of miserable religions. Krishna alone dances among the serious masters, and he alone rejoices in beauty and joy. Whatsoever is written about Krishna and all the commentaries on the Gita are one-dimensional. No one has been able to accept the multi-dimensional aspects of Krishna except Osho. Reading Krishna through the eyes of Osho I could finally understand him. Osho says, "Although Krishna was born many centuries ago, he belongs to the future. It was unfortunate that we did not allow Krishna to influence our life in a broad way. He remains a lonely dancing island in the vast ocean of sorrow and misery that is our life. Krishna has great significance for the future. And his significance will continue to grow with the passage of time. When the glow and the glamour of all other godmen and messiahs has dimmed, when the suppressive religions of the world have been consigned to the waste basket of history, Krishna's flame will be heading towards its peak, moving towards the pinnacle of its brilliance. It will be so because, for the first time, man will be able to comprehend him, to understand him and to imbibe him. And it will be so because, for the first time, man will really deserve him and his blessings."

KABIR

" Kabir's words blazed with fiery truth. He spared neither Hindus nor Muslims in his rebelliously insightful verses. "

Around five hundred years ago there lived a famous Vaishnava saint called Ramanand in Banaras. A Brahmin devotee came to meet him with his daughter who was a widow. Ramanand blessed the woman and said, "May you give birth to a son."

In due course, the woman fell in love with a man, and became pregnant. It was unthinkable to raise a child born out of wedlock in those days. So, to avoid disgrace, she wrapped the child in a lotus leaf and left him on the bank of the Lahartara Lake in Banaras. On the full moon night of June, Nima, wife of Miyanur Ali, was returning home from her mother's place, and saw the abandoned child. She took the child home and raised him. Thus, Kabir was raised in a Muslim family in Nirutila, Banaras. The place is now known as Kabir Chauraha.

However, it's hard to find an authentic account of Kabir's life. There is an ongoing debate as to whether the narrated story is an actual historical account or simply a metaphorical allegory to his life-long effort to unite Muslims and Hindus.

The spark of rebelliousness was evident in Kabir from his very childhood. Although he grew up in a Muslim family, he refused to eat meat or get circumcised. When he was ten years old, he went to Ramanand to become his disciple. But Ramanand didn't have the courage to initiate a Muslim child into the Hindu Vaishnava sect, as it would have created nothing short of a scandal in his community. Kabir tricked his way into disciplehood. Every morning, Ramanand used to go to Panchgangaghat, the holy bank of the Ganga, to perform his morning ablutions. One morning, Kabir wrapped himself in a blanket, and lay down on the steps leading to the Ganga. It was still dark in the morning, and Ramanand's feet hit Kabir's head. Seeing that he had unknowingly hit a child's head, Ramanand patted Kabir's head and said, "Ram! Ram!"

Kabir regarded this as his initiation and started chanting the name of Ram as his *Gurumantra*. This is how the rebellious life of Kabir started as a Vaishnava seeker in a Muslim household. Kabir was sent to a *madrassa*, a Muslim school, to study but he was disgusted by the attitudes of the *Maulbis* and was incredibly bored by the environment there. Thus, he escaped from the *madrassa*. Regarding formal education, Kabir has said in a song:

> *You tell me what's written in scriptures,*
> *I tell you what I see with my eyes.*

Kabir started writing fiery verses against the rigidity of the established religions. He sang:

> *The world is utterly mad, they travel far and wide to worship a stone idol*

But no one worships the stone grinder in their own home, which grinds their grain every day.

And,

Every morning the priest climbs the mosque made of stone and sand

And screams the name of God. Is God deaf?

Kabir's words blazed with the fiery truth. He spared neither Hindus nor Muslims in his rebelliously insightful verses. Soon enough, his poems became a luminous backdrop against which the hypocrisy of priests and Maulbis was revealed in all its atrocity. His couplets, composed in the local dialectic language, spoke directly to people. He avoided using difficult Sanskrit words and esoteric references, and wrote in simple language, making his words easy to understand. Gradually, his rebellious verses started spreading far and wide. But along with his fame came the public criticism by the enraged Hindu priests and Muslim Maulbis. Illiterate as he was, Kabir, however, was blessed with unrivalled genius. None could beat him in logic. When his rivals failed to counter him in logic, they made several attempts at his life.

During those days, Sikandar Lodi of the Lodi Dynasty was the emperor of Delhi. Both Hindu and Muslim priests went to him to complain about the havoc Kabir was creating. The Muslim priests said to Lodi, "Kabir is a Muslim and he chants the name of Ram, and he doesn't believe in the Koran, nor does he fast during the month of Ramadan. He doesn't even perform his daily prayers. He has converted many Muslims to Hindus. He is going to destroy Islam."

The Hindu priests had their own complaints. "He denounces religious texts and holy places, and ridicules priests," they said.

When he heard countless complaints about Kabir, Sikandar

Lodi became curious about him, and came to Banaras to meet him. In Banaras, Kabir was summoned by Lodi. When Kabir arrived at Lodi's audience, Seikh Taki, the master of Lodi, ordered him to bow down to the Emperor, and said, "Tell him that you will not talk against Islam again. Ask for his forgiveness and the Emperor shall spare your life." Kabir remained as fearless as ever. He said, "I don't bow down to anyone else except my Guru and God. And when death comes, the Emperor can't even extend his own life by a day. Who is he to spare my life?"

Infuriated by Kabir's statement, Sikandar ordered his men to execute him publicly. A mad elephant was released and set after Kabir. A huge crowd had gathered to see the execution. But to everyone's surprise, as soon as the elephant saw Kabir, it became still and docile. They also tried to kill him by setting fire to his hut, and drowning him, but miraculously Kabir came through these gruelling attempts on his life without a scratch. Seeing this, Sikandar Lodi and his Guru, Taki, realized Kabir was no ordinary man. Soon after, they became devotees of Kabir, and turned into two of his ardent admirers. From then, Kabir's fame rose throughout India. He continued his old work of denouncing all kinds of hypocrisy prevalent in society and religion.

In one of his songs he says, "The whole world is unconscious; they eat, and they sleep. But Kabir alone is sad as he is awake, and thus laments how foolishly people are wasting their life."

It is a curse to feel deeply in this insensitive world. To live in this world, one needs to either totally desensitize oneself, or live in complete isolation. For an awakened mystic like Kabir, there is no peace, no consolation.

Kabir famously wrote:

Kabira lives close to a slaughterhouse, drowned in a doom so deep,
He who sows must reap the fruit, why should Kabira weep?

Even if Kabir puts on a face of an apathetic observer in this poem, in reality, he felt deeply for the suffering and ignorance of the others. This song spoke to beggars and kings alike. His devotees ranged from pauper to prince.

Throughout his life, he did not leave his simple vocation of weaving cloth. His message was simple: Live a simple, natural life without making it unnecessarily complicated in the name of religion. He lived among the simple folk, and practiced what he preached.

He exposed all kinds of evil practice, carried out in the name of religion or tradition, by means of his songs. It is his genius that he could reveal the complexities of spiritual life in the common man's dialect.

He sings:

Oh seekers, the natural ecstasy is the best.
I don't close my eyes, pierce my ears or torture my body in any way.
With open eyes I look around, and smiling, I praise the beautiful.
Wherever I go, there is my temple, when I sleep, that is my prayer.

Kabir was contemporary with Nathpanthis, Tantriks, and Jains whose meditation techniques were arduous, and who preached various forms of self-torture as the means of reaching God. Kabir saw this as absurd practice, and sang vehemently against it. He propounded that living simply and spontaneously could take one to the path of *samadhi*, and called it *sahaj samadhi*. Once, the Rajasthani devotee of Krishna, Meera, came to Banaras to meet Kabir, and stayed in his house. The King of Kashi had also become a follower of Kabir, and so was invited to speak at the religious gathering of priests of Banaras. But Kabir told them he would come only if Meera was also invited to the programme. Inviting Kabir had been scandalous enough, and the organizers didn't want to extend the invitation and invite Meera as well. It was impossible to imagine a woman in a religious gathering. However, Kabir was not ready to compromise. So, the priests finally agreed to invite Meera. Once she was seated among the noted religious speakers of Banaras, Kabir asked her to sing her devotional songs and dance as she often did. The Priests immediately protested. It was sacrilegious to conceive of a woman dancing in the congregation of the learned scholars. But since Kabir refused to speak before Meera sang her songs, they had to give in unwillingly. The event caused a great debate among the scholars. Kabir's respect and recognition for Meera as a spiritual leader had been quite a revelation for the members of the chauvinistic dominion of Banaras priests.

Kabir was married, and had twins whose names were Kamal and Kamli. Many followers of Kabir, the Kabirpanthis, are reluctant to accept that he was married or had any children. In one of his songs he refers to Kamal and says, "Kamal, my son, didn't marry and ended the lineage of Kabir."

While Kabir's whole life was nothing short of rebellion, his death too was extraordinary. During those days, it was believed that those who died in Kashi would go directly to heaven, and those who died in Maghar, a town near Gorakphur, would be reborn as a donkey in their next life. This belief is still popular among Hindu fundamentalists. To shatter this age-old myth, Kabir went to Mahagar at the age of one hundred and twenty and left his body there. The governor of the area, Nawab Bijuli Khan, was a devotee and wanted to perform the last rites in the Muslim way. The Maharaja of Banaras, Birdevsingh Badhel also was a devotee of Kabir, and rushed to Maghar when he heard of his Guru's death. He wanted to perform Kabir's last rites in the Hindu way. Kabir was always for friendship between Hindus and Muslims, and disregarded all traditional divisions between them, but immediately after his death, Hindus and Muslims almost went to war to decide who had rights over his dead body. It is said that Kabir's body turned into flowers, and the Hindus took half of it and created a *samadhi*, and the Muslims took the other half and built a *majhar* in the Islamic tradition. The two *samadhis* of Kabir in Maghar is a unique example of how spirituality is above religions.

Kabir was a rebellious flower. He didn't live his life by predetermined rules. He lived his life in the light of his awareness, and encouraged people to break away from the hypocrisy of religions, race, nationality and similar false divisions. He shunned all rules and dogmas. He lived a simple, humane and natural life. Unfortunately, Kabirpanthis, the devotees of Kabir, couldn't keep the legacy of rebellion intact. Instead of contemplating upon and living his fiery message of universal brotherhood, they have confined him to a sect. I met many Kabirpanthis who have fallen prey to religious sectarianism and dogmatism. But there are still a few seekers who are receiving direct guidance from Kabir.

Just recently, I was conducting a meditation camp in Sravasti, India. There I met Bhagwat Das, who used to be the main priest of the Kabir *Samadhi* at Maghar. He was born in the Dhanusha district of Nepal. He is a friendly, honest man. He was devoted to Kabir. But after attending the meditation camp, he was filled with a great longing to be initiated into Osho Neo-sannyas. It was quite a courageous act, and he relented to his longing, despite chances of being denounced by those who ran the Kabir *Samadhi*.

When he returned to Maghar, his love for Kabir had increased manyfold. Osho has spoken extensively on Kabir. Through Osho's eyes, Kabir's teachings became even dearer to his heart. He continued his daily work at the *samadhi* along with the meditations he had learned at the camp. This news soon reached Kabir Chauraha, Banaras. He was, thereby, sent a letter of admonishment with a warning to drop meditation as soon as possible. Bhagwat Das argued against this by quoting Kabir, who encouraged his devotees to follow their heart. Of course, the argument fell on deaf ears, and eventually he was expelled from the temple. I knew that Bhagwat Das had great love for Kabir, and this event unsettled him.

These days, he runs Osho Kabir Meditation Centre near Maghar, where he practices his regular meditation and also teaches meditation to others who go there.

It is a great paradox of life that those who have regarded the most rebellious people as their leaders, have also become rigid with time.

Seeing such hypocrisy, Kabir's heart used to cry, and this is what he sang:

> *I see that priests of all sects and religions are phony.*
> *They talk about heaven but they themselves are going to hell.*
> *And,*
> *All try to look like a saint but hardly is anyone's heart saintly.*
> *All doors will open to him alone whose heart is that of a saint.*

In his time, enlightened masters such as Nanak, Dharmdas and Ravidas revered Kabir as their Master. Mahatma Gandhi's mother, Putlibai, was also a Kabirpanthi, and Kabir's words had a profound impact on Gandhi and his philosophy. Einstein, the scientist-mystic of our times, has said, "If the world has to choose one path then it should be the path of Kabir."

Osho has spoken extensively on Kabir. He praises Kabir as "a unique blend of wisdom and devotion, formless and form, the otherworldly and this world, nothingness and totality, experience and expression as well as poetry and music."

MAHARSHI PATANJALI

> "Yoga is not a religion, but a science of consciousness. The more secular the world becomes, more will be the popularity of yoga."

The *Patanjalyogpradeep* is one of the most important texts dealing with self-transformation. No one else has explained the spiritual path in such a decisive and scientific manner as has Patanjali.

Not much is known about him, but it is said he was a yogi from Kashmir.

Primarily there are five types of Yoga: *Rajyoga* or the path of meditation, *Gyanyoga* or the path of wisdom, *Nishkam Karmayoga* or the path of detached action, *Bhaktiyoga* or the path of devotion, and *Hathayoga* or the path of *yogasanas*.

It is wrongly assumed that the term *Yoga* only denotes different body postures and breathing exercises. This is *hathayoga*, the primary stage, in which one cleanses the body and opens its channels by a scientific and gradual process to prepare the body for meditation. *Hathayoga* refers to the *yogasanas,* or postures, and *pranayama,* the breathing exercises. It was started around a thousand years ago and its main text is *Hathayaga Pradipika*. Patanjali's text deals with *Rajayoga*, or the art of meditation. *The Patanjalyogpradeep* is divided into four chapters: *Samadhipad, Sadhanapad, Bibhutipad* and *Kaiwalyapad,* and has one hundred and ninety-five sutras in total.

As Krishna has presented the crux of spirituality in the second part of the Gita, similarly, Patanjali describes the essence of *samadhi* in *Samadhipad*. In this chapter, he gives the explanation of Yoga, the signs of an impure mind, the ways not to allow the impurities to take over the mind, or the ways to still the mind, the state of detachment, and the states where the mind is not disturbed by the impurities. At the end, he describes the state of ultimate union, or Yoga. The essence of these fifty-one *sutras* can be said in the following three *sutras*:

Yogascittavrttinirodah.
Yoga is the cessation of mind.

Tada drastuh svarupe vasthanam.
Only then is the witness established in itself.

Vrttisafupyamitaratra.
In the other states there is identification with the modifications of the mind.

The second chapter, containing fifty-five *sutras*, is called the *Sadhanapad*. This chapter is for the seekers who have started the journey and are struggling to calm their chaotic minds. It describes the types of impurities, the methods of *kriyayoga* through which one can purify these impurities, the source of habit-forming actions, their effects and the ways to be rid of them, the pure state of the soul or the witnessing consciousness, along with the various stages of yoga. In the twenty-ninth *sutra* of *Sadhanapad*, Patanjali has called his Yoga *Asthayoga,* or the eight-fold path. These eight stages are: *yama* (self-restraint), *niyama* (fixed observance), *asana* (posture), *pranayama* (breath regulation), *pratyahara* (abstraction), *dharana* (concentration), *dhyana* (contemplation) and *samadhi* (trance). The first five of these are called *bahiryoga*, the Yoga of the outside, and the last three are called *antaryoga,* or inner Yoga. But the last three stages also remain outside once the ultimate stage of Yoga, the absolute state of godliness or *nirjiv samadhi,* is achieved, which is the experience of being one with the whole. *Yama* includes the rules for behaviour. They include *ahimsa, satya, astaya, brahmacharya* and *aparigraha. Ahimsa* means not giving pain to any creature through one's mind, speech or body. *Satya* means to use your senses and mind to express your realizations for the benefit of others. *Astaya* refers to honesty or not stealing in any way. *Brahmacharya* means the transformation of sexual energy so that one's body, mind or speech isn't tainted by sexuality. *Aparigraha* means non-possessiveness.

The second stage of *Asthayoga* is *niyama,* which refers to the techniques of fixed observance. There are five different *niyamas*: *shauch* (purification of body, clothes, food and mind), *santosh* (contentment while performing duties, by not having expectations or feeling low due to difficulties incurred while performing them), *tapa* (to be able to accept difficulties while fulfilling your aim), *swadhyaya* (to study the tendencies and habit patterns of your own mind) and *ishwar pranidhan* (to be surrendered to existence).

Pertaining to the stage of *Asana,* to be able to stay comfortably in one posture for a considerable period of time is known as *aasansiddhi*. This state is useful in achieving a still mind.

To be able to achieve slow and even breath is the result of *pranayama* or breath exercises, the next stage. This helps the mind to be more focused.

The following stage of the eight-fold path, *pratyahara,* refers to the process of detaching energy from all senses, and concentrating on dissolving your consciousness within yourself.

The stage of dharana refers to the state of focusing your consciousness in one place.

The next stage, *dhyana,* is when you can achieve concentration without being disturbed by the mind.

The last stage, *samadhi,* is when you are liberated from the mind, and are totally established in your original consciousness.

Patanjali has explained *dharana, dhyana* and *samadhi* in *Bibhutipad,* the third chapter of *The Patanjalyogpradeep.* When the mind is still, many mysterious psychic powers start manifesting around a seeker. In Yoga, these psychic powers are called *siddhis.* Patanjali describes the various *siddhis* in the fifty-fifth verse of Bibhutipad. On the path of Yoga, the meditators are distracted by lust for these *siddhis.* Only the seeker who is free from the temptations of these *siddhis* can achieve the state of *Kaivalyapad.* The seeker who has reached this stage becomes one with God and is omnipotent, the most powerful and all knowing. This is the final destination of Patanjali. He describes this stage in the thirty-fourth *sutra* of *Kaivalyapad*, which is the last chapter of the *Patanjalyogsutra.* Mahavir has taken the *yama* of Patanjali, and calls it the *panchamahabrat,* which is the foundation of Jainism. The *panchasheel,* or five disciplines, of Buddha are also based on Patanjali's *yama,* but instead of *aparigraha* (non-possessivenes), Buddha has placed the rule of abstinence from the use of intoxicants.

Yoga is not a religion but a science of consciousness. The more secular the world becomes, the greater will be the popularity of Yoga. Today the Christian priests, Jewish rabbis and Islamic imams are all interested in Yoga. Yoga has also found a place in the prescription of Western doctors, who refer their patients to it for a healthy life.

# GURU NANAK

> "Nanak was loved wherever he went. He travelled all the way to China through Nepal and Tibet. This happened around the year 1517. While in Nepal, he stayed in Kathmandu for a while. He had stayed on the bank of the Bishnumati River near Balaju, where there is a small Nanak temple today."

Lone Seeker Many Masters

Guru Nanak Dev was born in a village called Talbandi near Lahore, which falls in present day Pakistan. The place is now known as Nankana Saheb. He was born on the full moon of the month of April in 1469. It is said that Nanak was born laughing.

There was a spark of keen intelligence seen in Nanak from his early childhood. Along with his local dialect, Panjabi, he learnt Sanskrit, Farsi and Arabic - the three most important languages of his time. Not only was Nanak blessed with intelligence, but also with a sense of detachment and fire of rebellion, the combination of which made him an unusually pensive and fiery child. He took a stance against social and religious injustice from an early age. He was sent to school, but felt suffocated by the education system which was based on superstitions, and promoted an unfair system of social hierarchy. Nanak showed no interest in learning a vocation either; he was more interested in knowing the meaning of life. He would spend his time with saints or meditate alone with nature. Seeing his lack of interest in learning a vocation, his father, Kalu Mehata, told him to look after their herd of buffaloes. So following his father's wish, he would take his cattle to graze, but always ended up meditating under a tree. While he was immersed in his meditation, his cattle would go and eat the crops of his neighbours. Nanak's father had to deal regularly with his neighbours' complaints about his, and Nanak would get scolded by his father as a result. As the complaints only increased, his father realized that Nanak was not fit for the job. He thought maybe it would be better if Nanak started a business of his own. Handing over twenty rupees to him, Nanak's father told him to go to the nearest marketplace and start a business that he felt was the most profitable one. Nanak went to the market with his friend, Bala. On the way, he saw a group of monks. The monks hadn't eaten for a few days and said to Nanak that he would be immensely blessed if he could feed them. Nanak felt that there could be nothing more profitable than feeding hungry monks, and fed them to the fill. He then donated to them the money that was left after paying for the food. He returned home fully satisfied. When his father saw he had returned empty-handed, he asked what exactly did he invest the money in. Nanak, feeling he had made the most profitable business deal possible, said, "What can be more profitable than feeding the hungry, and helping those in need?"

These words of Nanak seemed far-fetched and impractical to his father, who was constantly shocked by his son's crazy ways. So thinking that familial responsibility might knock some sense into him, he arranged for Nanak to be married to a girl named Sulakshana. Nanak was only eighteen years old then. Nanak accepted this scheme of his father without any protest, as he felt that liberation was possible by leading the life of a householder, and there was no need to renounce the world and become an ascetic. His wife gave birth to two sons - Srichandra and Laxmichandra. Although he lived as a householder, in his core, he always remained a renunciate. His heart remained undefiled by any attachment. In an attempt to make him more practical, his father sent him to his sister's place at Sultanpur. His brother-in-law held a high position at the palace of Nawab Daulat Khan Lodi, the Muslim governor of Sultanpur. Due to his brother-in-law's influence there, Nanak acquired the job of a storekeeper at the Nawab's palace. But Nanak would only count to twelve when counting the sacks of grain. Thirteen is *tera* in Punjabi, which also means "yours." So when he said "*tera*", he would remember God, and feel, "all is yours," and go into a state of *bhava samadhi*.

During Nanak's time, India was under Muslim rule, and the Hindus faced a great deal of discrimination. The strict caste system of the Hindus had made many people *untouchables*, who were treated as second-class citizens, and denied any dignity. In such a difficult time, Nanak disregarded all divisions of religions and caste, and gave out the message of love and unity through Sikhism.

Sikhism is the youngest religion in the world. Four important religions have emerged on the Indian subcontinent: Hinduism, Buddhism, Jainism and Sikhism. The three main religions born outside the subcontinent are Judaism, Christianity and Islam. All four religions of the subcontinent share the same basic concept of karma and reincarnation. They also stress the concept of *moksha* or nirvana, which means complete emancipation from the cycle of birth and death, rather than the concept of heaven and hell. From the fifteenth to the seventeenth centuries, many saints were born in India, and they led the path of devotion. They showed it is possible to attain enlightenment by singing, dancing and celebrating, and it was not necessary to be a renunciate and escape from life. Among the blissful saints of that age are Kabir, Nanak, Farid, Raidas, Dadu, Daria, Charandas, Chaitanya, Meera, Daya, Sahajo, Surdas, Tulsidas, Raskhan and Rahim. The path of devotion that was started in ancient times by Narad and Shandilya came to its flowering in Nanak's age. There are countless paths to enlightenment but each age gives birth to a particular type of saint and consciousness that reaches its peak through the path which is the most suitable for the age.

"*Sadho, sahaj samadhi bhali,*" "O seekers, the natural ecstasy is the best, there is no need for methods", said Kabir, who propagated the spontaneous path towards truth. Kabir hugely influenced Nanak. Nanak often stated that he was only the dust on the feet of Kabir. The *Guru Granth Sahib*, the priciple holy book of the Sikhs, contains the teachings of many saints, but Kabir's sayings and songs recur most frequently.

Nanak's closest friend was Mardana, a low-caste Muslim, who remained Nanak's close confidant throughout his life. Nanak used to sing his hymns just like Kabir, Meera and Surdas. Mardana accompanied Nanak with a stringed instrument called rubab.

One morning Nanak and Mardana went to the river to bathe. While bathing, Nanak went under the water and didn't re-surface. Mardana panicked and asked villagers to help him find Nanak. The frenzied search lasted the entire day and yet they couldn't find him. The villagers abandoned all hope of finding him and tried to console Mardana, who was overwhelmed with grief.

Three days later, to everyone's surprise, Nanak was seen meditating under a tree, close to the spot where it was presumed he had drowned. Nanak's energy had completely transformed. Having experienced *nirvikalpa samadhi*, Nanak was glowing with divine radiance. His heart, full of bliss and compassion, became eager to share his experience. Thus after enlightenment, Nanak left his job and travelled far and wide to share his love and vision.

Nanak was loved wherever he went. He travelled all the way

to China through Nepal and Tibet. This happened around the year 1517. While in Nepal, he stayed in Kathmandu for a while. He had stayed on the bank of the Bishnumati River near Balaju, where there is a small Nanak temple today. I have often visited this temple, which is still vibrant with Nanak's loving energy.

Nanak was loved by both Hindus and Muslims, and both groups claimed him as their own. He criticized the malpractices prevalent in both religions, and revived their positive aspects. He spoke against the caste system and the discrimination against women by both Hindus and Muslims. He especially denounced the *sati pratha*, where women died with their husband on the funeral pyre, and abolished it from his area. If people wanted to join his *sangha*, they had to stop taking intoxicants, and become hard-working and independent. He also started the tradition of donating ten percent of his *sangha's* income to the common kitchen called *langar*, where anyone could come and eat for free.

Nanak gathered all his friends and followers from every caste and creed, and all ate together in the *langar*. The tradition continues even today in all Sikh Gurudwaras. When I travel to Europe and America to conduct Osho meditation camps, I take my friends to Gurudwaras. They are often astounded by the generosity of Sikhs, and tell me, "Such graciousness, dedication, devotion, and service is possible only in your culture, not in ours."

Osho has explained the essence of the Japji Sahib, the first composition in the holy book of the Sikhs, in his book Ek Omkar Satnam. This book has revived the essence of Sikhism for the modern mind. After reading the book, the famed Sikh writer and intellectual, Khuswant Singh, said, "Till now I thought that Nanak was a parish saint. I didn't feel any flavour in his words. I listen to Osho's discourses every morning. After hearing Osho explain the essence of Nanak, for the first time, I feel love and devotion for him."

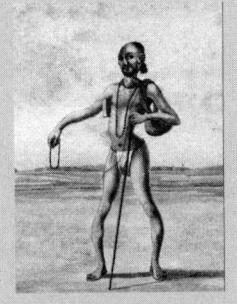

ASTABAKRA

> "IN THE CURVE OF A TEMPLE
> IS THE SKY CURVED? WHEN A POT
> IS SMASHED, IS THE SKY SMASHED?
> THE SKY IS BEYOND CHANGE.
> MY BODY IS TWISTED, BUT I AM
> NOT. LOOK AT THE ONE WITHIN."

A twelve-year-old child, crippled in eight places, arrived limping at the court of Emperor Janak. Janak was a seeker of truth, and in his kingdom the theologians and scholars were paid the utmost respect. The Emperor himself invited them to his court for philosophical discussions. It was in the middle of such a discourse that the boy appeared in the court.

As he walked into the court limping, everyone in the court broke into uproarious laughter. As they started to laugh the boy swept his eyes through the court and started laughing louder still. Perplexed, they stopped laughing and stared curiously at the boy. His laughter continued to echo through the court. Emperor Janak, unable to contain himself, asked him, "I can understand why they are laughing, but why do you laugh?"

The boy turned his majestic eyes towards the Emperor and answered, "I am laughing at your sheer ignorance."

Janak, even more surprised, asked, "Why do you think so?"

"I thought this conference was for scholars and philosophers, but these are all skin-traders. Their scholarship is only skin-deep, and they cannot see beyond the body. Your Majesty, in the curve of a temple, is the sky curved? When a pot is smashed, is the sky smashed? The sky is beyond change. My body is twisted, but I am not. Look at the one within. You can't find anything more straight and pure. Does wisdom only descend on those with grey hair? What kind of knowledge do you expect to gain from the company of such idiots? I couldn't help but laugh when I saw you fooled by such a comical congregation."

A cold silence descended in the king's court. The insult was too much for the Brahmins to bear, but Janak's heart opened up to the fearless and clear words of the boy. As though shaken awake from a long and endless nightmare, Janak got down from his throne, knelt at the boy's feet, and asked,

Katha gyan bapnoti katha muktibharbisyati.
Bairagya cha katha praptametadibruhi mama prabho.

"Oh Lord, how can one achieve wisdom? How can I become detached and liberated?"

The boy was none other than Astabakra. Astabakra was born to Sujata, the daughter of Uddhalak Rishi, and Maharshi Kahod, who was Uddhalak's disciple.

During those times, it was the royal tradition of Mithila to invite sages to the palace. Even kings sat humbly at the feet of sages and asked their questions. The title of the Nemibansha kings of Mithila was "Janak". The Janak we are talking about is Sita's father Sirdhwoj, the twenty-second Janak king. All Janaks were free from attachments and were enlightened. This is why they were also known as Videha, which means the one who has transcended the body. Likewise, Sita was also called Vaidehi, or the daughter of Videha. Mithila was also blessed by the presence of enlightened sages such as Yagyabalkya, Gagri, Lomas and Uddhalak.

There is a story that one of the kings of the Janak lineage attained the state of vairagya when he spotted a gray strand on his head while combing his hair. He then handed over the kingship to his son, became a sannyasin and went to the forest to meditate. He also made it a rule that as soon as the king spots the first grey hair on his head, he should leave kingship and become a sannyasin. This tradition of the Mithila palace continued for more than twenty generations.

Hearing the humble but intense plea of Janak, Astabakra said to him,

Muktimichasi chettata bishayan bishawatyaja.
Chhyamajajarwadayatosha satya piyushwad bhaja.

"If you want freedom, then shun the sensual experiences as if they are poison. Turn your attention to forgiveness, sincerity, kindness, simplicity and truth." Astabakra says, "Emancipation means that your obsession with desire is over. The world exists as long as you are governed by desire. Remaining in the world and working and enjoying it does not create bondage, it is the attachment that creates bondage. Detachment and witnessing bring freedom."

This teaching is the crux of the science of *moksha*, the ultimate emancipation.

In the next verse, Astabakra adds, "You are not the body made of the five elements, you are the consciousness that resides in the body. If you drop the fallacy that you are a body, and rest in your consciousness, then this very moment you will be peaceful, joyous and free. Right and wrong, pleasure and pain are all illusions of the mind. It will not have any effect on your original, innocent nature, because you are neither the doer nor the one who experiences, you are just the one that witnesses all that is happening. You are the light, you are innocent and are always free, but the same effort that you make to be free becomes your bondage."

As soon as Janak heard this, all his illusions were shattered, and he immediately achieved the state of God-realization. He then expressed his astonishment to Astabakra. "Oh Lord, I became omniscient and blissful as soon as I heard your words. The same way as my soul keeps my body alive, I am spread around the universe as consciousness and vibrate in each atom. Lord, now I find it incredible that I went on missing this simple truth for lives. There is neither beginning to me nor is there an end, neither is there any joy nor sorrow. I am bliss supreme. I bow down not only to you but also to my own self – *aho aham namo mahayam*."

The Gita is more of a debate than a conversation between Krishna and Arjuna. In the Gita, Krishna tries to explain the truth to Arjuna logically, but Arjuna keeps on questioning using counter-logic. The communion happened only at the end of the seven-hundredth verse of the Gita.

But the Astabakra Samhita is exeptional, because Astabakra does not need to make so much effort to get through to Janak, as he was a ripe soul. Janak's enlightenment is historic, as the very first utterance of Astabakra is enough to rekindle the flame of truth within him. He became free and content immediately. The remaining verses are simply conversations between a master and a disciple. They authenticate each other's experiences, and talk about the nature of the ultimate freedom and the indications and character of an emancipated person. There is no conflict or debate between

Astabakra and Janak, rather just an amicable conversation between two enlightened people.

The reason why the Astabakra Samhita would not become popular is well laid out by Astabakra in the first three verses of the fifteenth chapter of the book. Astabakra says, "Those with a pure mind will be satisfied by little wisdom. Those whose minds are impure enquire throughout their lives, but their lust for knowledge remains unsatiated. Those who are lustful are intelligent, hardworking and like to talk a great deal, but after self-realization, their worldly desire is also melted by detachment because their whole energy starts moving withinwards and refuses to go outward. They then become silent. This is why the words of wisdom regarding sannyas, freedom and detachment are not for those who are deeply attached to worldly things, or those who live too much in their minds and are very ambitious. Thus, wisdom should not be imparted to such people. My words are for people who have already seen the worthlessness of sensual and worldly pleasures; those who have already been through the alluring but bitter experiences, and are thoroughly frustrated with life. Only such people will be able to listen, understand and digest my words."

Such people are indeed rare. This is why the *Astabakra Samhita* did not become popular like the Gita, and there is no indication that it will be so in the future. In our time, Osho has explained the *sutras* of Astabakra in a series containing two thousand, five hundred pages. He calls the book the *Maha Gita*, which means the "Great Gita".

Speaking about the *Maha Gita*, Osho has said, "Man has many scriptures, but none are comparable to the Gita of Astabakra. Before it, the Vedas pale, the Upanishads speak with a weak voice. Even the Bhagavad Gita does not have the majesty found in the Astabakra Samhita — it is simply unparalleled."

MA ANAND MADHU

> "The name of my first sannyasin is Ma Anand Madhu -- a woman of course, because that's what I wanted. Nobody has initiated women into sannyas like me. Not only that, I wanted to initiate a woman as my first sannyasin, just to put things in balance and in order."
>
> -OSHO

Ma Anand Madhu

On the brink of Triveni Ghat in Rishikesh, a quaint Gujarati ashram houses a female mystic. Usually draped in her orange cotton sari and a thin shawl of the same colour, she looks like a Hindu female sannyasin. Her small, frail figure, chiseled face, stern voice and beatific smile gives her an otherworldly look. At the same time, her presence, her gesture, and her simple yet refined lifestyle gives an impression of sublime regality. The mystic is no other than Ma Anand Madhu, the first initiated disciple of Osho.

Ma Anand Madhu has been continuing her meditation practice since 1974, the first fifteen years of which she spent in total silence at Mayakund, Rishikesh. She only resumed talking after her self-realization. For the first five years of her silent years, she was practicing *kasthamaun*, which literally translates to "wooden silence". During *kasthamaun*, a seeker is as still as a wooden block, and separated from all worldly connections. The seeker neither reads nor writes anything, nor does he or she meet anyone, and remains confined in a room or a cave. During this tough period, Ma Madhu did not look at anyone else but the Ganga. The only thing she ate was wheat porridge in the morning and a glass of cow's milk at night.

My intimacy with her goes back a long way. We knew each other since the early 1970s, when she was initiated into Osho Neo-sannyas.

Ma Anand Madhu was born into a respected Gandhian family from Gujrat. Famed Gandhian leader and ex-Prime Minister of India, Morarji Desai, was her uncle, and her husband, Babubhai, was a well-known leader of the Gujrat Congress and a member of the Indian Parliament. Ma Madhu was the Principle of the Gandhian Women's College at Aajol, Gujrat. During this time she met Acharya Rajneesh who had arrived at Aajol to give a public discourse. Because of her meditation and good karma of her past lives, she felt instant recognition and love for Acharya Rajneesh. Later, both Ma Madhu and her husband devoted themselves to the teachings of Acharya Rajneesh.

In September 1970, during a meditation camp in Manali, Acharya Rajneesh initiated the first batch of his sannyasins. Against all tradition, Osho initiated Ma Madhu, a female, as his first sanyasin. Osho has said, "The Buddha, Mahavir, and Shankaracharya decided not to initiate women into sannyas. However, the Buddha was compelled to do so. After his father Suddhodhan's death, his stepmother, Mahamaya, shaved her head and left Kapilvastu for Vaishali, where the Buddha was staying. She pleaded the Buddha to initiate her. When the Buddha's caretaker, Bhikkhu Ananda, also pressured him to initiate her, the Buddha couldn't say no to his mother and unwillingly allowed women into the *sangha*. The

Buddha is reported to have said, "My religion would have lasted for two thousand, five hundred years, but now with the entry of women it will only last five hundred years.'"

Osho is very critical of Buddha's unwillingness to initiate women into the *sangha*. He says, "What's the point of a religion that lasts two thousand, five hundred years if it denies entry to half the world's population?"

According to Osho, religion may last just a year, but it should be open for all. If it can bring about transformation in the lives of only a handful of people, it is still better for religion than to survive for thousands of years on the crutches of irrelevant laws and order. Osho was particular about initiating a female disciple.

Osho's revolutionary approach to religion responds aptly to the need of a contemporary man. While Buddha unwillingly allowed women into the *sangha*, Mahavir went as far as to declare that enlightenment was not attainable through a woman's body. At most, a *sadhika* (a Jain nun) could earn enough good virtue to attain a male body in her next life. Osho was unwilling to continue the legacy of this flawed and biased view-point. Not only did he recognize women as equally worthy candidates, but even initiated a woman as his first disciple. And in his ashrams, all leading and decision-making positions were given to female sannyasins. Most of the Osho centres in Europe are also run by women. No other Guru has been able to give women the respect and recognition that Osho has given them.

Ma Madhu's husband had also wanted to be initiated by Osho. But when Osho decided to give initation to his wife before him, he was deeply hurt. He decided not to take sannyas. One of the main reasons why Morarji Desai persistently criticised Osho was because the family had been enraged by Ma Madhu's initiation.

After she took sannyas, Ma Madhu established the first Osho Ashram near the Women's College in Gujrat where she was the

Principle. Its name was Rajneesh Sanskar Tirth. After a while, she resigned from her job and started travelling around India, leading a *kirtan mandali,* spreading the word about Osho and his teachings. In 1974, when Osho's Ashram was established in Pune, he had wanted Ma Madhu to go to America to spread his work there. However, Ma Madhu expressed her desire to go somewhere in the Himalayas near the bank of the Ganga, and practice silent meditation. Seeing that the desire was intense and genuine, Osho allowed her to go, and said, "You have an intimate relationship with Ganga and the Himalayas. Your meditation will mature in that area."

Blessing her for her journey ahead, he gave her his shawl and said, "Never feel that you are alone there. Whenever you feel that you need my help, wrap this shawl around your body and remember me. You will instantly feel my presence and energy."

With her Guru's words as her only support, she has been meditating alone in Rishikesh since 1974. She has already achieved the highest state of *nirvikalpa samadhi,* or god-realization, during her fifteen years of silence. Because she spent such a long period of her life alone in silence, she prefers not to meet many people. But she remains available for seekers every afternoon between 4:00 and 5:00pm, and showers love and blessings on those who come to meet her.

It's very easy to write about Ma Madhu, but it must have been a difficult choice for an educated woman like her to leave a distinguished family, with all its comfort and facilities, and spend thirty-three years alone on the bank of the Ganga, her only strength being the faith in her master, Osho.

Mystcism lives in Ma Madhu in the most human form. She portrays divinity as a personal bearing, so human-like and yet so divine! The strong energy field around her influences everyone who comes into her presence. The undying love and devotion that she carries for her master is contagious, and she imparts it all in the form of love and blessings that she showers upon everyone who comes to her. Although grounded in the depths of life, her being lives in the open sky of boundless freedom. Ma Anand Madhu is a presence that can only be understood when one understands the absence that surrounds her.

IN SEARCH OF TRUTH

THESE CHAPTERS ARE DEDICATED TO ALL
THOSE SEEKERS WHO HAVE SACRIFICED
THEIR LIVES IN SEARCH OF TRUTH

MAHATMA GANDHI

In 1942, the whole of India was taken over by the Independence Movement. The fire of rebellion had engulfed the country. The news reached the Wardha Ashram that the British were on their way to arrest Gandhi. His assistants became anxious, but Gandhi was his equanimous self. Every afternoon, Gandhi used to take a ten-minute nap. That day before he retired for his usual siesta, he said to his assistants, "I am going to take a nap; please make preparations for gaol."

Gandhi woke up exactly ten minutes later. The British officers had already arrived. Greeting them courteously, he said to them, "Please let me drink my lemonade."

After drinking a glass of lemonade, he peacefully surrendered to the officers. The British were upset due to the ongoing revolution, and were very angry with Gandhi, too. There was fear amongst his followers that the British might torture Gandhi and keep him in gaol indefinitely. With teary eyes, they asked him, "Do you have any instructions for us?"

Gandhi said calmly, "This morning Ghanashyamdas Bidala has taken some goat milk from the Ashram. He still hasn't paid for it. Please take two paisa from him, and write it down on the Ashram's income sheet."

With these words, he namasted everyone around, and left with the British officers. This kind of unfaltering yogic mind is what Krishna calls a *steethpragya*.

Mahatma Gandhi was the first inspirational figure in my life. While I was still in school, I had an opportunity to read his book, *My Experiments with Truth*. In the last fifty years, my respect for Gandhi has only grown. I was inspired by many spiritual people and much spiritual literature, and became initiated by many masters. But my spiritual search came to an end when I met Osho. The quest that began with Gandhi found its contentment in Osho.

Although Osho is one of the harshest critics of Gandhism, his criticism has chiseled Gandhi's personality, scrapping off the rough parts to reveal its most profound aspects. The more I understand Osho, the more I realize his admiration for Gandhi.

Distinguishing Gandhi's political personality from his spiritual side is difficult. He never preferred being addressed as a Mahatma, the great soul. He didn't take initiation from any master or ashram. He repeatedly said the Gita was his mother and his master. The Bhagavad Gita and the Ramayana were the source of his inspiration and energy. His mother, Putlibai, was a Kabirpanthi, and we can trace clearly the influence on Gandhi of religious tolerance as preached by Kabir. Gujrat, Gandhi's home town, is largely influenced by Jainism. The concepts of non-violence, truth and celibacy that remain the cornerstone of Gandhism were inspired by Mahavir, the twenty-fourth *Teerthankara* (great master) of the Jains.

Gandhi has written in his autobiography that after watching the play of King Harishchandra, he was inspired to pursue the path of truth and honesty. Gandhi was contemporary with many renowned mystics. Meher Baba had been spreading his silent message from Pune. Thousands of seekers from India and abroad were coming to him. In Pondicherry, Sri Aurobindo was trying his best to manifest the divine consciousness on Earth. He was very much concerned with the freedom and development of India, and actively instigated an armed rebellion to release India from the clutches of the British Raj. But while he was locked up in Alipur Gaol, he had a vision, where Swami Vivekananda and Lord Krishna visited him and said, "Leave politics, and put all your energy into self-transformation, because God has chosen someone else for the task." Later, Sri Aurobindo found out that Mahatma Gandhi was the prophesized leader. After the vision, Sri Aurobindo abandoned all his political pursuits, and devoted all his time to spiritual transformation. Concurrently, two hundred kilometres away from Pondicherry, at Arunachal, another saint, Sri Raman Maharshi, had attained enlightenment. Many were being transformed by his silent presence.

Whenever there was conflict in his party, Gandhi used to send the leaders of the Indian National Congress to Raman Ashram to have Raman's *darshan*. Simultaneously, in Bengal, Paramhansa Ramakrishna had just left his body. His disciple, Swami Vivekananda, was spreading the vision of his Master far and wide, and was being received very positively. In Bengal, there was another great yogi, Yukteswar Giri, whose brilliant disciple, Paramhansa Yogananda, was spreading the message of yoga in the West. Annie Besant and Krishnamurti were busy experimenting with various esoteric practices. These luminaries lit the Indian spiritual sky. They all had respect and love for Gandhi, and all these enlightened Masters wanted to help Gandhi spiritually.

I am continuously surprised as to why Gandhi persistently refused to see any of them. The only Master Gandhi met was Swami Yogananda, who insisted and went to Wardha Ashram himself. Swami Yogananda spent two nights in the ashram.

Gandhi is one of the few people in the world who can claim their life to be their message. His response to every situation was filled with love. Gandhi did not have a political frame of mind. Cunningness, opportunism, fear of mass opinion or the desire to appease the masses, and the wish for power and position were furthest from him.

For the first time, through Gandhi, politics and spirituality were brought together. This gave politcs the solid base of honesty and compassion. This approach helped to purify the political atmosphere, which otherwise was based solely on competition and power-hunger.

The status-quo is always afraid to let go of power. There is no "peaceful" path to power. Often empires are built over dead bodies. Chinese saint, Lao Tzu, says, "The victory achieved through violence always ends in a funeral."

But sadly, most of our victories follow this course. By merely swapping the positions of oppressor and oppressed, we cannot bring about a meaningful change in our socio-political structure. At most, it will only interchange the roles of the ruler and the ruled, but the hunger for power and dominance remains the same. In fact, the vicious circle of the power-game only gathers more momentum. No-one is happy to lose. The defeated group will simply be waiting for the right opportunity to wage a war and overthrow the ruler. Therefore, despite fighting countless battles for equality and democracy, we see humanity is yet to find or establish an "equal" society.

In this context, Gandhi's peaceful approach to rebellion was a breath of fresh air. It was a very courageous act in itself. His protest was called Civil Disobedience. Many within his own party were not convinced that peaceful protest could restore Indian independence. But Gandhi had unshakable faith in non-violence. Gandhi heralded a new age in politics. His non-violent revolution became an inspiration for oppressed people around the world. Civil Rights leaders, Martin Luther King in the United States of America, Nelson Mandela in South Africa, the Democratic leader, Ang Sang Suki in Burma, and the Dalai Lama all used the path Gandhi had laid. In Nepal, B. P. Koirala gave up armed rebellion and returned to Nepal to start a peaceful protest. Krishna Prasad Bhattarai was in agreement with Gandhi when it came to non-violent political protest.

The beauty of non-violent protest is how one can achieve the desired result without compromising the universal human values such as peace, tolerance and kinship. This avails both parties to come to an agreement in dignity. Let's take India as an example. Even after the British left India, they still remained friends with India by becoming members of the Commonwealth countries. Both countries are still benefiting from it today.

The day Mahatma Gandhi was shot dead, Osho had wept for hours. He has said, "I pay him respect for his sincerity, and that he lived it whatsoever the consequences. He lost his life just because of that sincerity.

"With Mahatma Gandhi, India lost its whole past, because never before was anybody in India shot dead or crucified. That had not been the way of this country. Not that they are very tolerant people, but just so snobbish, they don't think anybody is worth crucifying...they are far higher.

"With Mahatma Gandhi, India ended a chapter, and also began a chapter. I wept, not because he had been killed, because everybody has to die, there is not much in it. And it is better to die the way he died, rather than dying on a hospital bed, particularly in India. It was a clean and beautiful death in that way.

"Gandhi had the capacity to know the pulse of the people."

Gandhi can only be born into a culture where there has been an unbroken tradition of enlightened masters such as Ram, Krishna, Buddha, Mahavir, Kabir, Nanak and Ramakrishna. Gandhi is a beautiful flower in the same lineage. According to Osho, Gandhi could not be spiritually liberated, and needs to take one more birth for his liberation. Maybe he has already taken the birth. Still, I don't regard him any less than an enlightened master. He postponed his own spiritual growth to free the country from social, political and economic oppression. Such compassion can only flower in the heart of a Bodhisattva.

RAMAN MAHARSHI & GANDHI

Whenever there was conflict within the Indian National Congress, Mahatma Gandhi would send his political leaders to have the *darshan* of Raman Maharshi. In this way, many important figures in Indian politics went to have *darshan* of Raman Maharshi, but what is surprising is that although Gandhi sent many people to meet Raman, Gandhi himself never went to see him.

Mahatma Gandhi also spent a lot of time in Pune. Another enlightened master of that time, Meher Baba, sent invitations to Gandhi many times, but he never accepted Meher Baba's invitation either. Both Raman Maharshi and Meher Baba were silent saints. Meher Baba had even written a letter to Gandhi in which he had said, "I have already found the path to emancipation and *samadhi* that you are searching for. I can help you to find it."

But although he was in Pune many times, he never met Meher Baba.

In 1930, Gandhi was delivering a public speech in a place

which was just three hundred metres away from Raman Ashram in Tiruvannamalai. The ashram was en route to the place where Gandhi was delivering his speech. Gandhi often appreciated Raman Maharshi publicly, so everyone in the ashram thought he would surely come and meet Raman. All the ashramites gathered at the gate of the ashram with garlands to welcome Gandhi. Gandhi's car arrived. In the open-hooded car, Rajagopalachari was seated with him. He was the organizer of Gandhi's trip to South India. Rajagopalachari later went on to become the first Governor General of independent India, and then the Chief Minister of Madras.

Gandhi's car stopped in front of the ashram gate for a while. The ashramites welcomed him by offering garlands. Gandhiji received the garlands and returned the courtesy by greeting them in return. All thought that Gandhi would get out of the car and have a *darshan* of the Maharshi in the ashram, but Rajagopalachari signaled the car to move ahead. Gandhi did not meet Raman, although he reached the gate of his ashram, which left everyone surprised.

One of the ashramites, Sundaresha Ayer, had gone to meet Gandhi at his event, and also had the opportunity to meet him, at which time he presented two books of Raman Maharshi. Instead of keeping the books for himself, Gandhi signed them and auctioned them right then and there, and deposited the amount in the Harijan Welfare Fund. The ashramites, not understanding Gandhi's behaviour, asked Raman, "Why didn't Gandhi come to have your *darshan*?"

Raman Maharshi answered, "Gandhi is a man of very high consciousness. Rajagopalachari had the fear that if Gandhi had my *darshan*, he would be immediately transformed. He could even reach the state of *samadhi* and leave active politics. This is why Rajagopalachari prevented Gandhi from seeing me."

Gandhi returned to Madras after a few days. An ashramite, Krishna Swami, went to Madras to invite him. Gandhi's reply was,

"I want to have the *darshan* of Bhagwan but I don't know when that time will come."

That time never came, because on January 30, 1948, Gandhi bid farewell to the world.

Similarly, Western psychologist, Carl Gustav Jung, also appreciated Raman, and would regularly write in his letters, "I will certainly come to meet Raman."

Jung came to India because he had great interest in Indian mysticism. He met many so-called saints, but didn't meet any of the enlightened masters of that time such as Raman Maharshi, Meher Baba, Anandmayi Ma or Sri Aurobindo.

I have witnessed this time and time again. When Osho came to Patna, Jayaprakash Narayanan would come to listen to Osho's discourses, but he would do so staying in his car.

Once I had asked Osho about Jayaprakash, Vinoba and Kripalini during his discourse. In that discourse, Osho had praised Jayaprakash as a man of saintly nature. Osho had said that while Vinoba is a saint from the outside but a politician inside, Jayaprakash only has politics on the outside but essentially he is a saint. This is why he never became successful in politics because he is a spiritual person by nature and always gets crushed in political tussles. I had given that recording to Jayaprakash when I met him in Patna. I had thought that after listening to the discourse, Jayaprakash would meet Osho, but that did not happen. Many renowned figures of India came in contact with Osho, but didn't begin their meditative journey. Some of these people include: Indira Gandhi, Rajeev Gandhi, Haribansharai Bachchan, Mahipal, Mahesh Bhat, Amrita Preetam, and Khuswant Singh among others. Although they all praised Osho, they could not come close to him spiritually. Similarly, when Osho came to Nepal in 1986, many spiritual people who read Osho and praised him, didn't come to meet him. Even today many famous people with spiritual potential come to Tapoban. They praise Tapoban, but save themselves from meditation.

Why does this happen? Osho has spoken to me in detail about this. Osho's analysis goes deeper than that of Raman Maharshi. He says, "Gandhi was not going to be stopped by Rajagopalachari . Gandhi is not a man who could be stopped by anyone. He was stopped by his own unconscious mind. Gandhi was an exceptional seeker, and his unconsciousness knew that if he met enlightened masters such as Raman or Meher Baba, his world would turn upside down. Similar fear of transformation stopped people like Jayaprakash Narayanan, Kripalini and Vinoba from coming close to enlightened masters. This is our story as well. We like to talk about truth, *samadhi*, and transformation, but our unconsciousness becomes extremely fearful when the actual time for our transformation comes. Thus, we run away from it, and later try to justify it logically."

The answer that Jung gave when asked why he returned to the West without meeting Raman Maharshi is worth contemplating. He said, "All kind of meditation is unscientific, and the Western and Eastern paths are separate. It is not necessary for the Western philosopher to meet an Eastern saint because they can deviate you from your path."

Similarly, famous Indian journalist, Khushwant Singh, praises Osho publicly, but when asked about sadhana he says, "Meditation is a waste of time."

These statements of great intellectuals such as Karl Gustav Jung and Khushwant Singh are baseless and only self-aggrandizing at most. In these words, the fear in their unconsciousness has manifested beautifully. But no matter how beautifully you craft your logic, one cannot alter the truth. Buddha, Mahavir, Shankaracharya, Kabir, those who have guided humanity through the dark nights of ignorance, remain our pathfinders.

SADHO SAHAJ SAMADHI BHALI

The places where a seeker attains the ultimate truth remain charged for years. The more receptive a person, the more he will be able to soak this energy. I have experienced this myself. Whenever I visit the meditation room of Paramhansa Yogananda at 4 Garapada Road, Kolkata, the place where he attained enlightenment, or when I am in Bodhgaya, under the Bodhi tree where Buddha attained enlightenment, I feel the same blissful wave of energy. And time doesn't make much of a difference either; when one is sitting under the Maulsri tree of the Bhawartal garden of Jabalpur, where Osho was enlightened, one can feel the same meditative energy as one feels under the Bodhi tree. Simply visiting those places can fill one with inexplicable joy and serenity.

The Himalayas, the ancient buddhafield of Amarkantak in

Central India, has been charged for years. Amarkantak lies in the area between the Bindhya and Satpura Hills, and is at an altitude of over one thousand metres. It is covered with dense forests and has many waterfalls and lakes. The place is also famous for various species of medicinal herbs that grow around the area. It is slightly cold on winter mornings, but otherwise, the weather is pleasant throughout the year.

Amarkantak has a special attraction for me because Shivapuri Baba, one of the most beautiful masters of our time, had attained enlightenment here. In the East, we have a belief that all places where an enlightened master lives are holy sites. But the places where they were born, become enlightened and leave their bodies, have a special significance. They are called *Mahateerthas*, the holiest of holy places.

Before I reached Amarkantak, I had often wondered what must have inspired Shivapuri Baba to choose it over the Himalayas or the banks of the Ganga, which are more popular destinations for spiritual seekers. However, after visiting Amarkantak several times, the obvious truth dawned on me. Unlike the Himalayas, Amarkantak has very pleasant weather all year round, which makes it easier for meditators to remain immersed in their meditation for longer periods of time. The forests of Amarkantak are full of various kinds of edible roots, tubers and medicinal herbs. Brahmani, a herb that grows in abundance around the area, is considered the best tonic for the brain. Regular consumption of this herb has been proven to sharpen memory and relieve anxiety and other mental illnesses.

Amarkantak is an ancient buddhafield. Adi Shankaracharya had been initiated by his master, Sri Govindapa, in the eighth century in Amarkantak, and meditated in the same place until he attained liberation. Along with him, ancient mystics such as Rishi Markandeya, Bhrigu, Durwasa and Kapil, and more recent ones such as Shivapuri Baba and Barfani Baba meditated here. Kabir and Nanak had meditated in the area and met each other at Amarkantak.

Even today, many yogis are meditating in the dense forest of Amarkantak. From among the yogis I met there, I would like to share a story of one such yogi who intrigued me.

Swami Shailendra Saraswati had completed his Masters in Quantum Physics, and went on to gain another Degree, this time in Management, from the Indian Institute of Management, Ahmedabad. He had already worked as a CEO of a reputed Indian business house. When he reached the peak of his career, he was haunted by a sense of emptiness and meaninglessness. He looked deeply into his life, and realized that the places where he sought contentment could never contain him. When the realization crystallized, one fine day, he just left everything and set out on a pilgrimage. He eventually reached a place called Tapoban, which is fourteen thousand, six hundred feet above sea level in the Himalayas.

Incidentally, while he was in the Himalayas, he met Maharshi Mahesh Yogi, who had already achieved fame in the West. They grew close to each other, and Mahesh Yogi took him on a world tour in his private jet to develop the Management Division of Maharshi University. He then worked as a Dean and Department Head in Maharshi Universities in Nairobi, Oslo, and America. But he was not happy in the West, and asked Mahesh Yogi if he could go back to the Himalayas to continue his meditation. Mahesh Yogi told him that the best place to continue his meditation would be Amarkantak, and advised him to go there instead. He had not even heard about the place. When he finally reached Amarkantak, Shailendra Swami met Baba Kalyandasi Maharaj, who gave him a comfortable room at Kalyan Sewa Ashram to continue his meditation. After meditating in the comforts of the ashram, he spoke with his master. Mahesh Yogi was not happy with the comfort Shailendra was enjoying.

Mahesh Yogi told him that meditation was not possible in comfort and by being in the company of others. He instructed Shailendra to continue his meditation in seclusion in a cave in the dense forest of Amarkantak. Following his master's instruction, he bade farewell to Baba Kalyandashji. He carried two blankets, two sets of ochre clothes and a bag of flour, and left for the forest. He tied one of his blankets to the trees and made a small canopy, and spread the other blanket on the floor. Since he did not have any cooking utensils, he used to knead the dough on his dhoti and roast it on the fire.

Years later, a manager of the Birla Company who had worked as Shailendra's subordinate many years ago, came to the same forest to survey for a mine. He was disheartened to see Shailendra Swami in such a state. He asked Shailendra to move to a windowless storehouse nearby, which had been constructed by the Birla Company to store gunpowder. I met him in the same storehouse. I had not expected to find such an accomplished person surrounded by secluded forest, leading the quiet life of an ascetic. Although he was not dependent on anyone or any modern amenities, and totally surrendered to existence, he had the countenance and confidence of an emperor. In our very first meeting, we became good friends, and an interesting conversation took place, an excerpt of which I would like to share with you here:

Q. Don't you feel like meeting someone or talking with someone as you stay here alone?

A. Sometimes I have to go to the bazaar to get supplies. It's a different story if I get to meet seekers like you. Otherwise, I find it torturous to be in a crowd. There is bliss in solitude.

Q. How are your needs met here?

A. For years, I have survived on chappatis that I make with my hands. When I am about to run out of wheat flour, someone brings it to me. When my clothes get tattered, someone brings me clothes. I have totally surrendered to God, so it is his responsibility to fulfill my needs.

(I have seen this kind of divine help in my own life and the lives of many other seekers.)

Q. Before you became a renunciate, you had been an academic scholar. Don't you feel like reading the newspaper and listening to the radio to find out what is happening in the world?

A. Not at all. The radio and newspapers only talk about negative things. I don't enjoy indulging in that sort of news anymore. If there is something that I really need to know, then a seeker like you will somehow come here and let me know about it.

Q. You must read a lot in this silent atmosphere. What kind of books do you read?

A. Until quite recently I used to read a lot of books. I mostly read spiritual literature. I also read Osho, which was a blissful experience in itself. I really appreciate him. But soon I realized that bookish knowledge is also just a mental addiction, and at a certain point in a seeker's life, knowledge gathered from the outside becomes a burden. Even if it looks helpful in the beginning, it is actually a hindrance to self-realization. When I realized this, I distributed all my books. I haven't read anything for years, and have no desire to read anymore.

(This was difficult for me to imagine because reading books is the ultimate pleasure for me.)

Q. Why don't you give discourses and teach other seekers?

A. It is written in my birth chart that I will attain self-realization in 2017. Before that, I have decided to devote all my time to meditation. If I start teaching now, my meditation will weaken.

Q. How do you spend your days?

A. I sleep around five hours. I wake up at three in the morning and start my meditation. After finishing the ablutions, I cook for myself. This takes me around three hours. The rest of the time I spend in meditation. Even the three hours feels like a waste of time. I feel it would have been better if I could spend those hours in meditation as well.

Q. What type of meditation do you practice?
A. I practice *Siddhiyoga*, the yoga of going beyond the grip of gravitation and hopping.

Q. Do you also levitate or just hop?
A. I only hop. Levitation requires a deeper state of meditation, and it is easier to levitate in groups of meditators. Just hopping and being released from the grip of gravitation for a brief period of time in itself is very blissful.

Q. Do you practice *Siddhiyoga* all day?
A. Yes, I do this whenever I get the opportunity.

I gazed deeply into his eyes. It lacked the confidence of God realization; neither did he claim to have attained it. Maybe he was waiting for 2017. It saddened me to see how without proper guidance even those people who have made a great sacrifice on their spiritual path are disillusioned by something as insignificant as *siddhis*. In the natural course of meditation, a meditator will attain many supernatural powers. But these are merely distractions on the path, and not the goal. They don't have any spiritual value.

I wanted to say this to Shailendra Saraswati, but out of courtesy, I kept my words to myself and respectfully bade him farewell. My own master constantly warned me against displaying any *siddhis*. He reminded me again and again that the *siddhis*, after all, belong to the realm of mind, and only strengthen our bondage with the world rather than liberating us. As I walked through the dense forest of Amarkantak, I kept remembering a beautiful line by Kabir– *Sadho sahaj samadhi bhali* (Oh seekers, take the easy path to liberation.)

SUVADRA MATA

Although there are many beautiful places on Earth, for the seekers of truth, the Himalayas are peerless. Especially the area of Garhwal in Northern India, with the fresh waters of the Ganga, Yamuna, Alaknanda and Mandakini, is unmatched in its purity. The entire range vibrates with meditative energy. I have been visiting the Garhwal Himalayas at least once every year since 1981. And since 1995, I have also been regularly conducting meditation camps in the area. Each time I visit the place, I encounter some interesting yogis there.

Of course, not everyone in an ochre robe is a genuine seeker. There are also runaway criminals and the lazy ones who are in the Himalayas to escape responsibilities. But every once in a while, I have stumbled upon very advanced seekers. The presence of such a meditator in itself is very healing and uplifting. These seekers are, by nature, very rare. But it is even more rare to come across a genuine female saint in the Himalayas. Our social construct discourages women from taking sannyas or devoting their lives to the search for truth. But I consider myself fortunate to have met a few women in the Garhwal Himalayas who were real seekers of truth. One of them is Suvadra Mata.

Suvadra Mata was born in Gujrat, but the love of the Himalayas eventually brought her to a place called Tapoban, which is situated at an altitude of fourteen thousand, six hundred and forty feet over Gomukh. From Tapoban springs the little stream of water, the source of the Bhagirathi River, which later turns into the Ganga. Tapoban is snow-clad throughout the year, and people can visit the place only during the warm summer months. A few courageous yogis are in silent meditation throughout the year in the caves around Tapoban. The Lalbaba Ashram of Bhojbasa, four kilometres below Gomukh, provides the seekers with their yearly supply of food.

Gangotri, at the altitude of ten thousand, three hundred feet, can be commuted to via off-road vehicles during the months of summer. Gomukh is a day's walk further ahead, and its height is twelve thousand, eight hundred feet. Tapoban is further up, approximately two thousand feet above Gomukh. Despite the allure, it is not easy to reach Tapoban, let alone meditate there. I find it incredible that a lone woman lived and meditated in those secluded mountains and under harsh conditions for years.

Although my destination was Tapoban, difficult roads and adverse weather prevented me from travelling beyond Gomukh. But the moment I stepped into Bhojbasa, I was filled with overwhelming joy. I forgot all about the world, and my mind settled in joyous calm effortlessly.

At Gomukh, I met a gracious Japanese yogi. He and his disciples had set up a few tents, and had been practicing arduous meditation in the area. I learned that they spent four months every summer meditating at Gomukh. After years of practice, he had achieved the ability to levitate at will. He showed me a photo album with various pictures of him in his levitating posture. The time I spent with this Japanese yogi and his young Japanese disciples at Gomukh is unforgettable.

I couldn't reach Tapoban to meet Suvadra Mata, and had to return to Kathmandu a little sad. But to my surprise, I met her at the Shivapuri Baba Ashram at Mrigasthali, Kathmandu, a few months later. She had come to Kathmandu to have a *darshan* of the Pashupatinath temple along with Dr. Sanjaya Shah, who was the head of the hospital run by the Ramakrishna Ashram at Haridwar. Dr. Sanjaya was also a strange fellow; both he and his wife were MDs and could have been earning millions, but instead, they chose to surrender their lives to serve the Ramakrishna Mission. Dr. Sanjaya had immense reverence for Suvadra Mata. He had brought her to Kathmandu at her request so she could visit Pashupatinath temple. When I asked her to come and stay at Osho Tapoban, our ashram at Kathmandu, she agreed and stayed with us for a few days.

During the stay, she shared a few stories from her life in the Himalayas. To take her daily bath, Suvadra Mata had to climb down for two hours to reach Gomukh. There, she would break the ice to collect some water from the Ganga. After that, she would climb up to her cave and perform the daily chants and meditation, and then she cooked her food. This is how her days passed. Whether she would live to see the light of the next day was for God to decide.

While travelling to the area, if someone becomes ill or has their path impeded, they are at the mercy of God. The arrangements for the winter months have to be made by the end of August. The biggest challenge there, according to Suvadra Mata, was to keep the matches dry and functioning. If the matchsticks became soggy, there was no way to make a fire or cook food. So one had to resort to either eating raw rice or to sleep hungry. To keep the matchboxes dry, they were kept near the fire and later wrapped carefully in a piece of dry cloth and placed inside a sack of rice.

The bigger danger was the lack of oxygen in caves. The snowfall would usually cover the mouths of the caves in the night. As the oxygen depleted inside the cave, one would be awakened abruptly in the middle of the night, and have to break the wall of ice. One had to be careful not to pull down the ice-wall completely, as it helped to keep the cave warmer. The trick was to make just the right sized hole. And of course, there is always the danger of avalanches.

It is much harder to live in the Himalayan caves than to write about it. One has to be constantly aware and alert so as not to fall into the death traps that manifest in many different ways. A moment of unawareness, and one slips into oblivion! The constant remembrance of death creates a milieu, where one can contemplate deeply on the nature of impermanence without much effort.

Undaunted by the fear of death, Suvadra Mata continues her meditation in the Himalayas. I have been deeply touched by her dedication and courage. I am sharing her story with the hope that it will fuel your quest as brightly as it has fuelled mine. I haven't known a greater joy than to inspire others to walk the path of truth. I thank Suvadra Mata for keeping the torch of inspiration aflame.

RAM BOMJON

Nepal has been a fertile ground for seekers since ancient times. Mystics such as Astabakra, Yagyavalkya, Gargi, Maitri, King Janak and Buddha were born here and lived here. In keeping, at the beginning of this century, the world witnessed the miracles of a teenage meditator from Nepal, who drew an incredible amount of attention for the miraculous powers that manifested through him. He soon became an international sensation. The renowned international news channels started reporting on the mysterious young mendicant meditating alone in the forests of Central Nepal. When the pictures and videos of the sixteen-year-old Ram Bomjon, with his beautiful unruly locks that haloed his calm and radiant face, sitting cross-legged against a large gnarled tree in Parsa, started floating on the social media, it seemed as though Buddha himself had taken birth again. The world media was taken by the story of this young seeker, who didn't eat, drink or move and was immersed in deep meditation uninterruptedly for ten months.

We live in an age of doubts. Not surprisingly, different conspiracy theories soon began to ferment around the boy. A few skeptics said he was being fed at night behind a curtain; some suspected that his Guru was building himself a temple with the donations that poured in. Some went as far as to declare that the whole Buddha-boy hoax was planted by the Maoists to gather donations.

The fact that the team of doctors, sent to authenticate the event, could not tell for certain from the blood test whether the boy was consuming any food, only thickened the fog.

As Bomjon moved deeper into the realms of his uninterrupted silence, the vista around him was exactly the opposite. The site was being overrun by pilgrims, thousands a week, who were calling this boy "The New Buddha." A big bazaar unfolded around the silent seeker. Along with tea and snack stalls, a few car and bicycle repair shops, too, appeared in the otherwise wild and secluded area.

Instead of taking inspiration from Bomjon's honest effort of self-exploration and his unwavering quest for truth, people made him an object of entertainment, and a crowd of curious folks, who had not much to do with spirituality, started to gather around him.

I was also approached by different journalists, who wanted to understand the spiritual aspect of the phenomenon. They wanted to know what I thought of the boy. It is often difficult to put the experience of spirituality into words because these experiences are too subtle for words. I could only forewarn them not to disturb the ambience of peace and serenity around the area just to dig up more saleable news, because it might cost the young meditator dearly. I had expressed my fear that the burgeoning crowd could eventually force the boy to abandon the forest. And that was exactly what happened.

I haven't seen Ram Bomjon with my own eyes, but I have keenly followed the news about him with great interest. From his early childhood, he showed the traits of a spiritually inclined soul. Many incidents were narrated about his childhood which reflected this inclination.

Ram Bahadur Bomjon was born into a family where meat was the staple diet. Somehow, when Bomjon's mother was pregnant with the boy, she was repulsed merely by the sight of meat, let alone to consume it. When he was only a toddler, Bomjon was against the consumption of meat and alcohol. He also showed eager inclination towards Buddhism. His mother noted with some surprise how he never asked for a second helping. He only ate as much as he was served. While most of his friends were busy playing games, he wandered alone along the forest trails and sat cross-legged in meditation. Bomjon also had a particular fascination with the Peepal tree. He often offered an oil lamp to the Peepal tree in his village. As he grew older, he started fleeing to Lumbini and Dehradoon to participate in religious sermons. In the beginning, he had gone to Pokhara to search for a place to meditate.

Bomjon's childhood stories bear an uncanny resemblance to the life of the South Indian mystic, Raman Maharshi. Raman Maharshi, too, had left his home at the age of seventeen, and spent many years meditating alone around Arunachala Mountain. He, too, had forsaken food or drink and had moved deeper into seclusion when troubled by the crowd. Most likely, Ram Bomjon's fascination with Buddhism continues from his past lives. The depth of his meditation and silence testify his innate understanding of the teaching. Of course, the most intimate truths of spirituality are best left to mystery. And if the need arises, Bomjon himself might explain his past-life association with Buddha, and the purpose and inspiration behind his meditation.

All I can say for certain is he has shown an enviable dedication and thirst for enlightenment. I salute his willpower, determination, and fearlessness. If he had any greed or ambition, he would have accepted the title of "The New Buddha," which his devotees conferred upon him. He has refused to be addressed thus, and confessed he was yet to attain enlightenment. By disappearing from the forest of Ratanpur, where a fanatic crowd and a considerable amount of donations had amassed, he showed how little he was interested in pursuing the path of fame or prosperity. I have a feeling that if he had been left in the forest of Ratanpur to complete his meditation, then that forest would have become a world renowned *teertha* just like Arunachala.

Most of the accusations that were made against Bomjon were either baseless or malicious. There are many examples of seekers who have lived for years without food or water. The Pawahari Baba of Gajippur, Uttar Pradesh, India, that Swami Vivekananda met during his Indian tour, had survived for years on air. Swami Vivekananda was so impressed by him that he was ready to become Pawahari Baba's disciple. It is said his master, Ramakrishna, who had already left his body, gave him *darshan* and instructed him not to be carried away by miracles or a show of spiritual power.

Similarly, Paramhansa Yogananda has recounted the story of Giri Bala in *The Autobiography of a Yogi*. Giri Bala had not eaten anything since the age of twelve.

The sun and nature provide all the nutritional needs of plants and vegetables. They can directly break down the essential nutrients. But human have to consume these plants to assimilate the nutrients. New research is surfacing, which proves that a human being can survive for an indefinite period of time without eating anything. But this fact is not new to the yogic tradition. In the high yogic state, the human body can receive the energy it needs directly from the sun and nature. There is no need to rely on plants to get necessary nutrients. However, this state is the byproduct of an advanced state of meditation, and people should not try to emulate the feat without the guidance of a Guru.

Of course, Ram Bomjon is a rare phenomenon, but the rarity doesn't mean he is not genuine. My earnest wish and prayer is that Ram Bomjon succeeds in his endeavours, and is able to attain the ultimate truth.

Glossary

Acharya: A preceptor or instructor in religious matters; founder, or leader of a sect; or a highly learned man or a title affixed to the names of learned men.

Advait: Non-duality of the universal spirit

Anshaavatar: Partial descent of a deity.

Anima siddhi: The ability to disappear and appear at will.

Arhattva: The highest state of meditation achieved by one who has destroyed the foes of affliction.

Astasiddhi: Eight divine powers.

Badshah: An emperor.

Baisakh Purnima/Buddha Purnima/Buddha Jayanti: Buddhist festival that marks Gautama Buddha's birth, enlightenment and death. It falls on the day of the full moon in April/May.

Banke Bihari: The twisted and the joyous one.

Bhav samadhi: The state in which a person experiences oneness with the universe through the path of love.

Bhikkhu: A Buddhist monk.

Bhikkhuni: A Buddhist nun.

Bodhi Tree: The Bodhi Tree is a large and very old sacred fig tree located in Bodh Gaya, India, under which Siddhartha Gautama attained enlightenment.

Brahmachari: A celibate

Darshan: An opportunity or occasion of seeing a holy person or the image of a deity.

Dasain: The 15-day-long national festival of Nepal that falls in October. It is the longest and the most auspicious festival in the Nepali annual calendar. It is celebrated by Nepali people throughout the world.

Dharma: The principle of cosmic order. The teachings of Buddha.

Dhoti: a garment worn by male Hindus, consisting of a piece of material tied around the waist and extending to cover most of the legs.

Dipawali: A Hindu festival of lights, held in the period of October and November. It is particularly associated with Lakshmi, the goddess of prosperity.

Ektara: A single-stringed instrument most often used in traditional music from Bangladesh, India, Egypt, and Pakistan.

Ganji: A cotton vest used as an undergarment.

Garvagriha: Garvagriha is the sanctum sanctorum, the innermost sanctum of a Hindu temple where resides the idol or icon of the primary deity of the temple. Literally the word means "womb chamber".

Gopi/Gopini: Cowherd boy/girl.

Guru Mantra: Special mantra given to a disciple by their master.

Gyan Yoga: The path where reality is discovered through insight, practice and knowledge.

Jal samadhi: Consciously drowning the body so that one attains the ultimate union with the divine.

Janau: A holy thread that is worn by the Hindu Brahmins.

Kamandalu: An oblong water pot made of dry gourd or coconut shell, metal, or wood used by Hindu ascetics or yogis to store drinking water.

Karma: The sum of a person's actions in this and previous states of existence, viewed as deciding their fate in future existences.

Karma Yoga: The discipline of selfless action as a way to perfection.

Kasthamaun: Total secluded silence, where one retracts all sense organs for a considerable time.

Kirtan mandali: The dancing procession.

Kumbha Mela: A Hindu festival and assembly, held once every twelve years at four locations in India, at which pilgrims bathe in the waters of the Ganges and Jamuna rivers for the purification of sin.

Kurta-pajama: A set comprising a long shirt and pants that are everyday wear throughout India, Nepal and Pakistan.

Langar: The term used in the Sikh religion for common kitchen/canteen where food is served in a Gurdwara to all the visitors without any distinction and for free.

Leela: Divine playfulness.

Leela bhumi: The land where the deities/ enlightened beings enact their divine play.

Leela sahachari: The group of disciples who are regarded as the extensions of the divine consciousness of the master and are indispensable in fulfilling his mission.

Lungi: A length of cotton cloth worn as a wraparound sarong.

Mahaparinirvana: End of the circle of birth and death.

Maitreya Buddha: The Bodhisattva who is to appear as a Buddha 5000 years after the death of Gautam Buddha.

Majhar: Tomb of a Muslim saint consecrated in the Islamic tradition.

Maulbi: A Muslim priest.

Naga: A naked wandering ascetic.

Namaj: The ritual prayers prescribed by Islam to be observed five times a day.

Nirvikalpa samadhi: The highest state of samadhi.

Panchayat system: The Panchayat is a South Asian political system found mainly in the nations of India, Pakistan, Bangladesh and Nepal. It is the oldest system of local government on the Indian subcontinent. The word raj means "rule" and panchayat means "assembly" of five. During the panchayat days of Nepal, the king had absolute power.

Pooja: The act of worship.

Prana: Breath, considered as a life-giving force or vital principle.

Pranam: The joining of palms and bowing of head in reverence and submission to God.

Pranayama: Yogic breathing awareness and regulation exercise designed to help control one's vital energy.

Punya: Good and auspicious karma or a virtue that contributes benefits in this and the next birth.

Punya salila: The companion in the path of truth.

Purna avatar: The complete manifestation of the divine.

Purnayoga: An evolving system using a wide variety of inspiring and effective techniques to address our physical, mental, emotional, and spiritual needs.

Rishi: An inspired poet who invokes the deities with poetry. Post-Vedic tradition regards the Rishis as prophet, sage or saint.

Rubab: The rubab is a short-necked lute whose body is carved out of a single piece of wood, with a membrane, covering the hollow bowl of the sound chamber, upon which the bridge is positioned. It has three melody strings tuned in fourths, three drone strings and 11 or 12 sympathetic strings.

Sabikalpla samadhi: Deliberate evocation of the state of samadhi induced externally

Sadhak/Sadhika: A meditator, a seeker on the path.

Sadhu / Sadhu Baba: A holy man, sage, or ascetic.

Sagun Bhakti: Love and devotion to God manifested in physical form.

Samadhi: The highest stage in meditation, in which a person experiences oneness with the universe.

Samadhi: A tomb or a burial site of the enlightened beings.

Sangha: The community of monks, nuns, novices, and laity.

Sankha: Trumpet formed from a white conch shell.

Sanskar: Predominant habit pattern accumulated from previous past lives.

Satsang: A spiritual discourse or sacred gathering.

Siddha: An advanced meditator who possesses special supernatural powers.

Siddhi: A special set of supernatural powers possessed by an advanced meditator.

Shivalinga: A stylized phallus worshiped as a symbol of Shiva.

Shloka: A religious verse.

Shrotapanna: The first level of enlightenment.

Siddhi diwas: A particularly blessed day, which is conducive for meditation.

Sthitpragya: A Sanskrit word for a person who is balanced and is in a constant state of mental and emotional equilibrium with his/her surroundings.

Sutra: A precept or maxim.

Swadharma: One's own right, duty, or nature; one's own role in the social and cosmic order.

Swapna darshan: Visions that occur during sleep.

Tathagat: An honorific title of a Buddha.

Teertha: A holy place or pilgrimage site.

Vairagya: A state of detachment.

Veena: An Indian stringed instrument with four main and three auxiliary strings. The southern type has a lute-like body; the older northern type has a tubular body and a gourd fitted to each end as a resonator.

Videha: One who has transcended the body.

Vaidehi: Sita, daughter of King Janaka.

OSHO TAPOBAN

Location: Easily accessible from the city of Kathmandu, Osho Tapoban is located 12 kilometres west of the Tribhuvan International Airport in Kathmandu. Situated on a thousand acres of beautiful, lush forest at the dramatic foothills of Nagarjuna Hills, Osho Tapoban is home to abundant wildlife and is a delight for nature lovers. The commune is a perfect destination for a relaxed spiritual retreat away from the fast-paced city life.

Uniqueness: The commune is a strong buddhafield inspired by the vision of Enlightened Master Osho and welcomes thousands of seekers from more than 80 countries. Tapoban provides an opportunity for a new way of living -with more awareness, sensitivity, relaxation, celebration and creativity. Many options for self exploration are available throughout the year in the form of meditation camps and therapies.

Meditation Programs: Year-round, Osho Tapoban offers a daily schedule of six meditation sessions (one hour each), morning yoga and evening *arati* in the Rajneesh Dhyan Mandir. Meditations include both active and passive Osho meditation techniques.

Osho Tapoban Transformation Intensive: From 1-21 of every month indulge yourself in an intensive holistic package at Tapoban for inner growth as well as physical and mental wellbeing. This uniquely designed package at Tapoban caters to the need of your body, mind and soul. It will not only help you explore the inner depths of your being but also help you cleanse your body and integrate and lighten the mind.

1st week : Shuddhi- 7 days of *Osho No Mind* along with *Panchakarma* detoxification at Osho Arogya Mandir and Spa.

2nd Week: Sadhana- 7 days of Intensive Tranformation Meditation Retreat includes more than 8 hours of intensive practise of Osho Meditation techniques per day.

3rd Week: Samadhi- 7 days of Osho Neo-Vipassana includes Vipassana practise with Osho intensive techniques that complement and help seekers in their silence and awareness practise. (It is also possible for you to join one week of any of the three weeks)

Group Therapies: Includes Osho No-Mind Therapy, Osho 21-day Mystic Rose Therapy, Breath - Bridge to existence group, 3-day Intensive Enlightenment, Sufi: the way of the heart and other therapies.

Osho Sannyas Celebration: Every Saturday and during every meditation camp, an unforgettable sannyas celebration is held when new friends are initiated into Osho neo-sannyas.

Spa Center-Osho Arogya Mandir: Osho Arogya Mandir is a fully equipped Spa with facilities for Ayurvedic and Naturopathic detoxification through *Panchakarma*, *Shirodhara*, and modern day spa treatments of sauna, steam bath, massage, and other body therapies. The packagaes offered include Rejuvenation, Detoxification, Weight Loss, Relaxation and *Kaya Kalpa* packages.

Osho Samadhi: The open air Osho Samadhi is a unique marble structure that encloses Enlightened Mystic Osho's sacred ashes. The samadhi is built around a beautiful tree under which the Buddhist mystic Nagarjuna attained enlightenment.

Shivapuri Baba Silent Temple: Adorned with traditional Malla styled bricks, this silent temple is dedicated to the enlightened mystic Shivapuri Baba. Open for silent sitting and meditation.

Cuisine: Osho Tapoban features three dining options for our guests.

The Sujata Kitchen: Our main dining hall serves three delicious meals a day, offering Indian and Asian vegetarian meals, featuring simple, fresh food, beautifully prepared.

Mariam: Fully equipped with modern amenities, this small kitchen is for our International friends who want to cook their own food according to their taste and preference.

Zorba the Buddha Restaurant: You can also enjoy Continental and Western-stlye food, snacks, and beverages at our Zorba the Buddha Restaurant open from dawn till dusk, seven days a week.

Osho Welcome Lounge: Visitors can uncoil themselves in the relaxing ambience of the Osho Welcome Lounge at our entrance. You can purchase all your basic personal care needs and toiletries along with a large variety of meditation products, Osho books and CDs on site at the Nagarjuna Gift Shop at the welcome lounge.

Shuttle Service: The Commune also provides a paid shuttle service for airport pickup and drop-off or for sightseeing around the ancient cities of Kathmandu Valley.

Internet and Library: Osho Tapoban has a Wi-Fi facility, available inside the commune premises for internet access. You may also use the cyber connection at the welcome lounge. The Osho Library and Study Centre has a large collection of Osho books along with audio and visual Osho discourses which are freely available to visitors and guests.

Accommodation: You have a choice of staying in our newly built Regal suite and deluxe rooms or beautiful and fully equipped modern rooms or our more rustic cottages, situated in separate residential blocks spread across the beautiful commune campus. As we say here: "You can come and stay with us for a night or for the rest of your life!"

Email: tapoban@wlink.com.np
web: www.tapoban.com

ALSO BY SWAMI ANAND ARUN

To date one hundred -two books of Osho, both in English and Hindi are published by Osho Tapoban. The whole set of 102 Books including Loan Seeker Many Masters by Boddhisattva Swami Anand Arun is available at Osho Tapoban at cost price at ₹ 8940 or $ 84.

For details:

Osho Tapoban
Nagarjuna Hills, Kathmandu, Nepal
P.O.Box 278, Ph: +977-1-5112012/13,
9841597788, 9841440335
Email: otpublication@gmail.com
www.tapoban.com